THE GREAT UN

C000220788

Thirty years ago, around 770,000 p...
– attended a university or polytechnic. Now there are over 2.3 million students in Higher Education – almost half of all school leavers.

For the last 30 years we've all been sold the mantra that 'the more people go to Uni, the better off we'll all be'.

But is this true? Has the huge growth in the number of people going to Uni – the Great University Expansion – really been the success the politicians and universities would have us believe?

After all, what's the point of having a degree if one in every two people has one? Why get a degree if only a small minority of university graduates – on some courses less than one in ten – will find jobs requiring a university education, especially if many graduates leave Uni with debts of up to £60,000?

In *THE GREAT UNIVERSITY CON* we expose the truth behind the massive expansion of Britain's university sector: pressure on school leavers to get to Uni whether they are likely to benefit or not; schools feeling they have to game the system to send as many of their pupils to Uni as possible; universities lowering entrance standards to fill up their ever-increasing numbers of courses; dumbing down of university courses; falling academic standards as lecturers no longer have time to deal individually with increasing numbers of students; universities trying to avoid failing anyone, however poor their work, given that they've paid so much for their degrees; rising student drop-out rates; graduates with unrepayable debts which will have to be picked up by taxpayers; a massive oversupply of graduates compared to available job opportunities and a university sector that has become huge, bureaucratic and self-serving and which is too often a burden on, rather than a benefit to, the country.

David Craig has written 9 other controversial current affairs books exposing dishonesty, incompetence, stupidity, greed and waste in government, the private sector, financial services and Britain's charity industry. These include:

The Great Charity Scandal

Don't Buy It! *Tricks and traps salespeople use and how to beat them*

Greed Unlimited: *How David Cameron protects the elites while squeezing the rest of us*

Pillaged: *How they're looting £413 million a day from your savings and pensions....and what to do about it*

Fleeced! *How we've been betrayed by the politicians, bureaucrats and bankers*

The Great European Rip-Off

Squandered: *How Gordon Brown is wasting over one trillion pounds of our money*

Plundering the Public Sector

Rip-Off *The scandalous inside story of the management consulting money machine*

Hugh Openshaw has spent 12 years working in the post-compulsory education system as a lecturer, manager and researcher. During this time, he has worked within several universities, a variety of Higher and Further Education colleges and one prison. His doctorate examined Higher Education policy.

THE GREAT UNIVERSITY CON

How we broke our universities and betrayed a generation

DAVID CRAIG &

HUGH OPENSHAW

Original Book Company

Text copyright © David Craig and Hugh Openshaw
All rights reserved

This edition first published in 2018 by:
The Original Book Company
21b Knyveton Road
Bournemouth BH1 3QQ

ISBN-10: 1-872188-14-1
ISBN-13: 978-1-872188-14-0

CONTENTS

THE NEED FOR THIS BOOK

Thirty years ago around 770,000 people – just one in six school leavers – attended a university or polytechnic. Now there are over 2.3 million students in Higher Education – almost half of all school leavers.

For the last 30 years we've all been sold the mantra that 'the more people go to Uni, the better off we'll all be'. Students will have a fun time, learn all sorts of useful things and then get good jobs. Our economy will be more internationally competitive. Society will benefit as these graduates pay more taxes and, being educated and responsible citizens, will be less of a burden on the NHS and social services. And universities also provide plenty of other societal benefits through their academic research and their contributions to the nation's intellectual and cultural life. After all, everyone would probably agree that the more educated a country's population is, the more prosperous and civilised that country will be.

But is this true? Has the huge growth in the number of people going to Uni – the Great University Expansion – really been the success the politicians and universities would have us believe? What's the point of having a degree if one in every two people has one? Why get a degree if only a small minority of university graduates – on some courses less than one in ten – will find jobs requiring a university education, especially if many graduates leave Uni with debts of up to £60,000?

A degree is now the second most expensive thing most graduates will buy in their lives. But is it worth buying if it ends up costing much more than it returns? And does society benefit from the Great Uni Expansion if taxpayers have to pick up the bill for billions of pounds each year for student loans that will never be repaid?

Normally, these are the types of questions that academic researchers in universities would excel at answering. However, these are not questions that anybody working (or, at least, wanting to continue working) in a university is thinking about, let alone answering. This is quite understandable. It is, after all, both rude and impolitic to bite the hand that feeds.

There are plenty of reference guides to support students' university applications, numerous campus novels describing life within fictional universities and a huge body of academic texts about universities, written by academics for academics (and generally lacking page–turning narratives). But, despite the massive costs of the Great Uni Expansion for students, their parents and all taxpayers, nobody has dared question why and how we have so massively and rapidly grown our Higher Education system and what effect this has had on students, their families, academics, the economy and society.

In *THE GREAT UNIVERSITY CON* we expose the truth behind the massive expansion of Britain's university sector – pressure on school leavers to get to Uni whether they are likely to benefit or not; schools feeling they have to game the system to send as many of their pupils to Uni as possible; universities lowering entrance standards to fill up their ever–increasing numbers of courses; dumbing down of university courses; falling academic standards as lecturers no longer have time to deal individually with increasing numbers of students; universities trying all sorts of tricks to avoid failing anyone, however poor their work, given that they've paid so much for their degrees; rising student drop–out rates; graduates with unrepayable debts which will have to be picked up by taxpayers; a massive oversupply of graduates compared to available job opportunities and a university sector that has become huge, bureaucratic and self–serving and which is too often a burden on, rather than a benefit to, the country.

We've been sold the myth that with universities more is always better. But we've been fooled and now it's time to expose the truth about the Great University Con.

PART ONE

THE SYMPTOMS

CHAPTER ONE

EXPANSION AND ITS DISCONTENTS

"The Millennium generation of UK children may have the most educationally ambitious mothers ever. No less than 97% of them want their children to go on to university."[1] Institute of Education, 2010

"...the number of recent graduates in non-graduate jobs has risen from 37% in 2001 to 47% in 2013."[2]

Over the last 30 years our Higher Education system has tripled in size. This has required a massive additional investment of money and time – billions of pounds from British taxpayers and millions of years from British students. As a result, universities now affect nearly every adult in Britain, whether as students, parents, employers, graduates or taxpayers.

This Great Expansion has been driven by two beliefs. Firstly, that Higher Education provides a range of social, cultural and economic benefits to us, either as individuals or as part of society. Secondly, that the more time and money we invest in our universities, the greater these social, cultural and economic benefits will be. And so we've ended up uncritically pouring ever greater levels of resource into universities in the expectation of ever-increasing benefits. Any attempt at analysing the actual, rather than the claimed, value of university expansion faces opposition from a complicit vested-interests triangle of graduates, government and universities. Each group has a deep-rooted financial and emotional investment in the perceived success of an expanded Higher Education system. As a result, few within these groups will even entertain the possibility of any negative consequences arising from expansion.

These well-entrenched vested interests are stopping us from realising that our universities are not delivering the range of benefits

that we expect. They are preventing us from seeing that this relentless expansion has also contributed to a series of negative social and
economic by-products. Moreover, they are prohibiting us from
identifying the lasting damage that we are doing to our universities
and their worldwide reputation.

The wilful blindness towards the potentially harmful consequences of the Great Uni Expansion is similar to the hysteria seen in
stock-market and housing bubbles. It also has unfortunate parallels
with the problems created by subprime mortgages. Despite warnings
from a series of authoritative sources, most notably Professor Alison
Wolf in her book *Does Education Matter?*, nobody who benefits from
this ever-expanding Higher Education bubble in the short term
(universities, student unions, academics or politicians) wants it to
be criticised. Against this backdrop, it is difficult to have a serious
and unbiased debate about the very institutions – our universities – whose core purpose should be serious and unbiased debate.
Maintaining this level of ignorance has required a colossal amount
of fudge, spin and self-deception amongst the bubble's beneficiaries.
This delusion cannot be sustained indefinitely, however.

Many graduates now see minimal or even negative returns
from their degrees. These graduates come disproportionately from
poorer and disadvantaged backgrounds. They have been encouraged to spend money that they didn't have in pursuit of graduate
careers that many will never achieve. Politicians, universities and
the media have been complicit in this mis-selling and this social
injustice. Unfortunately, it is not just these graduates who suffer
from the effects of the Great University Expansion. Many families
make significant financial sacrifices to ensure that their children
can attend university. They do this because parents and students
are made to feel that there is no alternative to university – that it's
'Uni or bust'.

Despite the intense public interest in universities, public debate
about Higher Education is normally restricted to a limited number
of questions about university funding: who is to pay, how much will

they pay and is this fair? These are valid questions. But they miss an opportunity for a much wider public debate, questioning not only the issue of funding, but also the assumption that every university degree is worth paying for and that university on this scale really is a benefit to our country. Such a debate could start by asking: why is there no escape from universities in modern Britain? When did "Uni" become a *de facto* national service? Is this ongoing expansion really a benefit or simply a collective failure of imagination on the part of successive generations of mostly university–educated politicians, civil servants, media commentators and vice chancellors? More importantly, we need to raise basic questions such as: just how much benefit does our university sector provide and to whom? Has the policy of expansion done harm and, if so, to whom? Finally, if our universities are not delivering what we need them to, then how do we rectify this situation?

WHAT DOES EXPANSION LOOK LIKE?

There are over 160 different universities and Higher Education colleges in the UK today, many with multiple campuses spread out over thirty miles or more. This means that nearly every city and town in the UK now has its own Higher Education institution. Given the size and complexity of our Higher Education system, it is quite difficult to describe it in detail. But it is possible to get a sense of its scale through these four headlines:

1. By 2018 the UK Higher Education system had a total of 2.32 million students

This is equivalent to the combined populations of Birmingham, Manchester, Liverpool, Nottingham and Derby. This figure includes more than 438,000 international students.[3] The majority of these students live away from home, creating a huge transitory population, all moving house annually. This level of population movement is broadly comparable with the mobilization and demobilization of troops over the two world wars, only with more abandoned shopping trolleys and looted traffic cones.

Every year around 47% of the UK's 18–21 year-olds enrol at a UK university or college. In 1980/81 the UK Higher Education system (universities, colleges and polytechnics) had a total of 827,000 students including 52,600 international students.[4] In 30 years we have roughly tripled the size of the UK Higher Education system (Figure 1).

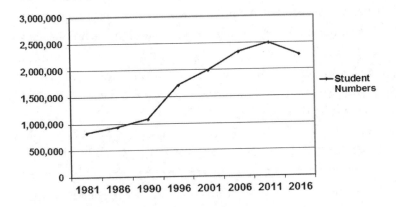

Figure 1 - Total UK student numbers 1980-2016[5]

Over the same period, we have increased the number of international students eight-fold from 52,600 to over 438,000.

2. UK universities employ around 400,000 people directly.[6]

The university workforce is equivalent to the population of a large city such as Bristol. This figure only includes people directly employed by universities. Students and employees combined total nearly 3 million people, or roughly 5% of the UK's population. Universities don't just employ academics and librarians now. It would be impossible to compile a full list but, to provide an indication of the range of jobs available within universities, they include caterers, cleaners, ICT support staff, administrative staff, printers, photographers, marketing staff, PR staff, gardeners, bartenders, drivers and electricians. If you can think of a job, then the chances are that UK universities employ a significant number of them.

3. A degree is now the second most expensive item that most people will buy.

Under the current loans systems, it is estimated that students could owe an average of up to £60,000 upon graduation.[7] This figure includes student loans for tuition fees and maintenance, an overdraft and, for many, credit card debts and additional loans. It does not, however, take into account the impact of compound interest (at an almost usurious government–set interest rate) on this debt.

4. Our Higher Education system is ranked second in the world

Higher Education is something that the UK is particularly good at. The prestige of our universities is one of the reasons that they can attract overseas students in such large numbers. The UK is currently the second most popular destination for students studying abroad. Our universities are ranked second only to the US in terms of their overall performance. UK universities produce a huge quantity of quality research in terms of journals, academic papers and books, second only to the US. Our oldest universities, Oxford and Cambridge, are iconic institutions and enjoy a special status at home and abroad educating countless domestic and international scientific, literary and sporting stars. At their best, our universities contribute enormously to society and help to define our national identity: they represent something to be proud of and something worth protecting.

WHY DID WE EXPAND?

The case for an expanded system of Higher Education has been an accepted part of UK political wisdom for over fifty years. Its roots lie in the *Murray Robbins* report of 1963, commissioned in part because grammar schools and the baby boom were producing too many qualified applicants for too few university places. At the report's heart was the *Robbins Principle*, which stated that:

> "Courses of Higher Education should be available to all those who are qualified by ability and attainment to pursue them and who wish to do so."[8]

Prior to the *Robbins Report*, university entrance had been guided by the principle of creating a national elite, with a limited number of places available to the brightest and the best school leavers. The adoption of the *Robbins Principle* by successive governments has ensured that the supply of university places since 1963 has broadly kept pace with the demand from students *"qualified by ability and attainment"*. The letter, but not the spirit, of this principle has been followed throughout the Great Uni Expansion.

Why has the *Robbins Principle* remained so influential through-out the last fifty five years? The answer lies in the benefits that the report associated with Higher Education, arguing that it provided a range of social, cultural and economic advantages not only for graduates, but also for the UK as a whole. These benefits included:

> "A skilled and educated work force" (paragraph 25)

> "(the production of) cultivated men and women" (paragraph 26)

> "Securing the advancement of learning through the combination of teaching and research" (paragraph 27)

> "Providing a common culture and standards of citizenship" (paragraph 28)[9]

The era of the *Robbins Report* was that of Harold Wilson's famous *White Heat of Technology* speech, which called for the British economy to capitalise on the opportunities afforded by emergent technologies. The most important contribution that universities could make to this putative national effort was to provide the skilled workforce necessary for the economy to adapt and profit from new technological advances. Then, as now, workforce development was the main driver for university expansion.

Since the *Robbins Report*, the economic rationale for expanding Higher Education has rested on this basic idea: that an ever-greater supply of graduates is necessary to meet the economy's need for a skilled workforce. But arguments about the less tangible social and cultural benefits, whilst de-emphasised, have also remained. These have gradually solidified into the commonly-voiced assumption that university is a "public good", in the same manner as flood defences, street lighting and clean air. By 1997, the idea of universities and expansion as a "public good" were so entrenched that the Dearing Review of Higher Education began by stating that:

> "Higher Education is fundamental to the social, economic and cultural health of the nation. It will contribute not only through the intellectual development of students and by equipping them for work, but also by adding to the world's store of knowledge and understanding, fostering culture for its own sake, and promoting the values that characterise Higher Education: respect for evidence; respect for individuals and their views; and the search for truth. Equally, part of its task will be to accept a duty of care for the well-being of our democratic civilisation, based on respect for the individual and respect by the individual for the conventions and laws which provide the basis of a civilised society." The Dearing Report 1997[10]

Examined critically, these claims and the language used to describe them are verging on the hyperbolic, brooking no argument or discussion about the value, worth or importance of an expanded system of Higher Education. The idea of universities as a public good is so obvious, so self–evident that no right–minded person could even think to argue or criticise it. Thirty four years on from the *Robbins Report*, this choice of language illustrated how important the idea of Higher Education had become to the UK establishment.

The most significant recent evolution of the case for expansion occurred as a result of New Labour's *Widening Participation* agenda and the introduction of tuition fees. Attempting to attract more students from non–traditional backgrounds – essentially those from working–class and ethnic–minority families – the expansionist argument shifted from the socio–economic benefits of a skilled workforce to the individual benefits that these new graduates would receive. Chief amongst these were the additional lifetime earnings that a degree supposedly bestowed compared with the earnings of a non–graduate: the so–called *graduate premium*. Allied to this were the opportunities that degrees provided for increased social mobility, in particular providing access to professional jobs. To address concerns over rising levels of student debt, the official mantra was loud and repetitive: that graduates earn more than non–graduates and that they enjoy improved life chances.

Unfortunately, this hard–sell of the graduate premium stifled any opportunity for a debate about the actual benefits of Higher Education expansion. Instead, all of the "benefits" of expansion were calcified into a self–evident truth for the UK's political class, media commentators and universities alike. This "truth" has become the starting point for any public discussion of universities. It includes the beliefs that university is always a public good, no matter who attends, what they study or how university is funded and that there can never be too much of this particular public good. Over time, however, a growing gap between these beliefs and reality has exposed the fault line between the original laudable intentions and the harsh reality of the implementation of the *Robbins Principle* during the Great University Expansion. Underneath this fault line are a series of social, economic and cultural problems that expansion has created and which our universities are now struggling to deal with.

DOES MORE MEAN WORSE?

"... more will mean worse." Kingsley Amis (1960) on the proposed expansion of UK Higher Education.

Over the last six decades this quotation has been roundly rejected by a long line of politicians, vice chancellors, academics and graduates. But to restate another, more famous quotation from the 1960s, it is hard to escape the feeling that "(they) would say that, wouldn't (they)?" In 2018, though, we can reasonably revisit Kingsley Amis's comment and ask whether or not he had a point. A good place to start is the gap between the intention and the implementation of the *Robbins Principle*.

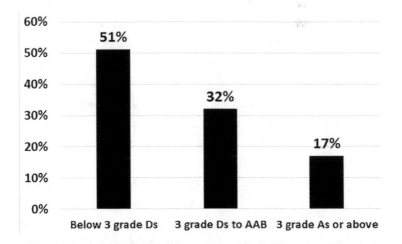

Figure 2 - **UK university undergraduates by entrance qualifications, 2010**[11]

This gap is evident in Figure 2. This shows the A–level grades (or equivalents) of domestic undergraduates enrolled in 2010 and reveals that the majority (51%) were enrolled with qualifications equivalent to **below** 3 grade Ds at A–level.

Were these really the students that Robbins envisaged when he referred to *"all those who are qualified by ability and attainment"*? This seems improbable, especially when we take into account 35 years of A–level grade inflation, with research suggesting that C grades awarded in the late 1980s were equivalent to A grades by 2008. Recently some universities, mainly the newer universities, have been so desperate to fill up their courses that the number of unconditional offers made to A–level six–formers shot up from just 2,985 in 2013–14 to a massive 51,615 in 2015–16.[12] A number of schoolteachers were concerned about how unconditional offers were being dished out "like candy" and how they removed pupils' motivation to work for their A–levels: "It affects performance. I would say students with unconditional offers drop at least a grade." Others saw these unconditional offers almost as a form of corruption: "I am worried about something that looks very much like bribery. 'Come here not somewhere else because you do not need any grades' they are saying."[13]

Whilst the entry requirements for undergraduates have been significantly lowered during the Great Expansion, there have also been dramatic rises in student complaints. In 2004, the government set up the Office of the Independent Adjudicator (OIA) to investigate complaints. In their first year of operation, the OIA received 300 enquiries and 120 official complaints. By 2016, this had risen to over 1,517 official complaints from students at 130 universities.[14] Complaints can only be brought to the OIA after a student has already exhausted the internal processes of their university without satisfaction. As such, these submissions represent the tip of a student complaints iceberg. To provide some idea of the scale of this problem, in 2014 the BBC sent Freedom of Information requests to 120 universities. The requests revealed that those universities had received over 20,000 internal complaints in the 2012/2013 academic year.[15] Many of these are settled internally. In other cases, the students simply give up or leave their university with debt but no degree.

Students unhappy with either shutting up or dropping out are increasingly taking legal action against universities. In 2012, a post-graduate student was awarded over £45,000 in legal compensation against their university.[16] In 2018, a student who got a First at Anglia Ruskin university launched a legal action against her *alma mater* for mis–selling the benefits and career opportunities her degree would bring. All of this raises another question: what are students complaining about?

In a protest at Bristol University in 2009, complaints were made about the quality and quantity of teaching. Students were incensed that they were paying more in tuition fees for less in terms of teaching and assessment. They have a point. Despite ballooning fees, UK undergraduates now receive notably fewer contact hours than their European counterparts. They also receive fewer contact hours than they would have done 30 years ago on a similar course.[17] Post expansion, students have lectures with up to 500 other students. Many seminars run with 30 or more students. These are often taken by postgraduates only a few years older than the undergraduates, usually without any doctorates or teaching qualifications.

This decline in Higher Education teaching standards became a political issue in 2009 when the House of Commons Select Committee responsible for universities took the matter seriously enough to undertake its own investigation. The resulting report and evidence base included 100 submissions from individuals, a total of nearly 800 pages. The evidence falls into two distinct camps. The first, provided by vested interests within universities, is gush-ingly positive, admitting to few, if any, of the problems created by expansion. The second camp, provided by individuals taught by or employed within universities, is negative, disillusioned and angry.

The Select Committee was highly critical of both the evidence about degree standards and of the universities' and sector bodies' attitudes during their investigations. The report declared: "... the system for safeguarding consistent national standards in England to be inadequate and in urgent need of replacement". It also accused vice chancellors of "defensive complacency" in their reactions towards evidence of falling standards within universities.[18]

All things considered, post–expansion graduates could have a good claim against successive governments for false or misleading advertising about the benefits of a degree. There have been few confirmed sightings of the £400,000 average graduate premium announced by New Labour in 2003. Later government estimates put the figure at £160,000, or more recently at £108,000.[19] Unfortunately for taxpayers and graduates alike, even this most recent estimate is a gross exaggeration and generalisation.

The latest official figures show an enormous discrepancy between the returns from different degrees. Whilst male doctors might expect a lifetime graduate premium of £403,353, arts graduates on average can look forward to £34,000 over their 40–year working life.[20] Male graduates in creative arts and design subjects receive, on average, **a net liability of £15,302,** in other words they will be £15,302 worse off during their lifetime than if they had only taken A–levels. It is worth emphasising that these latest estimates were calculated prior to the 2012 increase in fees from just over £3,000 a year to between £6,000 and over £9,000 a year and were based on data preceding the 2008 economic crisis.

Of course, getting a degree is not purely a financial transaction as students will receive other benefits such as making new networks of like–minded friends and hopefully some intellectual and personal development. However, one could question whether, with most universities charging the maximum of £9,000 a year increasing with inflation, these friends and this personal development are really worth accruing debts of up to £60,000 for three years at Uni.

As for the supposed economic benefits to our country, these have also been difficult to identify. There has been no step change in the UK's productivity or output throughout expansion. Our gross domestic product (GDP) and economic growth have broadly continued at the same pre–expansion rates. Productivity per head has failed to register even modest growth increases during this period. Taxpayers, parents, graduates and employers might question: where are the national financial gains that justify snowballing individual and national graduate debt?

It is certainly hard to understand who (beyond universities) has benefited from massive increases in the numbers of sports science, photography, gender studies and creative arts undergraduates churned out during expansion. Between 2002 and 2012, our universities more than doubled the number of sports science undergraduates from 15,000 to 34,000.[21] They similarly more than tripled the number of photography students from 5,000 in 2001 to 18,000 in 2012.[22] These increases have been offset by a few notable decreases. Despite the tripling in overall student numbers, engineering student numbers actually declined from 96,000 in 1994 to 84,000 in 2010. The number of chemistry undergraduates also managed to fall from 14,600 in 1994 to 13,800 in 2010[23].

Moreover, there is little evidence that ever more university has produced ever more people with inquisitive, independent, open, questioning minds. In fact, the opposite seems to have happened – the last decade has seen a worrying rise in the scale and intensity of university self–censorship and an increasing demand for 'safe spaces' where students will be protected from any views which might disturb their intellectual, political and moral comfort zones. During this period, we have seen institutions condoning gender segregation during events, banning some national newspapers, demanding the removal of statues they find 'offensive', stamping out anything that could be seen as 'cultural appropriation' even down to protests over the naming of dishes in university restaurants and refusing a platform to speakers as diverse as Germaine Greer and Nigel Farage. In 2016, the magazine *Spiked*, which monitors censorship on campus, found that 90% of British universities now place restrictions on freedom of expression.[24]

In summary, student numbers are up, but the numbers of engineering and chemistry graduates are down. Class sizes are up, contact hours are down and student complaints are increasing. The UK's rates of growth in GDP and productivity have remained bafflingly static despite continuous injections of drama, dance and sports science graduates into the labour market. Free speech is still tolerated within universities as long as you mind what you say or whom you invite to say it. Finally, graduate debt is soaring whilst returns on the investment in a degree are shrinking. These are just some of the results of the Great Uni Expansion.

CHAPTER TWO

ADMISSIONS: GREAT EXPECTATIONS

Many of us have our own individual memories of university. But we also share a number of *collective* expectations provided by books, films and television. Whilst it would take too long to list all of these, we could point to *Brideshead Revisited*, *University Challenge* and *The Young Ones* as three very different but enduring images of undergraduate life.

In *Brideshead Revisited*, the university is Oxford in the 1920s. It is a place of glamour and entitlement, populated by bright and beautiful youth expectant of bright and beautiful destinies. *University Challenge* presents a succession of (mostly) young and (mostly) studious faces "reading" a variety of (mostly) serious subjects in a quiz show with no prize money, just the chance to demonstrate knowledge. Then, in the surreal, anarcho–comedy of *The Young Ones*, student life represents freedom from domesticity and convention. These three images: entry into an elite, a few years of serious study and student life as one big (irresponsible) party, each suggest part of a wider expectation of what a university experience should be. We think of students progressing towards a brighter and more entitled future as the privileged elite of tomorrow. We think of them achieving a depth of understanding and the ability to think and learn independently. Finally, we think of students as having the best years of their lives. We wouldn't reasonably expect every undergraduate experience to meet each expectation in three years. Most students or parents would probably settle for a pinch of each, seasoned with some rites–of–passage experiences and hopefully some intellectual and emotional growth.

The reality of the Great University Expansion is that only a tiny minority of students will encounter anything close to these expectations. The *Brideshead* doors are closed to most students before they have even accepted their places at the wrong universities.

Beyond the walls of elite institutions, the brightest won't receive the level of intellectual stimulation that they need to shine. The least able won't receive the support that they need and will drop out or struggle through three demoralising years. Those in the middle, intimidated by the brightest and irritated by the less able, will shuffle largely silently through seminars and lectures, pausing only to ask *"will this be in the exam?"* The challenge for most students will be how to motivate yourself when you find it far too easy, far too hard or you're doing the absolute minimum needed to get your 2:1 degree. As universities increasingly become 'degree factories' trying to process as many students as possible with as few resources as possible, those students wishing to understand their subject in depth will gradually realise that just getting by – satisficing – is the name of this particular game.

As for having the best years of their life, the staggering levels of debt now required to finance a university education mean that a *"Young Ones"* party lifestyle is no longer free, nor carefree. Moreover, the sheer size and scale of many of today's universities is often alienating and isolating, whilst student accommodation is usually cramped, outdated and expensive. To cap it all, after graduation comes the realisation that a degree does not guarantee a graduate job. In the summer of 2016, 376,330 graduates arrived on the UK job market, *88,890 of them with first class degrees* and over 252,000 of them – around two out of three – with either a First or a 2:1.[25]

Whilst these three expectations of student life do still exist, they are only available to those limited numbers of students who do the 'right' courses at the 'right' universities. Without these golden tickets, the student experience is likely to be one long and expensive lesson in the gap between the great expectations raised by the politicians' promises and the universities' smart marketing compared to the harsh reality of a jobs market that has depressingly few opportunities for them.

The first challenge for the would–be student is how to navigate the pitfalls of the university admissions system. Success is generally dependent less on a person's intellectual capabilities and more upon years of informed pre-planning and preparation.

APPLICATIONS

Every year over 600,000 people apply for undergraduate degrees through the Universities and Colleges Application Service (UCAS).[26] Each applicant uses the same UCAS form, listing their choices of institutions and degree subjects and their personal data. They all include the dreaded personal statement describing the applicant's various qualities and the rationale for their choices. The applicant's school also provides a statement about the student with a prediction of their grades. UCAS sends this information to the admissions departments of the relevant universities. Decisions are made within those departments and offers or rejections sent back to the applicant. The candidate then chooses two offers, one "firm" at the grades that they are expected to reach and one "insurance" offer at lower grades, in case their exam results aren't as good as expected.

At the point of submission, all potential students are equal. What happens before and after submission, however, is radically different. Securing an offer for the right degree requires the right advice long before the admissions process. Without this, an applicant can find themselves ineligible for desirable degrees, swamped by information, lacking critical information or misled by inaccurate or dishonest marketing. With over 160 universities and higher education colleges, there is now a bewildering array of destinations for applicants. Many universities offer thousands of degrees, often with specific requirements for entry. Some requirements are obvious: to study French at university you need to study the subject at GCSE and A-level. Some are not so obvious: until recently you needed a GCSE in a modern language to apply to Oxbridge. Subject and qualification choices for specialist degrees such as medicine need to start when a student chooses their GCSEs. Students given bad or non-existent advice by their schools may encounter a glass ceiling preventing access to a particular course or university, of which they are often unaware until it is too late. The example below is typical:

> "A worried student called the Sutton Trust recently wanting a place on our university summer schools: *"I've just been told I need maths A-level for computer science at Cambridge – I had no idea,"* she said. She had been advised to take information technology instead, despite gaining a good grade in GCSE maths, because she stood a better chance of doing well."[27]

Students without a clear idea about a future career face information overload during application. Wading through a vast swathe of online and printed material to choose the right course can be time–consuming and bewildering for parents and students alike. In 2014, the Higher Education Funding Council for England's (HEFCE) own research in this area identified a "decision paralysis" created by cognitive overload which resulted in worse degree choices by applicants.[28]

Universities are largely responsible for this situation. They no longer provide objective course information. Instead, they offer promotional material. Many universities have large marketing and schools liaisons departments to recruit students – course fee fodder. This means multiple public–sector organisations spending hundreds of millions of pounds of taxpayers' money to compete against each other in a zero–sum game for a limited number students. It is estimated that university marketing departments currently employ over 2,000 staff and that their marketing and PR activities cost a total of £200 million a year.[29] In no other part of the public sector are organisations spending so much public money to compete with each other in this fashion. Speaking to the *Times Higher Education Supplement* about continuing increases in university marketing budgets in 2014, Roger Brown, Emeritus Professor of Higher Education Policy suggested that:

> "The truth is that almost all of this (spending on marketing) is a waste of money, as there isn't really any evidence that students are influenced in making their choices by university marketing strategies.... this is money that could be used to improve teaching."[30]

In addition, UK universities also pay around £60 million a year to international agents to help them to recruit students from overseas markets.[31]

University marketing material generally consists of glossy, corporate branded packs which look much like every other course's promotional pack. Designed to mimic a travel brochure, they are usually full of pictures of attractive lawns bathed in sunshine, happy students and impressive buildings – heavy on lifestyle elements but suspiciously light on such details as the hours of teaching provided, who will teach the course, the size of seminar groups and the average number of people in lectures. In 2009, the House of Commons Select Committee compared multiple online prospectuses and complained that:

> "... little or no information was provided about the nature or degree of contact which students could expect with staff or, for example, how many students would be in a group or who would teach them – academics or research students. Nor did universities appear to give students a clear idea about the work they would be expected to undertake ... in terms of numbers of essays, projects or assignments."[32]

The Select Committee argued that course information should be:

> "...presented in a consistent format, which facilitates cross-institutional comparisons, the time a typical undergraduate student could expect to spend in attending lectures and

tutorials, in personal study and, for science courses, in laboratories during a week. In addition, universities should indicate the size of tutorial groups and the numbers at lectures and teaching by graduate students."[33]

There was even less detail about employment prospects for vocational courses such as law. It is also far from certain that students should trust the information that universities did provide. A 2014 analysis of eight randomly–selected prospectuses found many actively misled applicants through a combination of selective data, exaggeration and dishonesty. [34] In 2017, the scale of this problem was underlined by the Advertising Standards Authority (ASA) upholding six complaints against individual universities. This was over misleading claims in their marketing materials about their performance in academic league tables and the student satisfaction survey. The ASA subsequently required the universities to withdraw material containing these claims. [35]

Of course, any negative information such as course drop–out rates or complaint levels were also notably absent from this marketing material.

COMPARISON WEBSITES

In response to this criticism, the Higher Education establishment has attempted to improve the information provided to applicants. By 2012, all universities were required to produce 'Key Information Sets' (KIS) for their degrees. These include course data about tuition fees, student satisfaction, assessment methods and employment destinations for graduates.[36] The KIS provided the basic information for several comparison websites, such as *Unistats* and *Which University?*, which were launched in 2012. These websites were designed to provide access to course information for thousands of degrees in one location, allowing applicants to select and contrast information for different degrees – their workloads, costs and economic benefits.

They were intended to provide neutral and accurate information enabling applicants to make informed choices.

In some ways these websites do assist applicants. Rather than spending days looking through dozens of individual university websites and hundreds of degree web pages, it is possible to use one or two websites. The information about course costs and earnings is a step in the right direction and is provided in a consistent format that is easy to read and compare. However, six years after their launch, it is not unreasonable to suggest that the websites have on balance failed in their mission. There are multiple reasons for this failure. The information that the websites provide is incomplete and inaccurate. It can also be misleading. This is especially problematic because this information is now being provided by nominally independent third parties. As such, it implies a greater level of trustworthiness than if it came directly from a university. At their worst, comparison websites act as a rubber-stamping extension of university marketing departments, validating rather than verifying their claims.

To understand this failure, we need to consider what information an applicant needs in order to make an informed decision about a specific degree. The most basic wish list would include accurate, evidence-based information about the costs and benefits involved in study. Such information should include:

- What is the likely starting salary post graduation?
- What is the total cost of the course?
- What are the chances that a vocational degree will enable a graduate to gain entry to its associated profession?

As an illustration, we can examine the information provided by two of the main comparison websites for a specific course – in this case a Bachelor's degree in psychology at Derby University. Why this specific degree? There are three reasons. Firstly, the subject has been a huge growth area during the Great University Expansion. Secondly, as a vocational subject, it nominally affords graduates entry into a well–defined career path. Thirdly, the university recruits 'floating voters' – applicants who might otherwise have considered not going to university. So, how effectively do the websites answer the three questions about salaries, costs and likelihood of entry to a profession?

1. What is an average salary six months after graduation?

The answer depends on which website we choose to believe; *Which University?* places the figure at £15,000. But *Unistats* (Figure 1) suggest £17,000.

£17,000

Average salary six months after the course ⓘ

Typical salary range: £13,000.00 - £20,000.00

ⓘ
Average salary across the UK after taking a similar course
£17,000.00 after six months (salary range: £14,000.00 - £20,000.00)
£21,000.00 after 40 months (salary range: £17,000.00 - £25,000.00)
More on Employment & accreditation ▸

93%

Go on to work and/or study ⓘ

This is what students are doing six months after finishing the course.

Figure 1 – *Unistats:* **Psychology at Derby University**

Unfortunately, neither website makes it clear how they calculate their starting salaries. Are these figures of £15,000 or £17,000 created by averaging the reported earnings of **all** course graduates in work or just those who have jobs directly related to their psychology degree? Moreover, whichever figure is correct, neither website provides any context to these salaries or how they compare to alternative options. For example, a **21 year–old non–graduate**, working 37.5 hours a week at the national minimum wage of £7.38[37] earns **£14,391** a year.

This suggests that this degree confers additional earnings of around £600 to £2,600 per year, compared with non-graduates working at the minimum wage. This estimate is likely to be somewhat generous though. If the non-graduate has been working for three years, then a combination of experience and non-degree qualifications are likely to have increased their hourly earnings significantly above the minimum wage. As such, it is entirely possible that many non-graduates of the same age would be earning considerably more than a graduate from this course.

There are three further problems with these figures. Firstly, whilst the survey on which these figures are based, the Destinations of Leavers from Higher Education Survey (DLHE), has a high response rate (around 66%), the 34% of graduates who don't respond are more likely to be unemployed or in part-time employment. Including data from these non-respondents would probably reduce the starting salaries. Secondly, the salary figure calculations don't include students who drop out during the course. The information for this course shows that 17% of students drop out in the first year. It is reasonable to assume that additional students will drop out in the final two years. If the average starting salary reflected the earnings of those who dropped out in their final year (having incurred almost the same level of debt as those who graduated) then it would probably be reduced still further. Finally, and most worryingly, there is widespread evidence that some universities are systematically manipulating the DLHE survey data to inflate the salary calculations for their degrees. The universities themselves are responsible for collecting this data and there are numerous reports of university employees being asked to remove or lose returns showing low salaries, not to contact graduates from degrees with low earnings or to mislabel employment categories.[38] All of this raises serious questions as to whether the salary information used by comparison websites can actually be trusted.

2. What is the total cost of the course?

Figure 2 is a screenshot from *Which University?* for the same degree in psychology at the University of Derby.

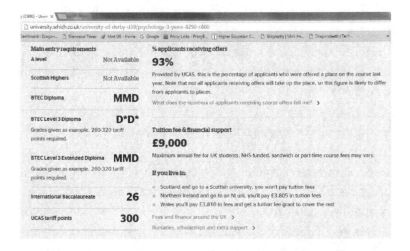

Figure 2 - *Which University?* **Psychology at Derby University**

Here, the main issue lies with how information about cost is presented. In the example from the screenshot, the comparison website notes that tuition fees for the course are £9,000. It could and should be much clearer that this degree incurs three years' worth of fees **(£27,000),** that the course fees will possibly increase each year with inflation and that most students will also be taking out the maintenance loans (probably **over £25,000** for three years living away from home at this university). All this would make the likely cost for the degree in excess of **£52,000**. These figures – more than **£52,000** of debt for a **£15,000** or **£17,000** starting salary – slightly above the minimum wage – would frame a decision about applying to this course very differently. These figures on total costs for the three–year course may seem obvious. But these presentational issues are problematic as many parents and students are likely to seriously underestimate the total cost of going to university. In 2012, a survey of prospective parents and students by Push (an independent university guide) reported that their estimates were **less than 50% of the actual cost.**[39]

3. How likely is a degree to enable a graduate to obtain work in a specific profession?

A quick visit will reveal that comparison websites and university websites provide little information to applicants about what *type* of employment they can expect after graduation. Applicants for vocational subjects such as psychology need to know how successful a degree is at providing entry to that profession. This is much more important than a course's overall employment rate post graduation. A psychology degree with a 90% graduate employment rate means little if 75% of those graduates are working in call centres or sandwich bars.

It is not impossible to provide this information. University psychology departments churn out about 15,000 graduates each year. Anybody intending to practice as a chartered psychologist after graduation has to complete a three–year specialised doctoral programme. The cost of this is prohibitive and, realistically, can only be undertaken via an NHS–funded place. Each year there are roughly 600 such training places available for Clinical Psychology and around 120 places for Educational Psychology.[40] Figure 3 shows this in graphic form:

Figure 3 - UK psychology graduates in proportion to funded training places

These funded places will go largely to psychology graduates from Russell Group universities with first class degrees. Graduates with lower degree classifications, degrees from non–Russell Group universities and with diploma conversions from subjects other than psychology are highly unlikely to be accepted onto these funded doctorates. The chances of obtaining one of these places with a psychology degree from Derby University, for example, are remote. Little of this is made clear in university marketing material. Whilst the comparison websites do note that these places are "Incredibly competitive", they fail to provide any ideas of numbers or that it really does matter where you do your degree if you want to get a place to train as a psychologist.

The problem around providing accurate and useful degree information reflects a conflict of interest between universities and applicants which is often not fully appreciated by teachers, parents and applicants. The primary incentive for universities is to recruit enough students to run their courses, rather than to ensure that the right students are matched to the right courses across the system. For elite universities, this potential conflict of interest is minimal. They simply select the most suitable candidates from a large pool of applicants. Recruitment can become murkier further down the academic league tables. These non–elite universities have fewer students applying, but they also have budgets to meet, staff to pay, courses to run and 'market share' to defend. Sharp practice can occur when students or parents ask about the employment prospects for a course post graduation. Sometimes the response involves the omission of pertinent details. Sometimes carefully–worded course descriptions can be misleading. The fact that a degree has been "accredited" by some professional body does not mean that it will provide students with a passport to a job in this area. Nor does the claim that a course is "designed" to train a student in, for example, forensic science actually guarantee employment as a forensic scientist. In fact, less than one in ten forensic science graduates will find a job in their chosen profession.

The mass–production factory scale of our university system has also depersonalised the university application process. Thirty years ago, nearly every applicant would expect an interview before receiving an offer or rejection. A system dealing with 600,000 applicants makes this impossible. Instead of interviews, universities now have Open Days. Instead of a dialogue with prospective students, there's a sales pitch to prospective students. Only Oxford, Cambridge and medical schools now require interviews. The rest simply make decisions on the information contained on the UCAS form. The natural conclusion of this approach to recruitment was the imaginative approach to choosing students adopted by Leeds Metropolitan and Huddersfield Universities in 2004. Faced with a massive oversupply of students (twenty applicants per place) applying for physiotherapy degrees, they turned the selection process into a lottery. Applications from students with similar grade predictions were placed into a software package and names selected at random. Leeds Metropolitan and Huddersfield were probably not the only universities which used this somewhat questionable process, but they were the only universities to admit to it.[41]

"UNI OR BUST!"

Stepping back from the operation of the university admissions process, there is a wider issue about how it frames the life choices young people make after school. As the Great Expansion has led to nearly half of young people going to university, it has increasingly felt like the only desirable or acceptable route, rather than one possible choice from a range of options. You'd like to start an apprenticeship? Wouldn't you be better off going to university? You want to set up your own business? Well yes, but after a degree. You'd rather start a band with your friends? But what about your other friends who are going to Uni?

There is a worrying amount of pressure now routinely placed on almost all school leavers to apply to university. The combined expectations of parents, teachers and peers make it difficult for any young person with even a minimum amount of academic ability to choose any post–school option other than "Uni". Ironically, this pressure to conformity is occurring at the very time when the average economic benefits of a degree are becoming less obvious compared with other routes such as apprenticeships. In 2013, the *Times Higher Education Supplement* reported on a survey of recent graduates of whom 76% said that they had not been informed of the alternatives to university before leaving school. 54% of these (or **41% of those surveyed**) then stated that they would have under-taken an apprenticeship or vocational training rather than attending university.[42] If the findings of this survey accurately reflect the wider pool of graduates, then this would be buyer's remorse on an almost unimaginable scale.

The pressure to apply to university has made it very difficult for anybody with ability to choose an alternative path, regardless of their intentions or wishes. Worse still, the brighter and more able the individual, the more unthinkable it has become that they should choose not to go to university. It is ironic that the one social institution which should promote freedom of thought and expression should have become such an engine for social conformity. Throughout expansion, the default setting – the aspiration which has been sold relentlessly to all young people – is that a university education is *de rigeur*. Few things illustrate this dogmatic inflexibility better than the university clearing process.

CLEARING

The pressure to apply to university reaches its climax in Clearing, a process which enables students without offers to apply to universi-ties with course vacancies. Clearing is supposed to provide genuine choice to students who have missed their offer grades. In some cases, it can and still does that. But there are indications that throughout the Great Expansion, the primary purpose of Clearing has been to dump students, who possibly shouldn't have been going to university, onto courses that shouldn't have been offered by universities.

Traditionally, what Clearing has offered are the worst degrees possible: the fag end of expansion, courses offering plenty of graduate debt but few prospects of a graduate salary. As the *Guardian* noted in 2010:

> "The great university crush is over while a few places remain, the University of East London still has space for podiatry and the University of Northampton could offer you a waste management degree that is pretty much it."[43]

Given what is on offer in Clearing, it is especially unfair that university applicants from disadvantaged backgrounds (in particular, mature students and ethnic minority students) account for a disproportionate number of those using the process.[44] This simply reflects, however, a much wider disparity in the university admissions process. There are significant differences in the chances of different social and economic groups obtaining a place on a golden-ticket degree.

Those who get a place through Clearing are often far from fortunate. They are more likely to drop out from their courses, wasting time and accruing debt for no purpose. In 2010, the independent student guide *Push* identified a strong correlation between universities heavily involved in Clearing and those with high drop-out rates:

> "Of the ten unis that take in the most through Clearing, all but one have drop-out rates at least three points above the national average of 19%. In fact, at four of them, **more than a third** of the students flunk."[45]

The fear fuelling Clearing is a typical symptom of the "Uni or bust" message we have been sold. Decisions about young peoples' futures are reduced to an existential panic about going to "Uni". It seems that any university and any degree will do as long as it happens now and they are not seen to be left behind by their family and friends. It is ironic that expansion has led to a situation that resembles the anxiety surrounding the old 11+ examination. What makes Clearing worse than the 11+ is that success in the 11+ did at least usually fulfil its promise of improving a young person's prospects. Clearing, on the other hand, holds out the promise of making the grade when what it has actually provided during much of expansion has been a substandard product charged at the standard rate.

It is worth mentioning that in the last two years (2016 and 2017) the picture involved in Clearing has improved somewhat. There has been a broader range of courses offered by universities, including a very limited number of medical school places and a wider range of places at Russell Group universities. This has been driven largely by a fall in the number of 18–20 year-olds due to demographics. Thus, whilst the bulk of Clearing remains a substandard product, there have been a limited number of golden-ticket places available.

But this temporary improvement has only happened because of a shortage of young people, rather than any concern from universities about the value of the courses offered in Clearing or the quality of the school leavers being tempted to go to Uni. From 2020 onwards, when this trend starts to reverse, the more typical Clearing offer made throughout expansion will resume. Or, as a head of outreach and engagement at one university put in in 2017: "A few years ago, Clearing was embarrassing." [46]

In a few years' time, it seems reasonable to suggest that the majority of the Clearing offer will be back to being embarrassing again, with students having to choose between courses such as podiatry and waste management. It seems unlikely, however, that the universities offering these dud degrees will be embarrassed enough to stop running them, well at least not while they can keep on banking the students' ever-rising tuition fees cheques.

Still, there is some good news for those who have to go through Clearing. With often third-rate degrees in less than useful subjects from often third-rate institutions, they're unlikely to ever earn enough to pay back even the rapidly-increasing interest on their student loans never mind the original loan. So they'll be getting three years of education and all their living costs – a three-year holiday of sorts – absolutely free. Britain's ever-generous taxpayers will have to pick up the bill.

CHAPTER THREE

STUDENTS: UNDER PRESSURE

"There are only two tragedies in life: one is not getting what one wants, and the other is getting it." Oscar Wilde

Forty years ago, it might have been possible to talk about one reasonably similar "student experience" at UK universities. If that was the case then, it certainly is not now. Our expanded university system provides an array of experiences. Exactly which experience a student receives depends on the university, the degree and their financial situation. It is important to be clear that *some* of today's students will receive an excellent education at world–class universities; *some* will enjoy their degrees and get all of the benefits that graduate status should confer. *Most,* however, will not receive an excellent education, it is far from certain that they will enjoy themselves and they certainly won't be walking into a graduate job. This is the most basic failure of expansion. To fully understand it we must consider student life before expansion.

The 1970's are not generally considered a golden era in British history, but for students they were something of a high–water mark. Firstly, there were no fees or loans but instead a system of grants. Undergraduates could also use the benefits system, claiming housing benefit during term time and unemployment benefit during holidays. Secondly, students had access to a series of new purpose–built universities with cheap, on–campus accommodation. Thirdly, relations between academics and students became more relaxed, as parodied in contemporary fiction such as Malcolm Bradbury's *The History Man.* This was partially due to shifting cultural mores and partially a product of the smaller scale of universities in the 1970s, where lower student/staff ratios enabled greater personal interaction. Finally, because there were a limited number of graduates, most if not all were able to secure graduate–level employment. Back then, degrees acted as a screening mechanism for employers and graduate status was supported by its relative scarcity.

Today, things are very different. The financial support provided to students has changed dramatically. Accommodation is expensive and scarce and graduate employment prospects are anything but guaranteed. Rather than a three–year party, student life can be expensive, difficult and isolating. Visions of intense intellectual debate quickly evaporate because other students often lack ability, interest or subject knowledge and because academics have neither the time nor the inclination to engage. Instead of opening doors and expanding minds, university today can be stressful, unfriendly and restrictive. It is hard to view any of these changes positively, yet they have resulted directly from the Great Expansion. Collectively, they have undermined what has traditionally been the foremost expectation of "Uni": that it will be an enjoyable and rewarding experience.

There are several reasons for this change. The sheer scale and size of universities has de–personalised the experience for most students. In 2009, the journalist John Crace revisited his old university, Exeter, 30 years after he graduated and noted that:

> "There are more than 15,000 students now, compared with the 5,000 or so in the 1970s. And it shows. The place is heaving, with long queues everywhere. If you want a coffee, you'd better want it bad." [47]

The long queues aren't just for coffee. Accommodation, sports facilities, student unions and lecture theatres are all now crammed. This is just the physical manifestation of the pressure that expansion has placed on nearly every aspect of student life. Now that almost half of young people attend university, pressure pervades every part of student life – there is pressure to get in, pressure to fit in, pressure to hold the right politically–correct views, pressure to get the right degree, pressure to get a graduate job, pressure to pursue a "career", pressure to start repaying your student debt.

Whilst each individual student experience inevitably contains peaks and troughs, there is a growing body of evidence suggesting that being a student today is less enjoyable and more stressful than previously. In 2015, a National Union of Students survey of 1,200 students reported that 80% felt stressed, 55% experienced anxiety, 50% suffered from insomnia, 10% had felt suicidal and 40% had felt "worthless" or "hopeless" at times.[48] It is well documented that students are accessing universities' counselling and academic support services in growing numbers. In 2015, Dr Ruth Caleb reported that:

"At Brunel University London, where I am head of the counselling service, the number of counselling clients has more than doubled in the last 10 years. We know, anecdotally, that this is repeated throughout the UK."

In 2015, a report from Higher Education Funding Council for England (HEFCE) examining student mental health found a rapid increase in the demand for counselling. It also suggested that the reporting of mental health issues by students to universities had more than doubled from 8,000 to 18,000 between 2008 and 2013. Crucially, the report identified that the problems reported had shifted from traditional student concerns about homesickness or relationships to more serious matters such as stress, anxiety or depression.[49]

The suicide rate of UK students increased by 56 per cent in the 10 years to 2016 to overtake the suicide rate of young people in the general population for the first time. Taking into account changes in the student population, the UK student suicide rate rose from 6.6 to 10.3 per 100,000 people between 2007 and 2016. The rate in 2016 was 9 per cent higher than in 2015, and 25 per cent higher than in 2012.

The factors underlying these issues are complex and the difficulties experienced by individual students are unique to them. It is clear, however, that there are collective problems affecting students, such as ballooning debt and worries about accommodation. We will return to each of these, but first it is perhaps useful to start by considering how the student body has itself changed during the Great Expansion.

THE STUDENT BODY

> *"The undergraduate system is so rigid – the English depart-ment are so stressed out and uptight...it's probably because they have so many people that they have to have such strict application of the rules and inflexibility. It's just like being kids at school again. I feel that the university views me as an annoyance."* English and Philosophy graduate

At the centre of the student experience is learning and at the centre of learning in a university is discussion with other students, both in class and outside class. A student's relationships with their peer group comprise one of the most important aspects of student life. Before expansion, students might have expected to engage with a collective of intelligent and motivated fellow undergraduates with an interest in their subject. Simply being at university put you and your fellow students in the top 15% of the population in academic ability. Today, such expectations do not apply in many universities. The student body has changed so much that this type of interaction is unlikely for all but a privileged minority. We can subdivide these changes into three areas: changes in scale, a widening ability range and a massive increase in international students.

1. Changes in scale
The student headcount has expanded by 300% during the last 30 years. This is an unprecedented growth for any major social insti-tution. Nonetheless, the systems and processes which underpin learning, teaching and assessment in universities (lectures, sem-inars and exams) have remained broadly unchanged. This means

that seminars that might have held half a dozen students now routinely hold 30 or more. Lectures that might have been for 200 students might now host 500. To operate on this scale, universities have adopted a mass–production factory model approach in their operations. This approach is, by necessity, focused on the needs of the *average* student rather than individual students. An academic lecturing hundreds of students has little chance of responding to them individually, let alone of developing relationships with individual students. The size of the student body provides limited space for personal interaction. For many students this is fine: they simply want to pass the module, bank the credits and move on. Studying is, for these students, an almost mechanical process in which the degree is a necessary stepping stone to hopefully a graduate job, rather than an end in itself. These students will generally seek to achieve their degree with the minimum of effort necessary to pass at the required grade.

For the bright student, interested in the subject, this factory approach to teaching is likely to be profoundly dissatisfying, affording them little encouragement to develop advanced subject knowledge or to achieve breadth or depth of understanding. For the less able student, this approach means that they can often receive little additional academic support to cope with the new demands of independent study.

2. A widening ability range

If students were once an intellectual elite, this is no longer the case. Given that the minimum entry requirements for some universities are equivalent to one or two grade Es at A–level, it is more remarkable if somebody can't gain entry. In 2012, the *Telegraph* noted that Leeds Metropolitan University offered entry to 97 degrees with two grade Es at A–level and waived the requirement on many degrees for GCSE grade Cs in maths and English.[50]

Because undergraduates were originally the most academically able, extending the university franchise has inevitably negatively skewed the overall ability range of all students. This means that, by definition, the average post–expansion student is less able. The effects of this can be seen across all UK universities, both in terms of a lack of essential background knowledge and a lack of ability amongst undergraduates (it can be difficult to disentangle the two). To illustrate this, we can return to the issue of undergraduate entry qualifications. Figure 1 shows undergraduate acceptances in 2010 by their UCAS tariff points. To put this into context, UCAS awards 140 points for an A* at A–level, 120 for an A, 100 for a B, 80 for a C, 60 for a D and 40 for an E Grade.

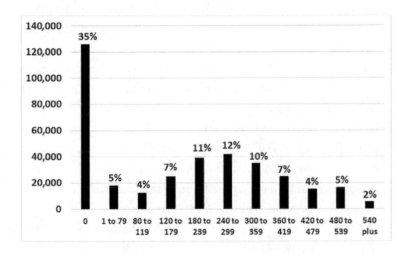

Figure 1 - 2010 UK undergraduate applicants enrolled by UCAS tariff points

These figures show that 35% of undergraduates enrolled with no tariff points at all and 51% of university undergraduates enrolled in 2010 with qualifications equivalent to a **DDD at A–level or worse** (180 or less UCAS points).

If we take into account three decades of A–level grade inflation, a massive increase in A–level retakes and the inclusion of AS–levels, 'key skills' and General Studies to boost an applicant's tariff points, then describing these students as DDD quality is being more than charitable. It is hard to put a positive spin on these students continuing to Higher Education. A minority of them might be more able than their exam results suggest as not all people perform to the best of their abilities in exams. But the majority have already spent their final two (or more) years at school demonstrating either a lack of motivation and/or aptitude for Higher Education.

The student ability range has not just widened at the bottom of the academic league tables, it has also blurred at the top. Due to grade inflation, it has become difficult for universities to distinguish between students holding similar GCSE and A–level grades. In 1980, gaining three As at A–level would have meant that a student was exceptional. Today, this is no longer the case. In 2006, Professor Mary Warnock of Cambridge University warned that: "The scandal is that not only are universities overwhelmed by the number of A grades, but that the possession of an A grade is no guarantee that its possessor can write intelligibly, read critically or think analytically." [51]

These problems of scale and a widening ability range interact with and amplify each other. Attempts to cater for a wider ability range and a lower average ability are often frustrated by the scale and size of the student body, which create further pressure towards uniform and worsening systems and processes for teaching, learning and assessment.

3. International students

UK universities have a proud tradition of educating international students who have gone on to great achievements in politics, arts and science. Expansion has seen a dramatic increase in the quantity of international students (Figure 2).

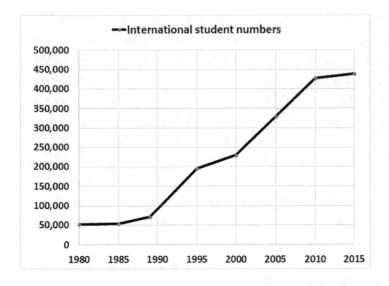

Figure 2 - The growth in international student numbers

However, there is ample evidence that the growth in the numbers of international students has been matched by a notable reduction in their average quality. This growth has not been driven by a desire to recruit the brightest and best from around the world. Rather, it reflects our universities' ability to charge these students whatever fees they wish and it has been achieved by lowering entry requirements – in particular, the standard of English as measured by International English Language Test (IELT) scores. In an investigation into IELTS in 2012, the *Telegraph* reported that:

> "... a combined 'band score' of 6.5 out of nine is needed in listening, reading, writing and speaking tests to play a full part in degree programmes. But it emerged that 58 out of 88 universities – including at least one member of the elite Russell Group – had a 'standard minimum' requirement for undergraduates of 6.0."[52]

This was corroborated by a *Times Higher Education Supplement* investigation which found that often linguistic "competence" was the best that could be hoped for from some international students.[53] Will "competence" really allow these students to read weighty academic books and debate and discuss complicated and abstract concepts at degree level? Further investigations from the *Telegraph* in 2012 suggested not:

> "… almost 66 per cent of institutions… are awarding places to undergraduates whose language skills are no better than 'competent'. Experts … suggested that the standard used to dictate entry to many universities was not good enough for academic courses."[54]

When the quality of international students declines, it affects the learning of other students in numerous ways. Some of these are obvious, as in this submission by a mature student to the House of Commons Select Committee in 2009:

> "I have taken modules where there are considerable numbers of students from all around the world. The varying abilities of the students, and their poor English, meant that I had the impression at times that things had to be pitched at the lowest common denominator. … one of my lecturers was being asked to slow his lectures down so that the significant number of Chinese students could follow what he was saying. His speed was fine for native English speakers, so I would assume that any slowing down will have an impact on the material covered."[55]

Other effects are less noticeable but more damaging. They can include a reduction in the complexity of material taught and a downwards pressure on the standard of assessment. Even more troubling is pressure placed on academics to mark weak but lucrative international students to less demanding standards.[56] The uncomfortable reality is captured in this comment from an understandably anonymous academic on the Guardian website:

> "...ask thousands of teachers and lecturers about what they think of IELTS indicators, as reflected in the quality of many international students coming into their courses, and you are likely to get the big thumbs down. At the same time, whole departments are kept open, and jobs are maintained, because of this cosy process."[57]

In 2012, Professor Susan Bassnet, a former pro–vice chancellor of Warwick University and an external examiner for other universities, described colleagues asking her to "disregard linguistic competence and focus on content". She noted that some students she encountered had such poor standards of English that they "wouldn't scrape a GCSE."[58]

Whilst UK universities still recruit bright and capable international students, they also recruit many who are neither. And this necessarily detracts from the overall learning experience. This situation is certainly not the fault of these students. If anything, they receive the worst value of any students. Though they'll still all get their degrees for which they, or much more likely their parents, will have paid so much.

MORE IS WORSE

Students who have barely squeezed through A–levels or equivalents or who have a limited grasp of English are now fed into a Higher Education system that is not designed for them. Because these changes have occurred over four decades, their effects have emerged incrementally and hence individually they have appeared to be relatively harmless. Taken cumulatively, however, their impact has been profoundly damaging, meaning that a student today is likely to have an inferior learning experience to a student on the same course 30 years ago.

MONEY

Not only does wealth improve your chances of attending the best universities, it also radically affects your experience at any university. Today, there are multiple student experiences and they often depend on what a student can afford. If you're poor, then you're more likely to study at your local university living at home for the three years and missing much of the *Young Ones* or *Brideshead* student experience on the grounds of cost. These students' choices are driven less by the reputation of a university or specific degree than the prospect of free accommodation with their parents and the relative cost and ease of commuting.

Students without financial support are also likely to work part-time during study or to undertake part-time study whilst working. Research by Universities UK in 2005 identified a growing trend towards a two-tier student experience: "Of those who worked during term time, 80% said they missed study time to do so, 51% said their assignments suffered and 42% missed lectures." The report described student experiences that were increasingly polarised by students' family background:

> "… higher income students … don't need to work in term time and do interesting work in holidays to enhance their CVs. Then there are those who have to work in term time and whose academic work suffers. The work they do is for short-term cash benefit rather than long-term career benefit."[59]

This fragmentation by ability to pay is even reflected at student union events. In 2009, for example, the Birmingham University Guild of Students offered Gold, Silver and Bronze Freshers' packages:

> "Students who can afford the gold package at £65 'don't miss a single thing!'. Bronze students (£45) miss out on

N–Dubz and Calvin Harris, but do go to the ball. Sadly,
there's no ball for the sub–bronze students who can only
stump up £9; …they get a trip to Cadbury World to see
how chocolate buttons are made."[60]

Students without financial support face a choice between racking
up more debt or largely opting out of a social life. Most, immersed
in a debt–fuelled university system, choose increasing debt. In
2014, research by the NUS found nearly 50% of students required
financial support from their parents, 11% relied on credit cards
and 2% made use of pay–day loans with enormous interest rates.[61]
Applying these percentages to the wider student population suggests
that over 200,000 students are using credit cards and over 40,000
students are using pay–day loans.

The full extent of parental support was revealed in a 2009
report on student spending by the Royal Bank of Scotland (RBS):

"More than half of all students (52%) are receiving the
same or more parental support than the same period last
year (2008). Of their children's weekly term–time income,
parents are contributing 61% (£69.51) compared with 58%
in 2008 (£64.12)"[62]

The reality is that today's students spend a lot more than they
receive in funding from the state and this gap needs to be plugged
somehow – the bank of mum and dad for those who have access to
such facilities or further debt for those who don't.

In 2013, the NUS reported that many students were struggling
to meet their daily living costs, with an estimated average annual
shortfall of around £7,600. At no point does anybody complicit in
this system (the government, universities, banks, student unions)
suggest that more debt might be a bad thing. The default option is
always to push another line of credit. After all, repayment can wait
until the graduate job arrives. The behaviour that this hardwires is

to spend without regard to the consequences – something that has potentially profound implications not just for students but for our society as a whole.

Financial reality generally sinks in after graduation, when graduates have debt but not the means to repay it, or worse when compound interest increases their debt faster than their repayments can keep up. Ironically, by cramming ever–increasing numbers of students into universities in the name of equality, we have also greatly increased existing economic inequalities in the nature of the student experience. Compared with the 1970's, when most students had their fees paid for them and received maintenance grants to cover basic living expenses, state funding is now spread more thinly across a massively increased cohort of students. Those with money can top this up, those without cannot avoid going into debt. Expansion has created a university experience that is nominally the same, but is in reality now segregated by the ability to pay.

ACCOMMODATION

With the exception of tuition fees, accommodation is the single biggest contributor to levels of student debt. Making new friends via the random allocation of students to halls of residence is a rite of passage at university. For many students, however, this experience is no longer available as their university's accommodation has been stretched past breaking point during expansion. Many universities no longer have the capacity to offer accommodation to all first–year students. Typically, those universities which have grown most have been those with the least money to spend on building new accommodation. The results can be seen all around the country every October:

> "Up to 800 students at De Montfort University in Leicester and 300 at the University of Hertfordshire have been temporarily housed in hotels and B&Bs because there

were no rooms left on campus. Aberdeen has put up 80 students in a Premier Lodge, while Warwick has booked 145 rooms in a private apartment block in Coventry."[63]

Some students find themselves in temporary accommodation for weeks on end. This could be caravans, university gymnasiums or even holiday camps:

> "Edge Hill University was scoping out a Pontins holiday camp in search of emergency accommodation for first-year undergraduates. A spokeswoman said that *'in a year when we have experienced increases in demand for our courses, there are a number of students looking for options off campus'.*"[64]

Often these students have to wait for other undergraduates to drop out, making places in student lets and halls available.[65] Perhaps this situation slightly resembles Stalingrad, where Russian soldiers, sent into the attack against German positions, were issued with one rifle for every two, or even every three, men – many had to wait till a fellow soldier was shot before they could get their hands on a weapon. On the plus side, in some universities they won't be waiting long. Drop-out rates for first-year students at some newer universities, where there is less available accommodation due to greater expansion, can be over 30% and tend to be much higher than at more traditional universities where student numbers haven't increased so much. Moreover, first-year students without a place in halls can find themselves living miles away from campus in expensive private accommodation. Late arrivals, such as clearing students, are particularly likely to find themselves in this position. This can result in social isolation and probably contributes to the higher drop-out rates amongst clearing students.[66]

The scarcity of student accommodation is now reflected in its cost. In 2016, a National Union of Students survey estimated

average weekly rents in university accommodation at **£134.23.**
Back in 2002, this figure was **£59.17.**[67] In 2016, private providers
charged an average weekly rent of £169.94. In 2009, this figure was
£112.[68] These are massive increases, well above the rate of inflation.
Research by the student housing charity, Unipol, suggests that these
increases are routinely outpacing the wider rental market. Between
2010 and 2013, student rents rose by 25%. In comparison, across
the rental sector as a whole the rise was 13%.[69] This is a key factor
in the mushrooming of graduate debt and a growing cost-of-living
crisis for students.

It isn't just the cost but also the duration of their accommodation contracts that cause problems. In the private sector, students
might want to rent a house for the 40 to 42 weeks of term time.
But demand often makes the best accommodation near campus a
sellers' market. Consequently, many students find themselves forced
to pay rent for a full year. The taxpayer, often via student loans, is
therefore paying to keep tens of thousands of houses and flats empty
for months during a national housing shortage.

At some point during expansion, many universities jettisoned
the notion of providing decent basic accommodation at low cost to
their students, relying instead on private companies to provide new
accommodation. In 2013, Unipol estimated that overseas investors
were responsible for around 80% of new student accommodation
built.[70] This accommodation is generally high-end, expensive and
beyond the means of students dependent on maintenance loans.
In Exeter city centre, for example, luxury student accommodation
can cost up to £10,710 per year and in 2018, purpose-built student
accommodation in Bournemouth ranged from around £6,000 a year
to £8,000 for a 40- to 42-week academic year. In 2018, the annual
student maintenance loan was £8,430 for a student living away from
home studying at a university outside London and £11,002 if living
away from home and studying in London. Out of this, a student is
expected to pay for accommodation, bills, transport, food, comput-
ers, social life and books.[71]

SAFETY

Money and accommodation are both issues that we would expect to directly affect student life. Something that we hear less about is student safety. University prospectuses might enthuse about the cultural activities awaiting young people in their host town. They are less likely to mention crime. It can be a major concern though. In 2008, the *Independent* reported that: "It is estimated that around a third of all of students will fall victim to some form of crime while at university."[72]

Gauging the full extent of this problem is difficult. In 2010, research from the NUS suggested that 40% of students had been subject to antisocial behaviour or crime.[73] Again, problems with crime are not experienced equally by students. Those studying in cities are particularly exposed as university buildings and student accommodation are often concentrated in areas within those cities with reputations for being crime hot spots:

> "Manchester has toppled Nottingham from pole position of most crime-ridden university city outside London. The city beats all others for the number of burglaries, robberies and crimes of violence put together. The second most crime-ridden city is Nottingham, followed by Liverpool, Bristol and Leeds."[74]

For those studying in more pleasant, green-leafed campuses, such threats are minimal. The *Independent* noted that the safest places to study were Lancaster, Canterbury and Bath – three "old" universities set apart from their cities on green campuses.[75] Student life in inner cities can be quite different, though. In 2000, the *Guardian* reported: "In Manchester, last year, there were 1,000 street robberies in a two and a half mile radius of the universities."[76] The situation had not improved by 2008: "100,000 students in Manchester make up a fifth of the *city's* population but are estimated to form between a quarter and a third of its robbery victims. One third of those who come to the university become victims of crime."[77]

Or for that matter by 2014 when *The Complete University Guide*, which publishes a list of crime rates for over a hundred universities and colleges, ranked Manchester as having the highest levels of student–relevant crime (robberies, burglaries and violent crime) in a city with two or more universities.[78] By 2018, students at Manchester, Bradford and the LSE were five times more likely to be affected by crime than students at York, Reading or Winchester.

The problem facing Manchester and other cities is that of "studentification", a social phenomenon in which areas become saturated with students and then act as a magnet for crime and antisocial behaviour. Students are the most expensive demographic group to insure, often arriving on campus with MP3 players, iPads, bikes and other high–value and easily–transportable items. For the enterprising criminal, this means that student accommodation contains multiple examples of these readily 'stealable' objects, as the website for the South Yorkshire Police noted: "Ten per cent of students are likely to be burgled, collectively having £34.65m worth of possessions stolen. As many as 38,500 people who are starting university this September could have their accommodation broken into... with items worth an average of £900 taken in each burglary."[79]

This information is only based on the items reported as stolen, the real figures for theft will be much higher. In some major cities, however, it isn't just a desire for financial gain that lies behind anti–student crime statistics. More concerning is the trend for students in these areas being mugged or even assaulted simply for being students. There is plenty of evidence of gang rituals in which assaulting a student is an initiation rite. To give an idea of the scale of this problem in Sheffield in 2014, within six weeks the South Yorkshire police recorded 43 violent crimes against students. Whilst this led to a student safety campaign in 2015, it still represented seven students being assaulted per week in just one UK city.[80] Unfortunately, some urban police forces are still perceived as viewing this type of violent crime as just part and parcel of the student experience.

Universities have also been criticised for failing to alert students to potential dangers, worrying instead about their reputations. As the *Guardian* noted in 2008:

> "Universities were nervous about highlighting the risks. *There is sensitivity around using the "crime" word because that worries parents,'* said Professor Alex Hirschfield, *'But you are importing a large cohort of potentially vulnerable people who are not used to living in inner-city areas. We would argue that universities are benefiting from fees and it would be positive for them to address the issue'.*"[81]

Whilst some elite research universities are located in poor inner-city areas, there is a greater preponderance of new universities in such areas, which explains why these universities are more likely to be found near the top of crime charts. This returns us to the two-tier student experience – because students from poorer backgrounds are more likely to attend such universities, they are also more likely *on average* to be affected by crime targeting students.

THE 'STEPFORD STUDENTS'

There is one other pressure on student life – a growing pressure towards social and political conformity on campus. Whilst university has traditionally been about individualism, exploration and discovery, today there appears to be a growing requirement for students to look, sound and even think alike. The journalist Brendan O'Neill, discussing his experience of students attempting to shut down debates or silence opinions that they deemed offensive, described what he was faced with as "*the Stepford Students*":

"…they look like students, dress like students, smell like students. But their student brains have been replaced by brains bereft of critical faculties and programmed to conform… anyone who's spent more than five minutes in their company will know that these students are far more interested in shutting debate down than opening it up."

Mr O'Neill's offence had been to accept an invitation from a student society at Oxford University to discuss abortion with another male journalist. After protests by feminist groups, the event was eventually cancelled. As males, it was apparently unacceptable to protestors that either should contribute to a discussion on this subject.

This experience is not an isolated exception. Instead it is a reflection of a growing norm of intolerance amongst students. This new norm only permits an increasingly narrow and politically-correct set of social attitudes and views and seeks to exile or silence anybody who would dare dissent. It is for this reason that the *"Stepford Students"* label has drawn such attention – it neatly defines a growing sense of totalitarianism on campus, coupled with a detachment from reality that is beyond satire. Anything which is deemed offensive – Red Indian head dresses, heterosexual men cross-dressing, a pop song with the 'wrong' lyrics, clapping, statues, the formation of a men's society – is banned in the name of creating 'safe spaces' for students. Moreover, student groups now regularly campaign for 'trigger warnings' on books which contain material that they might find or believe other people might find 'upsetting'.

Anybody who wants to speak at a university, but may say something that challenges this orthodoxy, is banned or 'no-platformed' with monotonous regularity. Student activists should be proud that the list of 'no-platformees' is becoming increasingly diverse. After all, where else might one hope to find Nigel Farage, Peter Tatchell, Germaine Greer and Nick Griffin (the former leader of the British National Party) keeping company?

There are many possible causes for this shift towards conformity and censorship – a lower average intellectual level of the student cohort, the pervasiveness of social media, a sense of debt-induced ennui or the troublesome notion that any institution adopting factory processes and scale is likely over time to become populated by and to produce drones. Whatever the explanation for this phenomenon, there is no justification for it in Higher Education. Students might not have much control over their high tuition fees, the accommo-dation on offer, the loans system or the size of the student body. But individually and collectively they either shape or are complicit in the shaping of their intellectual environment. If freedom of thought and expression is the lifeblood of the university, then conformity and censorship are pathogens.

Ultimately, it is students who promote these agendas and it is other students who let them, either by supporting them, ignoring them or failing to challenge them. That there isn't a greater backlash, a louder protest about such fundamental issues as the loss of free speech is perhaps the most significant and worrying illustration of today's campus conformity.

Being a student today doesn't sound like much fun. Shoddy or expensive accommodation, *de facto* segregation by income, dress codes, the prospect of getting mugged or, worse still, the censorious attention of the campus thought police. And then there's the prob-lem of overcrowding of most university facilities and decreasing face-to-face time with lecturers and tutors. To the casual observer, much of student life now appears to foster a sense of dependence, grievance, limitation and restriction rather than optimism, inde-pendence, personal growth and freedom. While many students will still thrive at university, there is little doubt that the Great Expansion has made student life worse for the majority.

CHAPTER FOUR

LEARNING: YOU'RE ON YOUR OWN

"A professor is one who talks in someone else's sleep."
W. H. Auden[82]

"The discipline of colleges and universities is in general contrived, not for the benefit of students, but for the interest, or more properly speaking, for the ease of their masters." Adam Smith, *The Wealth of Nations*[83]

Academics receiving criticism for their teaching is not a new phenomenon. During the 18th and 19th centuries the standards of teaching at Oxford and Cambridge universities were roundly condemned by many of their most illustrious alumni. Amongst the complainants were Adam Smith, Jeremy Bentham, Edward Gibbon, Shelley, Byron and Wordsworth. Byron's 1806 poem *Thoughts Suggested by a College Examination* captures the spirit of these complaints, caricaturing his teachers as:

"Dull as the pictures, which adorn their halls,
They think all learning fix'd within their walls"[84]

Similar reactions, encompassing the comic to the frustrated to the sad can be found dotted throughout the 19th and 20th centuries in the writing of Tennyson, Auden, Larkin and Amis, amongst others. During expansion, this tradition continued in the satirical campus novels of Malcolm Bradbury and David Lodge.

What these criticisms have in common is that they sprang from the same source – regular, prolonged, or even too prolonged, exposure to multiple academics and their assorted pedagogic and behavioural foibles. For most undergraduates studying today, however, it is unlikely that their university affords them the exposure required to develop either contempt or admiration for their academics. This is because many of the variables that determine teaching quality, such as contact hours, assessment quantity and quality, teacher experience and the size of seminars have worsened significantly during the Great Expansion. Undergraduates pay more but receive less on each measure than they did thirty years ago. In 2012, the *Times Higher Education Supplement* reported how students at Manchester University: "... used the Freedom of Information Act to obtain figures showing that social science students had half as much contact time as Manchester students 20 years earlier."[85]

This is now a serious issue for many students. In 2014, a report from *Which University?* noted that 32% of students felt that their courses were not providing value for money, a significant increase from 16% in a similar survey in 2006. The report also noted that students receiving relatively low levels of academic contact time were three times more likely to feel aggrieved about this issue.[86] Post expansion, it could seem that the higher course fees rise, the fewer hours of contact students have with those paid by those rising fees to teach them.

University apologists insist that contact hours are a misleading guide to quality; they mention the importance of informal learning and refer to the quality of teaching hours rather than the quantity. These caveats are, frankly, meaningless in a system where the size and quality of the student cohort has altered so dramatically. Effective informal and peer–to–peer learning is less likely to occur when many students have been pressured into going to Uni because they felt everyone else was going and when there is a very wide range of abilities amongst students. Moreover, huge courses with large cohorts of international students tend towards fragmentation along nationality and language lines preventing, rather than encouraging, integration. Equally, it is hard to see how academics teaching seminars the size of school classes can possibly provide a better quality of teaching than they would have done in seminars with half a dozen students prior to expansion.

The reality of expansion is that bigger means worse. In 1976, the average student-to-teacher ratio was 8.6:1 By 2013/14 this had almost doubled to 17.1:1. In newer universities, with fewer staff and more students, it can be higher still.[87] UK universities are also falling behind their international competitors on this important measure. The average student-to-teacher ratio at universities in the thirty member states of the Organisation for Economic Co-operation and Development was 15:1 in 2011.[88]

This ratio affects every interaction between students and academics. It increases the size of lectures and seminars and reduces the frequency and length of personal tutorials. Many students are now lucky to get two 15-minute slots with their personal tutor during an academic year. In 2011, the National Union of Students launched a campaign calling for universities to implement a *minimum* standard of every student seeing their personal tutor once a term:

> "All students are entitled to a personal tutor and should meet them *at least once a term*; the National Union of Students said this week. The union also calls for students to have the right to change their tutor, for all staff to be given full training on the role, and for published 'minimum requirements' in the area."[89]

The NUS charter asks that each student gets to meet their personal tutor at least six times during the course of their three-year degree. That the NUS offered the charter as 'an aspiration' underlines the fact that many universities currently fall below even this basic threshold. In 2006, the *Guardian* spoke to a final-year psychology student at the University of Manchester who stated that: "We never had one-on-one sessions with a lecturer. We didn't have seminars until this year – it was just lectures and occasionally a lab class, with 90 students there. We are paying all this money in tuition fees and we have had no one-on-one contact."[90]

A *Which University?* report from 2014 also showed major variations in academic contact time across universities. For example, despite paying the same fees for their psychology degrees, students at the University of Exeter received four hours of academic contact a week, whilst students at Durham University received ten. It is hard to square such variable contact hours with the identical fees charged by both universities – unless, of course, the psychology lecturers at Exeter are more than twice as good at teaching as those at Durham or their students are more than twice as intelligent as those at Durham.

Part of the problem, especially within research–intensive universities, is that increasing numbers of academic staff do little actual teaching. Instead, they are employed to generate more research funding for universities. Despite having minimal or no interaction with students, these academics are usually counted as teaching staff to improve apparent student/staff ratios. Clearly, reduced contact time leaves limited opportunity for students to build a relationship with academics in general and their personal tutor specifically. This is a key concern considering that personal tutors are usually the first port of call for a graduate job reference. By 2007, UK academics were complaining anonymously to the *Times Higher Education Supplement* about having to teach seminar groups of 35 students or more.[91] In 2008, 71% of academics surveyed by the University and Colleges Union said that they had seen seminar sizes increase in their institutions over the previous decade.[92]

Sadly, the Higher Education Statistics Agency (HESA) does not collect data on average seminar/class sizes. In 2008, Professor Bruce Charlton, then of Newcastle University, suggested why this might be the case: "I doubt that universities will publish class size data unless they are made to do so. University bosses probably feel too embarrassed to admit the real situation: nobody wants to be first above the parapet with shocking statistics."[93]

Problems of scale aside, there is widespread evidence that many students are very unhappy with the quality of teaching they receive. The experience of this graduate was common to many of those interviewed for this book:

> *"The teaching was horrendous in both schools of the university. The academics were not really teachers. They didn't have communication skills; they weren't there to teach us, they weren't good at teaching. Whatever I did to learn at university was done by myself; the teachers didn't help in any way."* Finance and management graduate

In the UK there is no requirement for academics to undertake any teaching training – a much greater priority is placed on the link between research activity and teaching on the bemusing assumption that teaching is always improved by research. This somewhat dubious proposition often dies a cold and lonely death in overcrowded lecture halls and seminar rooms crammed full of bored, fretful students. A student submission to the House of Commons Select Committee in 2009 noted:

> "In a lot of lectures, the entire year group are made to feel like an inconvenience. Complaints go unheard, student reps seem to be ignored even when the same complaints arise, and the bog–standard answer to most requests for help seems to be *'You should know it already, so I won't tell you.'* ….. if 10/20 students on a course of 80 (down from 130 in year 1) are all asking the same things, shouldn't this set off alarm bells?"[94]

This apparent disinterest in how the student receives and understands material and in how well the teacher transmits knowledge reflects the core belief within UK universities that an undergraduate has to make sense of a subject for themselves through independent study. But as a result of the Great Expansion, we are now sending many students to universities who have neither the capacity nor the motivation for this type of independent study. To successfully widen the pool of students attending university, either teaching methods or the new students needed to adapt. This did not happen and a system designed for a smaller cohort of bright students, who were genuinely capable of independent study, was scaled up without adaptation or proportionate resources to accommodate a much larger but less able, more dependent cohort of students.

The problems this causes were picked up by several students in the House of Commons Select Committee report in 2009. This comment is typical: "...university lecturers seriously need to take lessons from school teachers on how to teach. They are clever [...] but they are not skilled at conveying the message. They talk to us like we are fellow professionals who understand everything."[95]

Whilst seminars traditionally allowed students to ask academics questions about the lecture material they either didn't understand or slept through, they now rarely get this opportunity. Most seminar classes are taken by postgraduate students or researchers, rather than academics. These postgraduates are generally only a few years older than the students and unlikely to have either teaching or research qualifications:

> *"The seminar classes were predominantly held by research students who were not very old. They were not qualified to teach. ...."* Economics graduate

The postgraduates are also increasingly likely to be part-time and/or from overseas, often lacking subject knowledge, time and sometimes even a basic command of English:

> *"We had foreign language research students doing English, who were taking on first-year seminars about the structure of the English language and they couldn't speak it properly themselves."* English and cultural studies graduate

This is grim and tedious for the silent majority. It is desperately depressing for the motivated minority and, of course, the post-graduates themselves. This is the Great University Expansion in action – huge class sizes, inexperienced teachers and the majority of students exhibiting total disinterest:

> "*Often we would do presentations during seminars and you got the impression that was just the lecturer's or PhD student's way of avoiding having to do any preparation for the class themselves – it meant that many classes just felt unstructured.*" English and philosophy graduate

A significant number of individual submissions to the House of Commons Select Committee in 2009 painted a similar picture:

> "...the worst offenders are the PhD students ... employed to run lab sessions (in which they refuse to help), mark coursework (which is always carried out suspiciously quickly and inconsistently) and give lacklustre tutorial sessions (these involve a couple of half-baked PowerPoint slides and quickly deteriorate into having a chat)."[96]

UNDERWORKED AND OVERPAYING?

The reduction in hours spent teaching doesn't tell the full story, however. We must also look at how today's students are supposed to spend around half of their time – on self-directed learning. Research in 2007 by the Higher Education Policy Institute (HEPI) looked at the total workloads of UK students, including formal and informal learning. What they found was a growing variability for students studying the same courses at different universities:

> "Students on medicine and dentistry courses might be working for anything between 29 and 45 hours a week,

those studying biological sciences between 19 and 43 hours, while in history the difference ranged from between 17 and 18 to more than 32 hours depending on the university."[97]

Follow-up research in 2009, 2012 and 2013 found similar variations in workloads between different universities in the same subject areas: "In historical and philosophical studies, the loads ranged from 39.5 hours in the most demanding institutions to just 14 hours in the least."[98]

Graham Gibbs, former director of the Institute for the Advancement of University Learning at Oxford University, provided a commentary on the initial 2006 research, noting: "...a significant minority of UK students are enrolled full-time but studying part-time with their university receiving funding for full-time students".[99]

A 2013 *Which University?* survey supported this contention, suggesting that the average student workload appeared to be around 900 hours per year, 25% less than the 1,200 assumed by both universities and their regulatory body for academic standards, the Quality Assurance Agency. The *Times Higher Education Supplement* reported Richard Lloyd, executive director of *Which University?* asking whether this: "...raises questions over standards and whether students are being pushed hard enough."[100]

The same year, the *Times Higher Education Supplement* analysed data from the Higher Education Policy Institute/*Which University?* student hours survey. This revealed significant differences in student workload between types of universities, showing that students at research-intensive universities had higher average workloads than their counterparts at new universities.[101] Does this mean that the quality of teaching is so much better at some universities that they only require part-time learning for a full-time course? Or does it mean that less is taught and less is learned? It is hard to reconcile significant differences in workloads with the idea of a consistent standard and similar costs for UK degrees across all of our universities.

The only consistency that this research found in the workload of UK undergraduates was that they were on average significantly lower than those of their international peers:

"(UK) Students typically receive an average of about 14 hours tuition a week and spend 12 hours in private study. This 26-hour workload compares unfavourably with European figures suggesting 41 hours in Portugal, 35 in France, 34 in Germany."[102]

In other words, UK-based students do considerably less work for their degrees than their European counterparts (Figure 1).

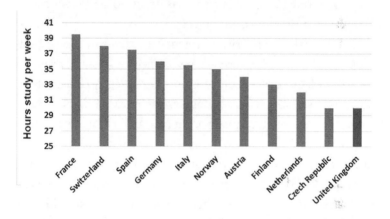

Figure 1 - European undergraduate weekly work (hours) CHERI project 2007 [103]

Perhaps UK-based students are more intelligent and/or UK academics more talented than their European counterparts? Alternatively, maybe UK degrees require less learning to pass and are therefore of a lower standard?

ASSESSMENT

"On an exam paper I answered less than half the questions, but still ended up with over 50% marks."
Engineering graduate

The ability range of students has widened, the average quality has declined and their workload has diminished, yet the grades that they are achieving have improved dramatically during expansion. Somewhat miraculously, this trend has occurred across almost all UK universities in almost all subjects.

Traditionally, universities provide two forms of assessment; *formative* and *summative*. Formative assessment (e.g. essays) relates to informal work that doesn't count towards a final degree classification. Summative assessment (e.g. exams) on the other hand does count. Formative assessment normally occurs through regular essays and coursework which are marked by academics and returned with advice and guidance to prompt further study and independent learning. Oxford and Cambridge still require formative assessment, but very few other UK universities do. This type of assessment **should** lie at the heart of learning within Higher Education, acting as an ongoing dialogue between students and academics throughout a degree.

Formative assessment is intensive, requiring a significant additional workload for academics and students alike. Classroom–based degrees at Oxbridge require students to produce (and academics to mark) an essay a week. Whilst this places more pressure on students, it also provides room for failure and experimentation and the opportunity to learn without worrying about grades. Professor Graham Gibbs describes it thus:

> "Students work hardest when there is a high volume of formative–only assessment and oral feedback – typically writing essays that don't count towards their degree result, but for which they have to cover a range of material. This

is the Oxford and Cambridge model and used to be the case at most universities 30 years ago."[104]

Failure and experimentation are incompatible with the factory–scale processes expansion has created within universities. The increasing number of students (who should be) attending seminars and lectures has spread university teaching resources ever more thinly, reducing time for marking and oral feedback. One of the easiest and least visible areas for universities to cut spending has been formative assessment. Because it isn't measured, it is simple to dismiss and easy to underestimate and understate its value. Academics might appreciate the importance of formative assessment. But how can they be expected to argue for it when they are already being asked to do more work for more students with fewer resources? Most students can't be expected to complain about reduced workloads either. As a result, formative assessment has mostly disappeared. Unfortunately, the weakest students at the weakest universities, who have the most to benefit from regular and consistent formative assessment, are probably the least likely to receive it.

The situation with summative assessment, which students undertake in the form of exams and coursework, is not much better. Even if students receive feedback on their summative assessments, it is often confusing and unhelpful, giving them little indication as to how they can improve their work. In 2006, the National Student Survey found that 49% of students were unhappy with the quality of assessment feedback.[105] Similar concerns were raised repeatedly in student submissions to the House of Commons Select Committee in 2009. This situation had not improved by 2013, when 78% of students in that year's Student Academic Experience Survey failed to describe their assessment feedback as prompt. In the same survey less than 25% of students described academics as "putting a lot of effort into commenting on their work".[106]

Whilst these findings are concerning, the real fault lies not with academics but with a university system which has failed to adapt or adequately resource its assessment processes post expansion. A three– (or, as is often the case now, a two–) hour exam is a rather primitive method of investigating how well a student has understood a subject, yet it remains the dominant model of assessment in universities. These exams were designed for bright academic students in relatively small groups.

The problems this poses become evident when we consider the mechanics involved in a student completing and an academic marking a three–hour exam script. The average student might write four A4 pages an hour over a three–hour period, many will write substantially more. This means at least 12 pages per exam script. In the worst case scenario, the exam scripts are for a module with 400 or more students, making a total of a minimum of 4,800 pages of marking. The normal academic week is 37.5 hours. The average exam marking turnaround time is two weeks. This means 75 hours (4,500 minutes) to read and mark 400 scripts comprised of 4,800 pages. This leaves less than one minute per each page to read and mark an exam script, assuming the academic doesn't take too many coffee or comfort breaks. Usually, the academic will put in a large amount of overtime during this period to mark the scripts. But even an extra 20 hours each week isn't going to make that much difference to the limited amount of time spent on each page. Moreover, the academic's other work will also continue during this period.

The subjects being marked and the marking criteria are also complex, making it difficult to read at pace whilst providing fair and consistent marking. How do academics cope with fatigue, stress or even RSI? One possible solution was proposed by a graduate interviewed for this book:

> *".... within a week you'd have your mark back and some exams have three or four hundred students sitting them. I asked to see my papers and on more than half of them there wasn't even a tick mark on them. I don't believe that these lecturers had actually read some of the exam papers. I think*

*that there was a lot of skim reading with no real structure
for the marks."* Finance graduate

Assessment is also probably easier when the majority (around 67%)
of grades awarded nowadays are Firsts or Upper Seconds. In many
cases, academics marking papers may just be asking: are the basic
points present in the essay, is the writing comprehensible, do the
answers contain references to reading? If so, then it's probably a
First or an Upper Second.

Learning, teaching and assessment lie at the heart of Higher
Education and expansion has seen a massive dilution in the quality
of each of these areas.

CHAPTER FIVE

STANDARDS: DUMBING DOWN

UK universities confer over 420,000 undergraduate degrees each year. These are awarded within one of five categories: Firsts, Upper Seconds (2:1), Lower Seconds (2:2), Thirds and General or Unclassified degrees. Firsts are the best grades and Unclassified the worst.

Many employers now specify a minimum requirement of a First or a 2:1 for potential applicants. As a result, most undergraduates worry constantly about whether or not they will achieve a 2:1. In a 2012 *Times Higher Education Supplement* survey, 72% of students listed achieving a 2:1 degree as among their top concerns.[107] Statistically speaking, today's students shouldn't worry too much. In 2015, the Higher Education Statistics Agency recorded that 67% of graduates achieved either a First or a 2:1.[108] So the majority of today's students will get one of these top two grades. This has neatly inverted the classification pattern from 1970, when roughly 33% of students achieved one of these two top grades.[109] Figure 1 shows the different proportion of degree classifications awarded in 2015 compared to 1994.

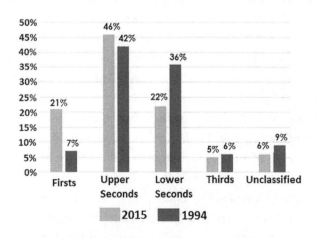

Figure 1 - Degree awards in 2015 and 1994[110]

The proportion of first class degrees awarded has **tripled** during this period from 7% to 21% and the proportion of degrees awarded at 2:1 or above has risen from 49% to 67%. For this to occur, whilst the average ability of students has declined and the average teaching hours per student have reduced, is a truly miraculous achievement and surely something to be celebrated. As one would expect, the grades at the bottom of the classification system have declined by a similar amount to the increase in top degrees. UK universities now award a lot fewer 2:2s than they did 30 years ago and slightly fewer third–class and unclassified degrees.

This pattern can be seen across almost all universities and almost all subjects, but the rate of degree inflation is most marked in elite universities. In a submission to the House of Commons Select Committee in 2009, Professor Mainz Yorke stated that:

> "...the period 1994–2002 showed that the percentage of 'good honours degrees' [...] tended to rise in almost all subject areas... the rises were most apparent in the elite 'Russell Group' universities."[111]

The trend towards better degree classifications is most pronounced at Oxford and Cambridge. Both universities now award around **25%** of their students a first class degree. This has not always been the case, as the think tank Civitas pointed out in a 2005 report: "In 1960, Oxford awarded 8.5% Firsts and 33% Thirds. In 2002, the number of Firsts awarded was 23% and Thirds, 8.5%."[112]

There are two possible explanations for this apparently admirable academic achievement. The first is optimistic. It could be the result of brighter students, better prepared to learn and absorb knowledge by schools and universities using improved teaching methods and new learning technologies. The second, more pessimistic explanation is that these performance improvements are nothing of the sort. Instead, they are just another result of the Great Expansion at work – a savage devaluation that creates a gap between the nominal value of these grades and the actual level of learning and understanding that students have achieved.

The evidence for the second explanation is convincing. It is not even that there are yearly variations around a general upward trend in degree classifications. Instead, as with A–levels and GCSEs, there is a year upon year incremental improvement, almost regardless of subject or university. Common sense might suggest that in some years the performances of staff or students would dip. Instead, we have near universal and constant improvement, an unlikely statistical phenomenon with all the authenticity of Soviet tractor production statistics. This raises the question as to who is responsible for the maintenance of degree standards.

Universities are independent organisations with the right to confer their own academic qualifications. They do, however, have nominal checks and balances on this right. Firstly, university courses are reviewed by the Qualifications Assurance Agency (QAA), a regulatory body set up by the government to monitor the standard of teaching in universities. Secondly, universities also have external moderators on each credit–bearing course that they provide. These are subject experts from other universities who moderate and validate samples of students' work and academics' marks, putting their stamp of professional authority and expertise on the university's grades.

The reality is that both the QAA and the external moderator system are paper tigers. At the parliamentary inquiry (17 July 2008) the chairman of the House of Commons' Select Committee on Universities condemned the QAA as 'a toothless old dog' and declared that the British degree classification system had 'descended into farce'. Neither the QAA nor external moderators have much power to safeguard against falling standards and grade inflation. This arrangement is not accidental. It operates the way that universities, funding bodies and the government intended it to – quality assurance in name rather than function. If it means that 67% of students now receive Firsts or 2:1s, then 67% of students and their parents are unlikely to complain. This perception is likely to change, however, when these same students start receiving rejection letters from company after company because they are now competing against so many other students with their own Firsts and 2:1s.

Complaints can certainly be heard from many graduate employers who find that our degree grades are not stable against time and certainly not consistent across universities. The Association of Graduate Recruiters has voiced concerns that the 2:1 has become devalued and is not trusted as a guide to a prospective candidate's ability:

> "Companies are dropping their requirement for graduate recruits to have a 2:1 degree because they believe the grade is being handed out inconsistently and can no longer be relied on to represent a high level of achievement."[113]

The same point has been made by Professor Alan Smithers, from the University of Buckingham: "...employers no longer fully trust degree results, and tend to look back to A–level results as a more reliable indicator. A First is no longer a First."[114]

The issue of degree inflation was first raised fourteen years ago in Parliament by Lord Matthew Oakeshott, a Liberal Democrat peer, who described these figures as:

> "...giving a sense of 'dumbing down' in Britain's universities. Students and prospective employers need assurance that degree standards are reliable and stable, not devalued currency."[115]

Perhaps the most compelling evidence of a problem can be found in the huge differences between the average marks required by different universities to achieve different grades. Traditionally, a student was required to achieve an average mark of 70% or above across all of their exams to achieve a First. This is no longer the case, as a Civitas report from 2005 outlined:

"...there is a large disparity between institutions in the marks required to achieve a first class degree, ranging from 68.7% at the University of East Anglia, to just 50.8% at Sunderland University. Moreover, on average, it is the newer universities that require lower marks for a First."[116]

In 2008, Peter Williams, the head of the Quality Assurance Agency, the organisation meant to safeguard academic standards at universities, admitted to the *Guardian* that: "...the current degree classification system is arbitrary and unreliable. The way that degrees are classified is a rotten system.... It just doesn't work anymore."[117]

In October 2009, a new Chief Executive was appointed and measures were put in place to strengthen the QAA's reputation. But in 2012, the Science and Technology Committee of the House of Lords concluded that the QAA was still not fit for purpose. However, in 2016 the Minister for Universities, Jo Johnson, declared:

"Our HE (Higher Education) system is internationally renowned........ Underpinning this reputation is our internationally recognised system of quality assurance and assessment, which we are updating to meet future needs in an increasingly diverse HE system. The UK Quality Code is central to this quality system and has been for many years."[118]

That should hopefully reassure anyone who was concerned about possibly falling standards in our degree factory universities.

DEGREE DEVALUATION

Grade inflation is just one aspect of declining standards within universities. In 2009, the House of Commons Select Committee responsible for Higher Education took this problem seriously enough to undertake its own investigation into university standards. The

Select Committee and its chairman, Phil Willis, were highly critical both of the evidence provided by Higher Education leaders and of their attitudes towards the issues raised during the committee's investigations. The report declared "… the system for safeguarding consistent national standards in England to be inadequate and in urgent need of replacement". It also accused vice chancellors of "defensive complacency" in their reactions towards criticisms about falling university standards.[119]

Interestingly, at the same time that the House of Commons undertook its investigation into university standards, the Higher Education Funding Council for England (HEFCE), the governing body of English universities, conducted its own research into teaching and learning quality. The HEFCE's findings could broadly be summarised as "nothing to see here, move along please". Phil Willis seemed unimpressed, declaring that this: "… proved the university sector's arrogance and refusal to accept independent criticism. I find it enormously dissatisfactory that the agencies are utterly complacent about challenging standards."[120]

This was more than a minor disagreement. Phil Willis, a senior politician with an in-depth knowledge of UK Higher Education was scathing not so much about the mismatched contents of the two reports. Instead, he appeared irritated by the underlying attitude of the Higher Education sector when genuine concerns about quality were raised with them. This "defensive complacency" meant that university leaders made few attempts to engage with the issues raised by the evidence submitted to the Select Committee. Instead, the standard response from university leaders was that these were clearly isolated incidents which wouldn't be found happening at *their* universities. The anger of vice chancellors was apparent at their annual conference in 2009. The head of Universities UK (the body representing vice chancellors) described the Select Committee as running "a sustained campaign of scepticism". Michael Brown, vice chancellor of Liverpool John Moores University, argued for: "…a consistent approach to try to head off the Parliamentarians' obsession, which is not based on great substance.... MPs have to be headed off at the pass before it gets too silly."[121]

Unfortunately, well before the Select Committee Report in 2009, there had been a long line of well-informed sceptics who had expressed concerns about UK academic standards. The standard response of universities has been to ignore them or attack the individual (perhaps the technical term for this is "heading off at the pass"?) rather than addressing the substance of their comments. In 2004, the historian Dr David Starkey claimed that:

> "We are introducing the slow corruption of our universities as heads of department are pushed by reduced budgets into lowering standards. Until 10 years ago British education was seen as the gold standard around the world and our institutions and examinations as incorruptible." [122]

The House of Commons inquiry in 2009 was initiated following allegations by Dr Geoffrey Alderman, a former head of quality at the University of London and Professor Roger Brown, the former chief executive of the Higher Education Quality Council. Both argued that evidence of deteriorating standards within universities was such that only an independent inquiry would reassure the public. In 2009, Dr Alderman described a Higher Education system in which standards were not so much in decline as freefall:

> "Students who would formerly have failed their degrees are being passed, and students who would formerly have been awarded... Lower Seconds are now being awarded Upper Seconds and even Firsts. Students are being admitted to commence their studies with levels of English so poor that universities are having to run remedial English courses to ensure that new entrants possess at least a basic level of literacy. Cheating is rampant, encouraged in part by lenient penalties."[123]

Senior politicians with links to universities have made similar complaints from across the political spectrum. Take, for example, the comments of Lord Chris Patten, the former Conservative minister and Chancellor of Oxford University in 2007: "... I am not in favour of social inclusion at the expense of academic standards. At its crudest the widening participation agenda has been reckless in its impact on standards."[124]

Alternatively, consider the views of Dame Shirley Williams, formerly of the Labour Party then of the Liberal Democrats, and someone who has worked in universities in the UK and the US. In 2002, she had this to say about British universities: "At the bottom end, there is a tail of colleges and universities which are not even second-rate. And at the top end, I doubt whether there are any internationally first-rate universities left in Britain; perhaps a few departments here and there..."[125]

It is worth noting that those voicing concerns about falling standards do not generally depend on the Higher Education system's collective goodwill for their continued employment, salaries and career prospects. Those inside the system want us to believe that any quality-related problems are isolated incidents that do not represent the wider reality within universities. The university insiders would also have us believe that anybody suggesting that these quality problems are representative of the wider system is clearly a crank. The difficulty for this argument arises when UK academics are asked anonymously about standards. Then they provide a similar response to that of the 'cranks'. A 2008 survey commissioned by the *Tines Higher Education Supplement* found that:

> "77% of academics said pressure on them to give better marks had increased. And 78% believed that student plagiarism was an increasing problem in their institution. A third (34%) believed reports of universities dumbing down were correct, while 82% said lack of resources were affecting academic standards." [126]

These results confirmed the findings of a previous *Times* survey of academics in 2004, in which:

> "71% agreed that their 'institution has admitted students who are not capable of benefiting from higher–level study'. Almost half reported that they had 'felt obliged to pass a student whose performance did not really merit a pass'. A worrying 42% said that 'decisions to fail students' work have been overruled at higher levels in the institution'. Almost one in five admitted they had 'turned a blind eye' to student plagiarism."[127]

This and other research suggests that, in private, many academics admit the reality of 'dumbing down'. It also suggests that they feel unable to say anything about this in public.

DUMBING DOWN

As the guardians of their own standards, universities can dumb down their courses in any way they see fit. But they have several preferred options. They can drop the marks required for different grades for an assessment. They can re–grade assessments after they have occurred to produce a more favourable result for all students. They can minimise the input and influence of the external examiners who are supposed to moderate and validate assessments. They can put pressure on staff to mark more generously. They can find methods for awarding marks that avoid assessment. Finally, they can simply give students the answers to their assessments.

At its worst, the Great Expansion subverts the assessment process into an informal collaboration between students and academics. This was encapsulated in a submission to the 2009 House of Commons Select Committee which was referenced in their final report:

> "Dr Dearden said that academic standards had been com-
> promised by, amongst other factors, management pressure
> on academic staff to fully utilise the range of marks and,
> in the extreme case, the threat of loss of teaching leading
> to staff priming students on exam content and he said that
> much of the compromise in standards was impossible to
> identify through formal monitoring procedures."[128]

So, how do these approaches work in practice?

1. Dropping the pass marks for assessments

Traditionally, universities have had standard requirements in exam
and assignment marks for degree grades. A First required a student
to score 70% or above, whilst a student needed to score 40% or above
in order to pass. However, the mark required for a First can vary by
more than 20% between universities. There is also no longer any
consistency about the threshold for failure. Susan Evans, a lecturer
at Manchester Metropolitan University, gave this evidence to the
Select Committee:

> "Under University regulations ...students could not be com-
> pensated in a unit where the aggregate mark was less than
> 35%. However, students in this situation were allowed to
> progress. In 2005, eleven students with marks between 16%
> and 33% progressed to Year 2. In 2006, seventeen students
> with marks between 14% and 33% progressed to Year 2."[129]

When students scoring 14% in an exam can achieve a pass grade,
is there actually any point in having an exam? Why not save time,
paperwork, ink and trees by removing the assessment altogether?

2. Re-grading assessments retrospectively

Sometimes re–grading can occur without the consent of the academic
who provided the original marks. In 2008, Professor Paul Buckland,

an academic at Bournemouth University, failed 25% of students on one of his courses. He later resigned in protest after the exams were re–graded and passed by another academic at the instigation of a university administrator. The case was eventually taken to an industrial tribunal at which Professor Buckland was found to have been unfairly dismissed.[130]

3. Reducing the influence of external examiners

The external examiner system involves a university inviting academics from other universities to scrutinise and moderate their exam and essay marks. This is intended to provide an independent and unbiased view of the quality of their students' work and the consistency of marking. Examiners are normally given a number of clearly–graded exams to provide context and then a number of borderline cases to adjudicate. They write a report on their findings and then sign off all of the course marks before they are awarded by the marking university.

Professor Trainor, then head of Universities UK, described the external examiner system as "a jewel in the crown of UK quality maintenance" during his evidence.[131] The Select Committee report wasn't quite so certain, noting that: "We received evidence that indicated that this 'jewel in the crown' had become tarnished."[132] There are, in fact, numerous ways to circumvent the system. One submission explained that: "External examiners are often friends of the module leaders and are frequently asked to scrutinise subject areas with which they are unfamiliar. They are not encouraged to pass adverse comments."[133]

If an informal approach fails to produce the results required and external examiners are not amenable to suggestion, the university administration can unilaterally change the areas of scrutiny that an external examiner has responsibility for: "The external examiner does not monitor the general level of the marks [nor] is given the opportunity to change individual grades, since all he/she is called upon to do is to arbitrate between first and second markers and/

or make a decision in borderline cases."[134] External examiners who don't sign up for rubber–stamping duties can simply be replaced with other academics who are happy to pick up a day out with expenses in return for their collegiate assent.

4. Preventing internal dissent

It was clear from the evidence submitted to the Select Committee that many academics were deeply unhappy with the types of behaviours identified above, correctly identifying them as an attack on academic culture and values. To prevent wider expression of dissent, university managers can take steps to warn and, if necessary, punish individual academics. Specific tactics vary: from this appeal to the academics' self–interest at Bournemouth University:

> "I would urge all academic staff to look very carefully at those students gaining marks in the 30s. If the mark is 38–39 then please, where possible, look for the extra 1–2 marks if appropriate... I often reduce the problem to one of money ... each student brings an income of approximately £4,500. You can all do the sums as well as me to work out the likely implications for the school."[135]

...to the 'stick with no carrot' approach favoured by Middlesex University which, as noted by the *Guardian* in 2004, had put in place a policy: "...of putting academic staff on the spot if 15% or more of their students fail a module. Staff have to explain the reasons for failure rates to a senior manager and report on remedial action. The university denied claims that it was putting pressure on staff not to fail too many students – particularly high fee–payers from overseas."[136]

Alternatively, there can be a gentle steer in the right direction from a 'more experienced' academic, such as described by an anonymous academic writing in the *Guardian*:

"When a module leader suggested to me that I re-mark a batch of work and add 5 or 10 marks on to the original scores, I thought he was joking. He wasn't. *'Look at it as encouragement if you like,'* he said. *'We give them good marks, they'll work harder and they'll achieve more.'* I wasn't in a position to argue – this man was the person who gave me my teaching contract at a UK university every term. I told myself it was probably a one-off.. .. Except it isn't a one-off. This kind of thing has happened again and again, at several Higher Education institutions." [137]

Given that speaking out against dumbing down can put an academic's career prospects in jeopardy, it is hardly surprising that this issue requires anonymity before people are prepared to voice concerns. Many of the academics who submitted evidence to the Select Committee were either at the end of their careers, outside the main university system, or already in serious dispute with universities. The Select Committee report noted that those at the beginning of their academic careers (i.e. those with much more to lose) were also those who were most pressurised to collude in dumbing down: "Dr Fenton told us that staff who were vulnerable, especially younger members or newer members to the profession, who had not got as much clout, standing or protection within the institution [were] very nervous about speaking out, or recommending that certain students should not be getting certain grades."[138]

5. Awarding marks to students in other ways

Some of the above unpleasantness is already being avoided by more forward-thinking universities. They award marks to students simply for turning up to classes and lectures: "…several universities had been found to be awarding 10% of marks if students attend all their lectures and seminars. They cited individual courses at Glasgow, Kent and Northampton universities."[139] Steve Smith, Vice Chancellor at Exeter University and then chair of Universities UK, defended these universities, stating that: "You don't want to be in the situation where people pass a seminar–based course without attending,"[140]

This rather overlooks the question of why such a situation could arise in the first place. How could a student be able to pass a course without attending any classes? Two possible explanations suggest themselves. Firstly, that the classes were so dire that they made no impact on learning or, secondly, that marking on the course was so slack that class attendance might not really matter anyway. Of course, if universities wanted to boost class attendances whilst avoiding the perception of dumbing down, they could simply dock 10% of a student's marks for not attending a percentage of classes, rather than awarding them for attending.

6. Giving students the answers

There has been a growing trend towards open–book exams in universities. In many cases, students can take in books and whatever other material they wish. This material is rarely checked beforehand by invigilators. With up to 500 students in an exam room, there simply isn't time. If students take in exam answers written by other people in response to broad hints from their lecturers about potential questions, there is little to stop them from merrily copying these answers out.

In fact, some universities are even happy to relieve their students of the onerous task of actually copying out pre–prepared material. Consider this submission to the Select Committee, again from Sue Evans at Manchester Metropolitan University:

> "In a computer–based statistics assessment that I invigilated the lecturer had already put some of the questions, together with the answers, on a common drive. Students could access the answers during the assessment and copy them into the document that they submitted for marking." [141]

On one level, we have to admire the entrepreneurial simplicity of this. If only a similar approach could be found for the delivery of lectures and seminars, then the whole resource-intensive business of Higher Education could be streamlined wonderfully. It is, of course, only one example. But perhaps it is indicative of a wider cultural shift in universities away from a community centred around learning and towards a bureaucracy centred on meeting its targets by any means necessary?

The above list does not include two other important aspects of dumbing down. Firstly, universities now routinely ignore industrial-scale cheating and, secondly, a dramatic reduction in the amount of material now studied in many degrees. Underlying each of these is a change in attitude within universities – a shift from traditional academic values and a search for knowledge towards a more utilitarian approach driven by financial considerations and a new corporate culture.

PART TWO

THE CONSEQUENCES

CHAPTER SIX

DEGREE FACTORIES

Unfortunately it seems that the attitudes and values of universities themselves have changed as a result of expansion. Many universities are themselves increasingly becoming mass–production degree factories focused on their own convenience, prestige and finances rather than on any abstract notion of spreading knowledge, educating the next generation and providing a 'public good'.

A number of UK universities have, for instance, put money ahead of principle in their choice of business partnerships. A notable example of this was the involvement of the London School of Economics (LSE) and the Ghadaffi regime. But this is not an isolated incident. At St Andrews University, significant donations from the Syrian government were alleged to have influenced research at their Centre for Syrian Studies, making it more favourable to a regime synonymous with repressive brutality.[142] While countries like Saudi Arabia, India and America have been traditional allies, during the last two decades we have also seen enlightened, forward–thinking, democratic countries such as Iran, Libya and Syria sending their children to study in the UK. There is a wide and obvious gulf between Mahatma Gandhi studying Law at University College London and Saif Ghadaffi receiving a controversial doctorate from the LSE. Possibly moving further into the realms of the satirical, the University of Nottingham happily accepted millions of pounds from British American Tobacco to set up a *Corporate Social Responsibility* centre.[143]

This 'degree factory' approach is also discernible in falling standards. After all, grade inflation and dumbing down both enable universities to achieve their objectives with the minimum of effort and resource. Similarly, curriculum shrinkage sees universities teach less material on their degrees, despite increases in student fees. The growth and tacit acceptance of plagiarism aids and abets falling standards, whilst simultaneously reducing the workload of universities by removing the need to catch or discipline cheats. There is also evidence of a new student hierarchy, based not on academic merit, but rather on the amount of money they bring into the university. This, in turn, determines their treatment by the university, with processes from admissions to assessment now often driven by financial, rather than academic, considerations.

Finally, the 'degree factory' university is increasingly corporate and litigious in its dealings with students. Expensive graduation ceremonies, the use of bailiffs to recover student debt and threats to prevent graduation over unpaid library fines all underline the changing nature of this relationship. Universities have been quick to complain about the rise of the "student as consumer", but they have rarely stopped to reflect on their own role in this transformation.

CURRICULUM SHRINKAGE

We are living in the information age. Our knowledge about the world is expanding faster than at any point in history. It is, therefore, ironic that many UK degrees are experiencing curriculum shrinkage. In other words, the total amount of subject material that they cover is diminishing.

Post expansion, undergraduates often arrive knowing less than they would have historically as a result of reduced A–level syllabuses (see Chapter 12 *Schools: Supplying Course Fee Fodder?*). They then learn less during their studies and end up graduating knowing less about their subject than they would have 30 years ago. This might sound hard to believe, but consider this quotation from a Russell Group modern languages graduate, describing their undergraduate studies: "We were studying French literature but in English translation and then writing about it in English."

All of these students will have studied French for *at least* seven years before university. But despite a course requirement of an A grade in A–level French, many students were unable to read literature in French and then write about it in French. It is notable that an elite university should accept students unable to study literature in the original language. It is even more remarkable that their language degrees should abandon the study of literature in the original language in order to accommodate these students.

This graduate's frustration is symptomatic of a wider problem identified in a 2009 Higher Education Funding Council for England (HEFCE) report.[144] This found that language courses in UK universities were being replaced by cultural studies courses, in which the literature and culture of a country are studied in English. Rather than addressing this problem of students arriving at university without sufficient language skills by actually teaching them, universities bypassed it by working in English. Universities might argue that the shift was ultimately driven by falling student demand for difficult, traditional language courses. Certainly, language courses have seen significant closures across the country, as the HEFCE noted:

"Between 2003 and 2008, the proportion of all students in the UK on languages degrees dropped from 3.3% to 2.9%. In England it was even more acute, dropping from 3.2% of the total to just 2.7%. The total number of full-time language students dropped 5% compared with an 11% increase in student numbers overall."[145]

To attract students, who otherwise might not have applied, universities downgraded their language courses to cultural studies courses. This created two problems. Firstly, students who expected to benefit from serious linguistic training didn't have the opportunity to do so. Secondly, language degrees were now misbranded meaning that employers, who expected a degree to equate to some fluency in that language, were likely to be disappointed. In the 1980s, a language degree would have been expected to ensure a reasonable level of fluency in verbal and written communication. This is no longer the case.

Curriculum shrinkage represents a reduction in the skills and knowledge provided by degrees compared with what has been taught in the past. It is driven by other Great Expansion symptoms. When contact hours are decreased, class sizes increased and the ability range of students widened, curriculum shrinkage is a natural and inevitable mechanism for preventing an unacceptable failure rate. It has been exacerbated by a similar process in the school exam syllabuses for GCSEs and A–levels, reduced to raise pass rates and provide greater numbers of undergraduates for university expansion.

This is not a new problem. In 2000, Dr Paul Taylor, writing for the *Independent,* claimed that many degrees contained around half the content that they had pre–expansion:

> "With the introduction of a modular curriculum, pro-grammes (were reduced) by combining two units into one or eliminating others altogether; within a few years, degrees were a fraction of their original breadth. In 1974, I started a degree, following eight subjects with 21 hours each week. Fifteen years later, I returned to the same university as a lecturer; the same degree course now consisted of four subjects taught in 10 hours. With increasing student numbers and no increase in teaching staff, vice–chancellors (had) two alternatives: a substantial increase in class sizes, or a reduction in curriculum. They chose the path of least resistance ... an undergraduate degree in 2000 requires about half the study time of its 1970s predecessor."

In 2002, the *Guardian* interviewed Dr James Anderson, a computer science academic at Reading University. He claimed that much of the undergraduate syllabus had disappeared during his ten years of teaching. He listed subjects that he no longer taught because the degree had shrunk. These included euler operators, morphing, fractals and radiosity:

> "It's my feeling that the curriculum has reduced by 50% during my time. People are still getting degrees but they

are studying half of what they used to. That experience is widespread across many universities, but no one will admit it."[146]

The head of Imperial College, Sir Richard Sykes, also noted in 2002 that most of his university's undergraduate degrees now required a four-year course to enable students to cover material that had traditionally been covered in three years. He identified the source of this problem as curriculum shrinkage in GCSEs and A-levels: "…because the standard of the A-level has fallen so much over 10 years that we have to bring them up to speed before they can get on with their courses."[147]

Geoff Parks, the director of admissions at Cambridge, made a similar point about his university's undergraduates in 2005, stating: "Cambridge had admitted 142 fewer undergraduates this year than last because of an increase in four-year degrees, which are now common in engineering and the sciences, the result of pupils knowing less than they used to."[148]

Whilst other universities have experienced similar problems to those faced by Imperial and Cambridge, they have decided to retain three-year science degrees. The reasonable assumption is that their three-year degrees now cover less material than previously.

In 2009, curriculum shrinkage was highlighted in numerous submissions to the House of Commons Select Committee investigation into universities. One was made by a mature student undertaking a Masters in Biological Sciences, whose son was taking the same A-levels that he had a generation earlier. Echoing Sir Richard Sykes, he noted the impact that curriculum shrinkage at school was having on universities:

"Swathes of maths have now disappeared from the school curriculum … much of what I had learnt at school now had to be taught at university, inevitably pushing out other material that would otherwise have been taught. This is …

why students will not be as advanced at the end of their
degrees as they were a generation earlier. Examples...
include vectors, matrices and set theory... which are now
only covered in optional modules at school."[149]

A lack of basic maths knowledge amongst school leavers is not just
affecting the curricula of STEM subjects (Science, Technology,
Engineering and Mathematics) degrees. In 2012, a report from the
Royal Society of Arts (RSA) warned that the numeracy problems of
the UK's school leavers were forcing other degrees to reduce their
mathematical content:

> "Universities are marginalising mathematical content in
> the delivery of degree courses because English students are
> not capable of studying it.... For instance, in the social sci-
> ences, quantitative research methods may be neglected....
> It also means English universities are not keeping pace
> with international standards."[150]

In fact, problems with numeracy were so acute that the RSA report
noted that some university degrees did not "...advertise the level of
maths needed to comfortably study particular subjects for fear of
hindering applications."[151] As with language students, the 'degree
factory' university's approach is not to help these students by
working with them to develop the necessary skills or knowledge.
Instead, it is to pander to them by making degrees easier to pass
and easier to teach. None of this actually helps the students in
the long run.

At its worst, curriculum shrinkage sees the 'degree factory' university providing the bare minimum amount of subject knowledge
that still qualifies as a degree. Many universities get away with this
because they are increasingly teaching students wishing to graduate
with the least possible effort. This creates a vicious and complicit
cycle in which the real victims are students with ability and a desire

to learn. Unfortunately, the 'degree factory' university not only helps students through its actions (curriculum shrinkage), it also assists them in what it ignores (plagiarism).

PLAGIARISM

"Over the past three years, more than 45,000 students at 80 institutions have been found guilty of 'academic misconduct' ranging from bringing crib–sheets or mobile phones into exams to paying private firms to write essays for them. Some 16,000 cases were recorded in the past year." *Independent on Sunday* (2012)

Plagiarism is cheating. It occurs when a student hands in somebody else's work as their own. It has always happened in universities and it always will happen. It is almost an expectation of academic life. It is also an expectation of academic life that, if detected, it will incur sanctions, with repeat or serious offences resulting in expulsion. The offence of plagiarism is at odds with academic cultural values. One core tenet that cuts across all subjects and all levels of study is that you give credit to ideas and thoughts of others by making reference to their work. To do otherwise, even unwittingly, is intellectual theft. If you want to understand how far attitudes towards cheating have changed during expansion then read the National Union of Students (NUS)' submission to the Select Committee in 2009. This claimed that: "Punishments' and 'penalties' are usually unhelpful in combating plagiarism and often take up significant amounts of valuable staff time. Institutions should instead focus their resources on deterrence through effective induction and training."[152]

This apparently soft and less than judgmental attitude to plagiarism could be seen to trivialize not just plagiarism but the whole academic process and it devalues the efforts of students who don't cheat. Every university and degree course provides copious guidance about plagiarism. If students don't understand this, then they are likely to struggle with some of the more advanced concepts that a degree will (hopefully) introduce to them.

It is difficult to estimate accurately the overall extent of plagiarism in UK universities, but it is clearly a widespread problem. In 2008, the University of Cambridge's student magazine *Varsity* reported on a survey in which nearly 50% of the university's students admitted to plagiarism. The figure was even higher amongst law students, with 62% admitting to cheating. Of those who admitted cheating, 82% confessed that they had copied material directly from Wikipedia. Only 5% of those who cheated reported getting caught.[153]

The *Times Higher Education Supplement* conducted its own plagiarism research in 2006, talking to over 1,000 students in 119 universities. It found that 33% of students copied material directly from the internet or books and that a further 16% copied work directly from their friends. A further 10% of students went that extra mile and bought essays online.[154] The research coincided with an admission from Oxford University's chief of discipline, Alan Grafen, that plagiarism was becoming so widespread that it was threatening to undermine the quality of the university's degrees. He had this to say in 2006:

> "There seem to be two reasons for the prevalence of simple copying. It is indeed very easy with online sources. A less obvious reason is that at British schools nowadays, a practice is encouraged of submitting work in class that is more or less cobbled together from the internet. Hard though it may be to believe, students type word–for–word and increasingly copy and paste from the internet, and submit essays containing whole pages of this verbatim material."[155]

When anti–plagiarism software was first introduced, the results were immediate. Coventry University found 237 students cheating, expelling 12. Nottingham University found 53 cases, but expelling just 1.[156] Since this initial burst of enthusiasm, universities seem to have changed either the settings on their software or their approach to dealing with the volume of plagiarism that the software was discovering. In one piece of anecdotal evidence, an engineering graduate interviewed mentioned that: "I know one guy who has chosen every module because they are the same as a guy in the year above him and he has every piece of coursework from him and he's copying it word for word."

Anti-plagiarism software used correctly will alert academics to this type of cheating as it stores copies of previous years' work, checking current submissions against these. The House of Commons Select Committee submissions from 2009 reveal academic after academic complaining about ever-escalating levels of plagiarism. What is also noticeable in these accounts is the extent to which unofficial university policy is criticised for complicity in ignoring plagiarism. This could take the form of discouraging academics from investigating suspicious work to lenient non-punishments for students found to have cheated. The same complaint is made again and again: that administrators in universities want neither bad publicity nor falling grades.

Equally alarming has been the rapid growth of essay-buying websites for plagiarists. These enable students to purchase specific essays written to order by subject, level and length and even grade. The website passes along the request to an academic who writes an essay. Then the website returns it to the student. These websites claim that they offer their services only as 'specimen answers'. But it seems implausible that students would pay for something to read rather than to submit. The benefit of this approach for the student is that it won't trigger plagiarism software as the essay will (hopefully) have been written from scratch rather than copied from the web. It also raises the grimly amusing possibility of academics moonlighting as essay-writers for their own courses, submitting essays to themselves for marking.

In 2006, the *Guardian* interviewed Barclay Littlewood, who ran one of these companies, ukessays.co.uk. In 2005, his company had a turnover of £1.6 million and he estimated the UK marketplace for online essays at £200 million (incidentally, a figure echoed in 2015, by Thomas Lancaster, one of the country's leading experts on plagiarism).[157] At the top end, Mr Littlewood mentioned one student who had spent £17,000 with his company. In the same article, the newspaper found that one online essay provider was able to supply a first class degree essay of 1,000 words, delivered the next day, at a cost of £320. They noted that: "Most bespoke essay–writing companies charge by the word, although some charge by the page. There is one company that bills students £30 per 250 words and another that charges at least £60 per essay."[158]

There is anecdotal evidence that essay–writing services are often used by international students. One company estimated that 60% to 70% of its work came from international students. This usage may reflect the now significant range in academic and linguistic ability of international students arriving in the UK. It might also be a reflection of the increased stakes for their study, created by the much higher fees they are charged by UK universities. If a student is already spending over £100,000 for a degree in terms of tuition fees, living costs and travel, then a mere £17,000 might seem a reasonable surcharge for the right grade. It also seems reasonable to suggest that the 2012 tuition fees rises will have replicated these incentives for domestic students.

A quick Google search for "UK Online Essays" reveals over one hundred UK–based companies with professional websites offering to provide virtually any level of material, from essay to thesis, on any subject. Given Mr Littlewood's estimate for the size of the online essay market, we can hypothesise at the scale of this problem in UK universities. For the sake of simplicity, we will stick to undergraduate essays. If ukessays.co.uk's turnover was £1.6 million a year and a 1,000–word essay cost £160, then that equates to sales of 10,000 undergraduate essays a year or 238 a week (if we look at the main academic year of 42 weeks). If the essay marketplace is worth £200 million, then this would be equivalent to around *1.25 million bought essays a year,* against a current student population of 2.3 million.

The financial inequalities of the expanded UK academic system mean that even cheating isn't a level playing field. If you can afford personalised essays written specifically for you, then there is little chance of the plagiarism being picked up by software. Academics might have their suspicions about how the barely articulate, unengaged student manages to produce a first class essay, but proving cheating requires significant amounts of time, effort and motivation on the academic's part. All of this is difficult to manage within a system where scale prohibits personal interaction and the university wants all students to pass and their grades to improve every year. For the less well–off plagiarist, however, it's a case of taking their chances with Google, Wikipedia and software detection. These students shouldn't worry unduly though; research in 2005 found 51% of academics took no action at all if they suspected their students of plagiarism.[159] It also showed great diversity in what academics actually considered to be cheating across different universities and subjects.

By 2017, a *Times Higher Education Supplement* survey of 1,000 academics found that 61% has discovered their students committing plagiarism at least once and that 26% suspected that their students committed plagiarism regularly. One social work academic who responded to the survey noted that: "…there are some cases where I think students have paid for essays or dissertations to be written… It is virtually impossible to prove these cases, even when a student, who usually gets poor marks, suddenly gets a 70 per cent – I think the university gets frightened of appeals, too."[160] Another academic provided the following context for how his university dealt with plagiarism: "I have seen a student found guilty of setting off a fire alarm by smoking in his dormitory receive a far harsher punishment than a student found guilty of the most arrant plagiarism."[161]

In a time of escalating workloads, increased student numbers and pressure from the university to pass students regardless of the quality of their output, it has become difficult for academics to swim against the tide. Perhaps it is better to think about cheating as a training issue as the NUS suggests. It's probably a whole lot less stressful...

THE NEW STUDENT HIERARCHY

The 'degree factory' university manifests two distinct attitudes towards its students. The first is a lack of interest bordering on contempt. The second is a desire to please to such an extent that this undermines academic standards. Which attitude a student encounters is likely to depend on what they pay the university. This has created an informal hierarchy in which treatment is closely linked to income at every stage of the student lifecycle. For example, in 2012 the *Telegraph* discovered that international students are regularly offered lower entry criteria to degrees:

> "The official agent in Beijing for the elite Russell Group claimed that it could secure over-subscribed places for a Chinese student purporting to have scored three C grades in their A-levels – when British students are required to have at least A, A and B."[162]

This was corroborated by headmasters of leading public schools, who stated that: "...some of their foreign pupils were being offered places with lower entry requirements than their British counterparts."[163]

Universities can even retract a lower offer if they discover that a student will not be paying international fees. Andrew Halls, headmaster of King's College School, mentioned: "...a boy who was made an offer dependent on him being a non-EU candidate, and when he clarified that he was a UK candidate, they said that the offer doesn't stand."[164]

The same preferential treatment is visible throughout Clearing, when universities offer a much broader choice of degree places to non–EU students paying higher fees. In 2012, the *Telegraph* found: "70 law courses in Scotland were taking applications from foreigners yesterday but just 25 had vacancies for British or EU candidates. Almost 150 maths courses were available for international students compared with 38 for home students, while 76 chemistry courses had foreign vacancies but only 28 (for) British candidates."[165]

We've already seen examples of how universities can and will try to influence academics in their marking of overseas students, especially if they form an important source of income for the university. This malaise goes much deeper, however. Since 2000, UK universities have developed close links with regimes with some of the worst human rights records in the world; Iran, Syria and Libya. Privileged students from these regimes have been welcomed by these universities with reduced entry criteria and enhanced academic support that is unavailable to ordinary, especially domestic, undergraduates. The exact form this transaction takes varies from case to case. But the basic ingredient reported would appear to be that universities provide huge additional support to students to gain qualifications that they might not be able to obtain through their own efforts. In some cases, it may mean allowing entry to unqualified students and supporting them through their studies. In other cases, it may mean doing some or all of their academic work for them whilst the students avail themselves of other, perhaps more pleasurable, activities than studying. If these allegations are true (and they are numerous), these universities are essentially providing a more exclusive boutique version of the services offered by essay–writing services.

Perhaps one of the most memorable examples of this is Saif Ghadaffi's enrolment at the London School of Economics (LSE). After five years of study Mr Ghadaffi successfully completed a Masters and a Doctorate at the university. Later, questions emerged from a number of quarters over allegations of plagiarism, the level of support that he received and the integrity of the university's assessment process. These questions linked Mr Ghadaffi's treatment to a £1.5

million donation from the Libyan government to the LSE and the high volume of university training purchased from the LSE by the Libyan state.[166]

Oxford University had rejected a previous application from Saif Ghadaffi. But they ran into difficulties with the former Iranian President's son, Mehdi Hashemi Rafsanjani. His thesis proposal had been accepted by the university originally, but later it was subject to investigation after claims that university insiders had helped to push this through the system and that his English was not of a sufficient standard to have undertaken doctoral work. A subsequent university investigation found that nothing untoward had happened in the admission. Mr Rafsanjani had in fact been allowed into the University with a 'let off clause' with regard to his language skills, something permissible under university regulations. Exactly why the university chose to exercise this clause for Mr Rafsanjani is perhaps a question best directed to the university's finance department.

THE 'DEGREE FACTORY' UNIVERSITY AND THE INDIVIDUAL STUDENT

> "The university views me as a source of funding."
> Engineering graduate

Many of the above issues can be viewed as victimless crimes from the student perspective. A large number of students are undoubtedly happy that many degrees now require less study. A large number of students are probably also pleased that plagiarism is now generally ignored within universities. The silent majority of the undergraduate body are also likely to be disinterested in where or how their universities find additional funding.

The possibly less than academic attitude of many of today's universities doesn't just apply to these areas however, it also affects the manner in which universities interact with individual students. Sometimes this behaviour is the result of scale, sometimes it reflects the increasingly bureaucratic nature of universities post expansion. Often the behaviour can seem selfish in its desire to wring the last available (usually borrowed) penny out of its students. For example, language courses which would have been free to students pre–expansion now cost full price.

The bureaucratic rigidity of universities becomes clear when a student wants to do anything that falls outside normal operating parameters. If, for example, a student wants to change course within the first few weeks of enrolment, universities generally offer little sympathy to such requests. University departments will similarly obstruct students who wish to take modules of courses external to their school. Transferring credit between universities is also far more difficult and arduous than it should be.

Some of this inflexibility is a problem of scale. Most popular courses are so oversubscribed that there are literally no spaces to move students to even if the university wanted to. It is also a problem of culture though. Post expansion, too many universities interact with their students through factory processes in pursuit of top–down targets. The student is a unit of funding and the modules that count towards their degrees are simply outputs. The intention is to convert funding to outputs as cost–efficiently as possible. Often, the result is that a university is set up to do the bare minimum possible in pursuit of this end, churning out a certain quantity of graduates rather than graduates of a certain quality.

Each university is also a monopoly supplier to its students and monopolies can treat their customers as they see fit. How many undergraduates are going to leave, if this means debt but no degree or even credit towards a degree? If a student does exercise the one choice available to them, of leaving, they should not expect any refund policy. One graduate interviewed mentioned that she had dropped out of a degree at her first university, unhappy with their standards of teaching. She complained several times and eventually left after six miserable weeks:

"... unfortunately it was past the point where I could get a refund on my tuition fees and I had to pay the full amount... The university got a debt collector in and I got this horrible phone call after I'd left." English graduate

She soon discovered that she was still liable for the full year's fees. The university had, in the student's view, failed to provide the expected quality but, despite this, the student remained liable. Despite no suggestion of default, the university involved the bailiffs, adding significant extra distress to the student and their parents.

This is not an isolated incident; it is what many students can expect when they drop out. Given that around 18% of undergraduates – tens of thousands every year – drop out of their degrees before completing them, it is a fairly widespread phenomenon. For these students there is no flexibility, no empathy and no special consideration. Instead, they are faced with the university seeking to enforce its side of a transaction through the legal system.

Complaints from the NUS over this type of university behaviour were serious enough for the Office for Fair Trading (OFT) to issue a warning to the Higher Education sector in 2014. Having analysed the terms and conditions laid out in the student contracts of 115 institutions, the OFT found that 75% contained provisions to stop students from enrolling for a new year or even from graduating if they owed any debts to the university for accommodation, childcare or even library fines. The OFT made it clear that such behaviour was disproportionate and put universities in breach of consumer protection law. [167]

The 'degree factory' university is nothing if not consistent in its approach, right up until graduation ceremonies. This final act of student life is meant to be a celebration of achievement and a significant event for student and university. Sadly, many universities don't view graduations in these terms, instead approaching them as a final chance to make money; or at least until they start their e-mail campaigns asking for alumni contributions. For example, in 2008 one of the authors attended a Russell Group university graduation which charged £20 per ticket. Graduates were allowed two family members to attend the event. Additional tickets were available on a "first come, first served" basis. Children older than two years were charged the full rate. Gown and Mortar hire was £50. A standard pack of photos with card frames another £50. By 2013, the *Guardian* estimated the average cost of a graduation for a UK student at £220.[168] In 2014, the average cost of a graduation ticket was £68 and several universities now charge students for the ceremony **even if they choose not to attend**.

Given their taxpayer–funded resources (photography departments, sports halls, catering departments) there is no good reason why all of this – outfits, tickets, catering, photos and DVD – could not be provided free by every university, especially in view of the massive tuition fees now charged by most universities – both the elite institutions and those which are far from elite. It is this relentless need to profit from the student that highlights the 'degree factory' university at its worst:

> *"They make you pay for your graduation after you've spent £40,000 already over three years...to me that's horrendous. It's not even the expense, it's the principle."* Finance and management graduate

That there is a principle at stake here is correct. But the 'degree factory' university doesn't do principles. So students are crammed in like sardines, forced to pay through the nose and bored rigid. In this, at least, graduation provides a fitting finale to an undergraduate degree at one of these degree factories.

But what happens after graduation?

CHAPTER SEVEN

GRADUATES: 'GIZZA JOB!'

"If you haven't got a degree nobody wants you, but when you've got it nobody cares." Engineering graduate

Prior to expansion, it was assumed that almost all graduates would find graduate jobs. Some might have to send off more applications than others, but eventually everybody who wanted it would find employment at this level. Graduates were in limited supply and, consequently, possession of a degree was a gateway to a career. However, employment data released by the Office of National Statistics (ONS) made it clear that this was no longer the case by 2011: "...25% of 21–year olds who had completed university degrees were unable to find (any) job, compared with 26% of 16–year–olds with no qualifications other than GCSEs. The unemployment rate for 18–year–olds with A–levels was lower, at 20%"[169]

The reality of life post graduation can come as a shock to graduates who expect to walk straight into a well–paid job. In 2011, the Higher Education Careers Service Unit (HECSU) found that 67% of undergraduates surveyed six months before graduation felt that their degree had been worthwhile. Eighteen months after graduation this number fell to 50%.[170] It's not difficult to understand how this disenchantment occurs. It is the result of interaction with the labour market in which the actual value of a degree is generally less than the anticipated value. This is a long–term trend that has been driven by expansion and its relentless oversupply of graduates into an already saturated job market.

Research into graduate employment confirms a pattern of increasing numbers of graduates working in non–graduate jobs. A 1997 report by the Institute for Employment Studies, which tracked 1991–93 graduates, found that by 1995 **just 22% of them were in low skilled (or non–graduate) jobs**.[171] By 2001, data from the ONS showed that the number of recent graduates working in non–graduate jobs had risen to 29%. By 2013, the same ONS figures had reached an eye–watering **47% of recent graduates**.[172]

What many of today's graduates slowly discover is that securing a graduate job depends on a variety of factors, many of which were beyond their control after they had started their degree. Particularly important amongst these factors are – which university a graduate attended, which subject they studied, where they live after graduation and what year they graduated.

1. Which university?

All the available evidence suggests that the university a graduate attends is a key determinant of their employability and future earnings. Research in 2008 by the 1994 Group, an association of eleven smaller, research–intensive universities, found that:

> "A third of science and technology graduates from (elite) universities earn between £30,000 and £49,999 three years after leaving university. This compares with 12.4% of graduates from less prestigious institutions."[173]

These findings were supported by ONS figures published in 2015 showing that graduates from elite universities (Russell Group) were 14% more likely to be employed in a high–skilled role and earned on average 20% more than other graduates.[174]

This pattern intensifies the higher up the pay scale you go. Research from the Sutton Trust in 2008 suggested that top earners were four times as likely to have attended elite universities:

> "A fifth of people (19%) who graduated from elite universities in the 1990s are now earning more than £90,000 a year, compared with only 5% of those who went to former polytechnics."[175]

Unsurprisingly, these unequal returns start immediately after graduation. Research in 2014 from the Sutton Trust, identified that the average starting salaries for Oxbridge graduates were around 42% higher than those of graduates from new (post 1992) universities.[176]

There are also huge differences in the ability of the graduates of different universities to find employment. A Higher Education Statistics Agency (HESA) survey of 2012 graduates showed that the average unemployment rate six months after graduation was 8%. For Aberdeen's Robert Gordon University – a university with one of the lowest rates of graduate unemployment – this fell to 2.3%, whilst for graduates from the London Metropolitan University it was 18.6%.[177]

Elite universities have significantly lower unemployment rates than new universities. In 2012, the Council of Professors and Heads of Computing Council found that universities such as those in the Russell Group had graduate unemployment rates of 7.2%, whilst the rate at new universities was 10.2%.[178] Despite these differences in outcomes for employability and future earnings, nearly all universities currently charge the same fees.

2. Which degree subject?

There is also huge variation in graduate starting salaries depending on degree subject. The 2014 Higher Education Careers Service Unit (HECSU) survey reported that graduates studying dentistry had the highest average starting salary at £30,348 a year, while those studying ophthalmics had the lowest at £15,546.[179]

Even for graduates from elite universities, their choice of degree subject can make a massive difference to their future earnings. Science, Technology, Engineering and Mathematics (STEM) degrees and some language subjects pay much better than arts or humanities subjects. Research in 2008 suggested that three years after university, graduates in science and technology subjects from elite universities were twice as likely to be earning £30,000 or above than their counterparts studying arts or social sciences. STEM graduates from these universities were also 10% more likely to be employed in graduate rather than non–graduate positions.[180]

These differences in starting salaries for subjects are only the tip of the iceberg. Later in graduates' working lives, there is an earnings gulf between different subjects. The cyclical nature of the employment market also means that many degrees which might have been considered good investments upon application, such as computer science, can turn out to be anything but after graduation. In 2009, nearly one in six (16.3%) of ICT graduates were unemployed six months after graduation.[181]

One of the most interesting pieces of research in this area was provided by the *Daily Telegraph* in 2012. This examined the percentage of graduates working in barista–level jobs six months after graduation, by their degree subject. The worst five subjects were fine arts (29%), media studies (26.7%), performing arts (23.5%), design (23.1%) and sociology (22.7%). The five best–performing subjects were civil engineering (4.7%), mechanical engineering (4.7%), architecture (7.9%), economics (7.9%) and electrical engineering (8.8%). If only it were possible for governments, universities and potential students to discern a pattern in these results and learn something from them...

3. Which location?

Another major factor in graduate employment is the region where the graduate lives. In 2012, the Local Government Association's research into graduate destinations found: "...huge variation in graduate employment levels across the country with some areas seeing around one in three (36 per cent) graduates in full–time employment while two in three graduates (60 per cent) are in work in other parts of the country. This reflects variable job opportunities in different towns and cities"[182]

In 2015, ONS figures showed that graduate unemployment rates in Outer London were, perhaps surprisingly, nearly double that of regions such as the South West and the East of England, possibly reflecting the relative oversupply of graduates (and universities) in the capital.[183] There are also significant variations in the levels of pay, quality and diversity of work on offer in different regions. None of this variation is reflected in the cost of degrees from different universities. Supporters of expansion have consistently argued that graduates still fare better than non–graduates in regions of high unemployment. Whilst these graduates might enjoy improved rates of employment, it is often in unskilled or administrative work. An improved prospect of a job in a call centre seems scant reward for the graduate debt that it often occasions.

4. The year of graduation

As recent graduates have discovered, in a recession the pool of graduate jobs can dry up for nearly all applicants. In 2008, at the beginning of the economic crisis, blue–chip employers reduced their employment criteria down to just five universities. Malcolm Grant, provost of University College London and chair of the Russell Group noted that: "Firms are already narrowing their search to a small number of universities: Oxford, Cambridge, the LSE, UCL and Imperial, and I think that's a shame."[184]

This meant that graduates with Firsts from other Russell Group universities found their CVs and application forms simply resulted in polite letters thanking them for their applications rather than inviting them for interviews. This situation hadn't changed greatly by 2012 when the Minister for Universities, David Willetts, criticised graduate employers for focusing their recruitment activities within *six* UK universities.[185]

Unfortunately, this initial period post graduation can be more critical for new graduates than they realise at the time. If they can't get the right job, or in some cases the right unpaid work experience, their CV becomes less attractive to top employers, degrading over time. Six months after graduation, graduates without employment find themselves competing in interviews with younger and more confident final–year undergraduates. Due to expansion, universities produce increasing numbers of graduates, regardless of how their previous graduates are faring in the job market.

In 2010, the think tank Demos noted that young people who were unemployed during recessions often suffered lasting damage through reduced lifetime earnings and a greater chance of subsequent unemployment. Their report also noted that graduate status did little to prevent or mitigate this effect:

> "Professor Lisa Kahn, a labour economist at Yale University, has demonstrated that graduating from university into a 'bad economy' has a significant negative and persistent effect on wages with earning over a lifetime substantially lower for individuals graduating into a poor job market."[186]

A final point is that some degree subjects are more vulnerable than others to the effects of the economy. Research into the variability of returns for different degrees between 1993 and 1999 found that graduates in law and architecture were particularly vulnerable to changes in wider economy during this period. Architecture graduates could suffer variable returns of up to 40%+ depending on what year they started their degree, for lawyers this figure was up to 50%+.[187]

GRADUATES AND THE UK LABOUR MARKET

The specific difficulties facing those graduating into a recession are a sign of a much wider problem facing all graduates. Namely, that the supply of graduates post expansion bears little relation to the labour market's demand for graduates. Until the economic crash in 2008, the problems facing UK graduates in the job market were generally ignored by the mainstream media. Such issues were effectively masked by a long period of relative prosperity and high levels of employment. Following the economic downturn, however, the problem of graduate oversupply started to reach the national news.

By 2013, the Association of Graduate Employers (AGE) was warning of **85 graduates competing for each available graduate job**.[188] In the most competitive fields these ratios were much worse, with 154 graduates applying for each position in the retail industry and 142 graduates applying for each investment banking post.[189] In 2010 Carl Gilleard, the AGE's chairman, advised graduates unable to find work that: "Any employment is better than no employment [even] if it's about flipping burgers or stacking shelves rather than being sat at home feeling sorry for yourself and vegetating."[190]

For many UK graduates, flipping burgers and stacking shelves is exactly what they end up doing and not just in the short term. Figures released in 2015 by the government department responsible for universities showed that 43% of recent graduates (aged 21–30) were either in low–skilled jobs, which by definition carry no graduate premium, or unemployed.[191] It's not what they were promised by teachers, politicians, careers advisers and glossy university marketing prospectuses.

It is hard to escape the conclusion that expansion has progressively swamped the UK labour market with a quantity of graduate qualifications far outstripping demand. In fact, it has been clear for well over a decade that universities are pumping out far more graduates than the UK economy either wants or needs.

In 2004, the Teacher Training Agency found that over 25% of graduates under thirty five in various jobs were bored and felt that they had started on the wrong career. Over 50% of graduates interviewed for the research admitted that they fell into jobs rather than planning them and that these jobs had not met their pre–university expectations. These graduates were relatively lucky though, bored maybe, but at least they were in work.

Five years later, figures from the Higher Education Statistics Agency (HESA) highlighted a significant number of graduates who weren't so lucky. Looking at graduates from 2005, HESA found that **nearly 25%** of these were not in full–time work by 2009. A **fifth of those working** (part–time and full–time) were not in graduate level jobs and 11.7% had been unemployed at least once since graduation.[192] Those graduating in 2005 did so when the economy was growing and jobs were readily available. They also graduated when there were 25% fewer graduates. The three years in which 40% could not find full-time graduate-level work were good years to be looking for employment. If these boom years were leaving 130,000 graduates a year in this position four years after graduation, then what should future graduates realistically expect from the labour market when they enter?

Moreover, many of the professions which traditionally have been high-volume employers of graduates, such as law, medicine and actuarial science, are projected to suffer the effects of deskilling through the ongoing digitalisation of many areas of process and expertise. This could have a significant impact on the scale and scope of graduate roles both within these professions and the labour market as a whole.

As a final point, it is also worth noting the recent trend for graduate salaries to either fall or stagnate. During the last seven years for which data is available, the average graduate starting salary has fallen significantly from £24,293 in 2007 to £22,057 in 2014.[193] These figures include sharp falls for some of the highest-earning professions such as medicine, dentistry and law. All of this signposts a growing gap between expectations and reality; between what students are told to expect from a degree and what, if anything, most of them actually get. What expansion has really meant for all graduates is a deteriorating labour market with less likelihood of a graduate job, falling starting salaries, less chance of finding any job at all and, for all but a fortunate few, the evaporation of New Labour's much vaunted so-called 'graduate premium'.

WHERE IS THE 'GRADUATE PREMIUM'?

> "Any politician that dangles the carrot of a graduate pre-mium on future earnings to justify increases in student fees, interest rates on loans, or adjusting student loan repayment thresholds, should be challenged for gross mis-selling" Angus Hanton, Co-Founder, Intergenerational Foundation[194]

The 'graduate premium' is a relatively recent term which purports to describe the additional average earnings that a graduate "might" expect to earn during their working life compared with a non-graduate. Throughout New Labour's *Widening Participation* era of university expansion, it was claimed *ad nauseam* by politicians that a graduate would earn, on average, £400,000 more during their working lifetime than a non-graduate. It was no coincidence that this term first entered the public consciousness during the intro-duction of top-up fees by New Labour. These additional earnings, this 'graduate premium', were introduced as the spoonful of sugar that would supposedly make the medicine of top-up fees more palatable for domestic consumption.

The graduate premium was essentially a marketing gimmick. The government wanted to keep on expanding Higher Education, sending more and more students to university from a broader range of backgrounds to hit its 50% of school leavers going to university target. It also wanted to transfer some of the cost of study onto the student through the introduction of tuition fees, but at the same time not to discourage would-be applicants. The idea of the graduate premium allowed politicians to make the case that, whilst a degree would now cost more money, it was a worthwhile investment because it would enable a young person to earn more money in the future. This sense of *quid pro quo* is what lies behind the concept of the graduate premium. The idea ignores the intangible value of Higher Education, of learning for its own sake, and fosters a sense of expectation amongst applicants. Through its constant repetition, the graduate premium has become dangerously close to an implicit guarantee that all students will see a financial return on their loans.

It is now painfully obvious that many graduates will see little, if any, of these additional earnings. Their degree will often result in a net economic cost – a graduate liability. To protect the policy of expansion, government and universities have been extraordinarily quiet about the fact that many degrees should carry financial health warnings, as cigarette packages carry physical health warnings:

> *"People planning to do arts degrees really need to be told that they have to have some sense of direction as to what they are going to do after they graduate. That there aren't going to be these great prospects for them."* English and philosophy graduate

The most recent estimate of the graduate premium was produced in a 2011 report commissioned by the Coalition government. It proposed a premium of £108,000 – a 'mere' 73% reduction from the original £400,000 premium outlined by Blair's and Brown's New Labour. This new estimate would suggest that, on average, a graduate can expect to earn roughly £2,455 a year more than a non–graduate during their working life. Unfortunately, the problems with the graduate premium do not end with this dramatic reduction. It is worth highlighting that the 2011 estimate was produced **prior** to the massive fee increases in 2012. These added in the region of £18,000 worth of additional debt onto the average graduate and that's before compound interest takes hold.

Even more significantly, there are two basic problems with the graduate premium. Firstly, the underlying concept is not fit for the purpose for which it was intended. Secondly, each estimate of the graduate premium suffers from fundamental flaws in their method of calculation.

The first problem is that the concept of the graduate premium groups together universities and degrees with wildly different returns, providing an average that is meaningless for individual graduates. For example, based on the government's 2011 figures, degrees in medicine and dentistry return **£403,000** (to male graduates) and **£339,511** (to female graduates). On the other hand, mass communications and documentation subjects (media studies, if you wanted to know) return **£5,437** (to male graduates) and **£33,483** to female graduates. This is certainly not a new point; it was made quite forcefully in a 2004 paper by the academics Andrew Robinson and Simon Tormey:

> "The government is taking what is only an average figure, and turning it into a universal benefit. Nursing is now a graduate profession, yet nurses are paid abysmally low wages. Financial benefits do not 'generally' follow at all; they follow only for some students, only in some cases."[195]

We can see this problem quite clearly in Figure 1 (taken from the 2011 report on the graduate premium). This shows the huge variations in returns (graduate premiums) for graduates according to their degree subjects and gender.

In Figure 1, the premiums for male graduates in medicine are the only ones matching the original New Labour £400,000 estimate for the graduate premium. There are also a large number of subjects where the premiums for male and female graduates fall significantly below the current government–estimated average of £108,000: biological sciences (including psychology), creative arts and design, mass communications, non–European languages, history and philosophy.

Subject	Male Premium	Female Premium
Medicine and dentistry	£403,353	£339,511
Biological sciences	£77,197	£54,379
Veterinary sciences	£164,859	£127,503
Physical/environmental sciences	£108,020	£76,206
Mathematical and computer sciences	£151,507	£121,751
Engineering	£157,124	£99,116
Architecture	£169,545	£81,128
Law	£214,626	£108,246
Business and administrative studies	£130,165	£100,424
Mass communications	£5,437	£33,483
Non-European languages and lit.	£67,226	£23,103
Historical and philosophical studies	£1,395	£42,291
Creative arts and design	(-£15,302)	£27,192
Education	£89,634	£142,051

**Figure 1 - Expected graduate returns by degree subjects
(2011 estimate)**[196]

At the extreme end of this, what exactly is the point in being a male
creative arts graduate, when a degree in this subject will leave you
worse off on average than if you never attended university? On the
plus side, the report's estimates do appear to confirm what has long
been suspected – that funding tens of thousands of undergraduates
to study mass communications is not quite the critical investment in
the nation's youth that media studies lecturers would have us believe.

The estimates also identify major discrepancies in the returns to male and female graduates in both different subjects and average premiums. Official estimates for the average male premium are **£120,512** and for the average female premium **£82,371**. This imbalance is even more pronounced in subjects such as architecture and law where there is a rough ratio of 2:1 between the average male and female premiums. In addition, the 2011 report also notes that degree classifications significantly influence graduate premiums. For men graduating with a First, the average premium is £144,000; for men with a 2:2 the premium is £80,000. Interestingly, female graduates with a 2:1 degree actually achieve a higher premium (£87,486) than female graduates with first class degrees (£79,206).

These patterns around degree subjects, gender and degree award are not just evident in the 2011 report, they have been identified and described in all of the literature on the graduate premium. Anybody who has read any of the literature around the graduate premium must be aware of this and the problems inherent in the concept of an average graduate premium. The bottom line is that the idea of the graduate premium is not just nonsense; it is mendacious nonsense, leading applicants to commit to debt for returns that were never feasible. **Graduate returns vary hugely depending on an individual student's sex, university, degree classification and subject**. Even were we to accept the estimate of £108,000 (which we should not), there are graduates from many universities for whom this average premium is simply a statistical sleight of hand. Unfortunately, the devil in this particular detail is rarely (if ever) spelt out to potential university applicants.

The second problem facing the graduate premium is a number of flaws in its calculation. The 2003 estimate of £400,000 was based on a sample of the Labour Force survey. This data was un–weighted and based on the reported earnings of people in full–time employment. It later became clear this type of premium was something that only male graduates in the highest earning careers might reasonably expect (for example, male doctors). When asked how they had arrived at this figure, the government department responsible for the estimate (the DfES) declined to provide any further detail.

In 2005, the Royal Society for Chemistry and the Institute of Physics commissioned the accountancy firm PricewaterhouseCoopers (PwC) to investigate the graduate premium. In their report PwC identified a "gross graduate premium" of £160,000. A subsequent study by PwC in 2007 for Universities UK (the membership body for vice chancellors) conveniently arrived at the same figure. Universities UK argued that their estimate provided a strong case for the continuing value of a degree in the face of future tuition fees increases. This sponsorship is a key problem for the graduate premium. Research into the graduate premium has always been commissioned by organisations with a vested interest in attracting the maximum number of students to university. If we take fast–food providers' research into the health benefits of their products with several pinches of salt, why do we accord any more validity towards the conclusions of research published by university trade bodies promoting the financial health benefits of attending university?

Moreover, the reports on the graduate premium published in 2005 and 2007 (which had estimated the graduate premium at £160,000) used data from long–term studies of graduate returns based on graduates from the 1990s or earlier. This data was taken from periods with fewer graduates, much stronger prospects for graduate employment and fewer degrees with low employment prospects and pay. Projecting this data forward into a future where there were twice as many graduates fighting for a similar number of graduate jobs is at best specious. Similarly, the 2011 government report, which provides the estimate of £108,000, uses labour force survey data from 1996 to 2009 – again a period with significantly fewer graduates and, as a result, when there was more employer demand for graduates. This data is also drawn from a period of relative economic prosperity and growth, which ignores the dev-astating effect that the economic crisis will have had on graduate earnings and employment from 2008 onwards. The calculations also overlook the fact that earnings in a whole range of so–called graduate careers are also open to non–graduates via other routes, including law, banking, retail management and so on. The difference in earnings between graduates and non–graduates is therefore hugely and dishonestly over–estimated.

There are several other problems with the way the graduate premium is calculated which would have any statistician tearing their hair out. But in summary we can say that any politician or university cheerleader, who continues to make use of 'the graduate premium' to advertise the benefits of Higher Education, should be sued for mis–selling.

STUDENT DEBT

What about the other side of this transaction, the *quids* for this dubious *pro quo* – namely student debts? Well, they now mount up very quickly. In 1994, Barclays estimated that students graduated with an average debt of £3,190. In 2010, the student website Push's debt survey suggested that students graduated with an average debt of £19,562, Push claim that students graduating from 2015 onwards will have an **average** debt of £59,100.[197] (Figure 2)

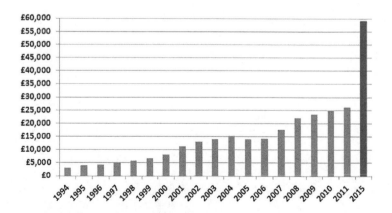

Figure 2 - The increase in average graduate debt 1994-2015

At the time of writing, a graduate earning under £25,000 a year won't have to pay back their student loan debt at all. But this debt will keep accruing compound interest at the rate of inflation (RPI which is usually higher than CPI) plus 3% (again, at the time of writing). Whilst debt is more widespread and socially accepted than 30 years ago, it still has implications that run far beyond the financial. Massive generational debt at this level will have serious psychological and social impacts for these graduates.

On an individual level, such debt constrains and even removes individual choice. Those rich enough to avoid most or all of this graduate debt can still take the time to "find themselves" or wait for the right job after university. Those without this luxury have a choice between "nose to the grindstone" to tackle this debt before the compound interest rides it over the horizon, or mortgaging their future to enjoy the present. It won't take many graduates choosing the latter option before student loan non-repayment becomes a serious issue for the taxpayer.

CHAPTER EIGHT

THE FINE ART OF MISMANAGEMENT

The Great Expansion has been massively funded by students, their families and the taxpayer and that expenditure has often been justified by politicians and universities as investment in the future of the country. But when we look at things like which universities or groups of universities have grown the most, which degree areas and subjects have increased in number and the financial results of the universities which have expanded most, we discover that this supposed 'investment in the future' has been mismanaged on an almost epic scale. And this mismanagement is going to be horrendously expensive for students, their families and taxpayers and extremely destructive for our Higher Education system and even for our country's economic future.

1. Which universities have expanded most?

The first point to make about expansion is that most of it has occurred in the universities and degrees that provide the worst returns for graduates and taxpayers alike. In other words, it has occurred predominantly in new universities, rather than elite universities. For example, the UK's two strongest universities, Oxford and Cambridge, have hardly increased their domestic undergraduate student body at all during expansion. The Russell Group* of elite research universities increased its intake of domestic undergraduates by around 7% between 1995 and 2010. Over the same period, Oxbridge increased its intake of domestic undergraduates by only around 0.95%.[198] For the rest of the university sector, the average rate of expansion during this period was closer to 70%.

Since 2001, 31 new universities have been created, normally

---

* This does not include Manchester University as its merger with UMIST in 2004 would distort rather than reflect the underlying pattern.

by changing the title of an existing college of Higher Education to 'University'. Chichester, Worcester and Cumbria all now proudly host their own 'universities'. From the perspective of the students who enrolled at university during expansion, it is worth remembering that these new universities were and are significantly under-resourced compared with their more established counterparts, something which is reflected in much worse ratios of staff to students and in higher student drop-out rates.

Another issue worth noting about expansion is the changing proportions of domestic and international students studying at the UK's elite universities. These universities may have barely increased their undergraduate intake of UK students during expansion, yet the number of international students enrolled at these universities has doubled in the last decade, correspondingly reducing the opportunities for domestic students. As the *Telegraph* commented in 2015:

> "Official figures show the number of international under-graduates has jumped from around 39,000 in 2005/2006 to over 75,000 in 2013/2014. Out of the 24 Russell Group universities, Exeter saw (a) jump from 685 foreign students a decade ago to over 3,200 – a 378 % increase. At Sheffield University, the number of students from China has gone from 580 in 2005 to over 4,000, a 590% increase." [199]

From the perspective of these universities, recruiting a greater percentage of non-EU students who can be charged fees at the international market rate (often triple that of domestic students) makes a great deal of financial sense. Viewed from the perspective of a national investment in Higher Education, this type of recruitment strategy is nonsensical.

2. Which degree subjects have increased most?

A further aspect of expansion to consider is in which subject areas it has occurred. Before we do this, it is worth reiterating that all of the available evidence suggests that degrees in science, technology, engineering and mathematics (STEM) subjects, on average, offer the best returns to graduates (and taxpayers) and that arts or humanities degrees, on average, offer the worst. It is also evident from all of the available research that STEM skills are in greatest shortage in both national and international labour markets. These statements were true at the start of expansion and they remain true today. Therefore, it seems reasonable to expect that expansion, as a national investment in the UK labour market, should have concentrated on providing a greater absolute and relative proportion of STEM graduates. So has this happened?

The short answer is "no". Instead, universities have focused on providing degrees which are cheap to run, quick to expand and which they think will attract students – essentially arts and humanities degrees. Taken at the level of individual institutions, this means an unbalanced cohort, top–heavy in arts and social science students. Considered at the national level, it is even more problematic. In 2004, a Higher Education Policy Institute (HEPI) report suggested that: "Current arrangements have resulted in institutions taking decisions based on their own self–interest which collectively may often result in suboptimal outcomes for the country as a whole."[200]

Unfortunately for Britain, British students and British taxpayers, expansion has mainly occurred in degree subjects for which there is little or no demand from employers. Figure 1 shows a list of full–time undergraduates across a number of the major areas of university study for the academic years 1994/95 and 2012/13.

	Number of students		
Subject	1994	2013	Difference
Medicine & dentistry	26,544	45,280	+70%
Subjects allied to medicine	60,239	133,770	+120%
Biological sciences	49,939	141,000	+180%
Agriculture & related subjects	11,159	8,850	-21%
Physical sciences	51,282	64,530	+26%
Mathematical sciences	15,528	30,040	+93%
Engineering & technology	96,118	93,945	-2%
Architecture, building & planning	29,489	26,230	-11%
Social studies	77,488	128,710	+66%
Mass communications & documentation	10,120	53,965	+430%
Historical and philosophical studies	32,847	53,105	+62%
Creative arts and design	62,835	134,250	+114%

Figure 1 - UK Full-time undergraduate study by subject area[201]

We can see the following main trends:

- A major increase in students studying subjects allied to medicine. This has largely been driven by nursing becoming a degree subject

- A huge increase in biological sciences students, driven by rises in the numbers of psychology and sports science students

- A large increase in undergraduates studying mathematical sciences. This is probably driven by a number of the less prestigious

universities offering degrees in 'mathematical studies' which
tend to be easier than pure maths degrees

- A drop in engineering and technology students

- A large increase in social sciences students

- A massive increase in mass communications and documentation (media studies) students. (The same 2011 research
  estimates suggest a £5,437 lifetime premium for male graduates
  in these subjects – just over a hundred pounds a year)

- A huge (114%) increase in creative arts and design students.
  (The government's own 2011 research into the graduate premium estimated that male graduates in these subjects were
  projected a net liability of £15,302 after graduation)

Nursing aside, expansion has mostly occurred in creative arts
and design, mass communications, social sciences and biological
sciences subjects. The number of students studying STEM subjects
has mostly declined in absolute or relative terms. Even in STEM
areas such as the physical sciences, where there has been growth,
it has been about half of the average growth across the sector as
a whole.

There are numerous other statistics available which reveal that
expansion has not occurred in the STEM subjects which we have
been told are so vital for our national economic competitiveness,
but primarily in new subjects (media studies, photography, sports
science, forensic sciences), for which there are few recognised career
paths, limited graduate–level jobs and minimal or even negative
graduate premiums. Expansion has also dramatically increased the
supply of graduates in law, psychology and journalism – professions
where there is no evidence of increased demand for these subjects
in the labour market.

In 2011, a search for "sports science" undergraduate degrees on the UCAS website identified 24 different courses at 13 different universities. A query for undergraduate courses in "sports studies" now produces 468 courses at a total of 69 universities. Despite the hoped–for boost in participation in sport promised from the £9.5+ billion 2012 London Olympics, it seems questionable whether we British have really become so athletic and sporty that the UK labour market actually needs the huge number of sports studies graduates that the universities are so enthusiastically producing.

3. What is the availability of key subjects?

There is one further issue which should be mentioned about the nature of expansion: that it has resulted in an overall reduction in the geographical availability of key subjects such as STEM degrees. Despite the massive growth in the Higher Education sector, the availability of these key subjects is actually reducing, at both the individual institutional and regional levels.

In 2006, the Institute of Physics noted that 30% of UK university physics departments had been closed or merged since 2001.[202] In the same year, a Universities and Colleges Union report showed that a total of 10% of maths and sciences courses had been scrapped across the Higher Education system between 1996 and 2006.[203] This reduction and concentration of STEM courses compounds many of the issues involved in equality of access. State–school pupils are statistically less likely to apply to or obtain places at elite universities. Disadvantaged students are much more likely to study and live at home, such that, if their local universities don't offer courses in these key subjects, which employers and the economy need, then realistically they can't or won't choose to study them.

EXPANSION OR JUST GETTING FAT?

Most expansion has occurred in the newer universities in cheap, easy–to–run subjects for which there is little demand in the labour market and, as a result, these are more likely to provide graduate liabilities rather than premiums. Moreover, the students who are studying these degrees at these universities are generally from state schools and have low levels of academic achievement. Many are from poorer and disadvantaged backgrounds and, in the name of expansion, they have been promised a mirage for which they are having to borrow up to £60,000 with compound interest to follow. It is hard to see how expansion of this type has benefited the majority of these students or their families. It is even more difficult to sustain the argument that expansion has provided the UK labour market with the skills that it needs. Finally, it is virtually impossible to identify what exactly taxpayers have received in return for footing a significant part of this bill.

There is one group of people and organisations that must have benefited from expansion, however, universities and their employees. At the very least, expansion must surely have been good for them?

UNIVERSITY CASH-FLOW PROBLEMS

Despite a massive increase in resources during expansion, the reality for many universities has been a hand–to–mouth existence, with the very real prospect of financial meltdown. In 2008, Tony Dickson, a former deputy vice chancellor at Northumbria University, describes many universities' financial problems thus:

> "Most universities operate with a year–on–year revenue surplus considerably below the 3 per cent of turnover that HEFCE recommends as a minimum. As a result, the sector is undercapitalised and under–invested. Another way of saying this is to point to the fact that the UK government spends less on Higher Education as a proportion of GDP than most other OECD nations." [204]

Throughout expansion, dozens of universities have flirted with insolvency – some yearly and some monthly. The reasons for this instability are complex. However, the scale of these problems shows that they are systemic in nature. In 2001, the Association of University Teachers (AUT) produced research showing that nearly half of UK universities and colleges were running annual deficits:

> "44% of Higher Education institutions were in deficit for 1999–00 – up from 28% in the previous year. Among universities £5m or more in the red were: Edinburgh (£11m), Aberdeen (£6.1m), Liverpool John Moores (£6.1m), Sunderland (£5.8m), Queen Mary College, London (£5.5m), and Ulster (£5m). The proportion of funding spent on teachers and staff had fallen from 70% in 1976–77 to 58% in 1999–00."[205]

A quick glance down this list shows that deficits were not confined to new universities, but also affected major research universities such as Edinburgh. This issue reappears every year, but with ever-larger debts. The names on the list might change, but the underlying message does not – many universities regularly operate at a loss. In 2009, data showed that:

> "Several universities had accumulated deficits of more than £4m by the end of the academic year 2006–07. Those with debts include the University of London (£6.9m), Manchester University (£12.4m), Nottingham Trent University (£7.4m), Thames Valley University (£5.8m), and the University of Sunderland (£4.2m)."[206]

This financial situation further reduces the resources available within these universities for teaching and learning. Paying 5% interest on £4 million costs £200,000 annually, equivalent to the cost of employing six junior academics. Moreover, the greater the deficit of a university, the worse its interest rates will be. The effects of this financial instability are visible in crumbling buildings and antiquated laboratories at some of the UK's elite universities. A 2010 report into the state of buildings across the Higher Education sector presented depressing findings:

> "LSE had 41% of their lecture theatres and classrooms deemed unsuitable for current use, Imperial College had 12% of its non-residential buildings branded 'inoperable'. More than 90% of Higher Education institutions had at least 10% of their buildings judged below the 'sound and operationally safe' category. One in 10 had at least 10% of their estate judged at serious risk of major breakdown."[207]

The LSE and Imperial College are two of our five top universities, institutions we rely on to attract the brightest and best students and academics from across the world. Worryingly, the same issues had been raised in 2002, as the *Guardian* noted at the time: "Universities need £5.1bn more to bring out-of-date equipment and crumbling buildings used for teaching up to scratch, a consultants' report advises today."[208]

Systemic financial instability has also been evident in round after round of redundancies at universities throughout expansion. As soon as a university gets into financial trouble (and many of them do) the first thing they do is reduce their biggest expense – staff. These redundancies often fail to reach the national news as they are salami-sliced over a hundred universities in tranches of 300 or less. The cumulative effect is significant staff churn, driven by crisis management rather than strategic planning. This approach can provide short-term financial relief whilst causing long-term operational damage. The Universities and Colleges Union (UCU) regularly reported on the scale of redundancies during the economic downturn. In 2009, they estimated: "... 4,593 jobs cuts expected in universities and 1,298 in colleges. According to UCU's survey of 45 universities, more than 2,000 jobs could be lost in London alone, with large Russell Group universities including University College London and Kings College London potentially cutting nearly 900 posts."[209]

In 2002, similar problems with university finances were evident, only without a wider financial crisis as a backdrop. Our universities are consistent in their instability. Post expansion they face financial crises in good economic times and bad economic times alike. In 2002, the *Guardian* reported that: "Universities are axing at least 1,400 jobs after a raft of poor budget settlements and falls in student numbers on some courses. Compulsory and voluntary redundancies and retirements in more than 20 institutions could ultimately reach well over 2,000."[210]

We can track regular financial crises at universities by looking for large–scale redundancies. Here is a very small sample:

1. In 2007, the University of Manchester needed to clear a £30 million debt created from a merger with UMIST. Part of the solution was 400 redundancies across the university.[211]

2. In 2008, the University of Plymouth made 220 staff redundant as part of a cost–cutting exercise aiming to save £10 million to "correct an historic overspend".[212]

3. In 2009, Leeds University was looking to save £35 million a year. Its union estimated that this would translate in up to 700 jobs being lost.[213]

4. Between 2010 and 2013, Salford University made around 400 staff redundant. This proved so expensive that in 2013 the university announced plans to reduce redundancy terms in a bid to save money.[214] The same year it announced plans for a further 95 redundancies.

5.   In March 2015, it was announced that Aberdeen University would cut 150 jobs to reduce its budget by £10.5 million.[215] Two months later Exeter University came forward with similar plans to cut over 200 jobs.[216] In April, Surrey University stated that it would cut around 100 jobs. Queen's University Belfast staff faced around 142 redundancies in November 2015.

6.   In 2016, Northumbria University announced plans for 112 redundancies to save £15 million over two years.[217]

This chapter could simply have been a list of the same story repeated with different names and dates involving multiple universities and redundancies running into the thousands each and every year. During expansion, universities throughout the UK have faced continual financial difficulties. Fortunately, many institutions have no shortage of takers for voluntary redundancy. The working conditions in cash–strapped universities can be abysmal and there is also a large contingent of skilled academics who can take redundancy and quickly gain employment at another university.

But whilst individual universities might make short term–savings in operational costs, they still face large redundancy payments. Considered in its entirety, the UK Higher Education system (and by this we really mean the taxpayer) suffers a net loss from these redundancies. Moreover, the staff most able to leave will take voluntary redundancy; those who aren't able are more likely to stay *in situ*. The net result of this is that financial crises often prompt an exodus of the most talented and mobile staff from universities.

Perhaps the best indicator of the instability of the expanded Higher Education system is the existence of a Higher Education Funding Council for England (HEFCE) "watch list". This includes all universities that HEFCE *knows* to have serious or possibly critical financial situations. The list is divided into two categories: Category 1: where an institution's health is at immediate risk; and Category 2: where an institution's health is likely to be at risk in the near future without urgent action. Category 1 means exactly what it says. In 2010, the University of Cumbria was in this watch list category with a £30 million deficit. In April 2010, the UCU reported that the university was uncertain whether it would have the financial means to pay its staff that month.[218] This was not an isolated incident. In recent years Gloucestershire University ran up a £31 million deficit and London Metropolitan University a £56 million deficit. That *at least* 30 universities out of 130 universities in England have been on the watch list since its inception testifies to the penny–pinching manner in which expansion has been carried out.

Crumbling buildings, a financial watch list, huge deficits and revolving–door mass redundancies are all results of the Great Expansion. Underlying each is also an unwillingness on the part of the Higher Education system to publicly acknowledge any of these problems.

In 2007, the Higher Education Funding Council for England (HEFCE) used legal action in attempt to prevent the *Guardian* from publishing the "watch list" of universities at risk of financial meltdown. The HEFCE was quite prepared to let students apply to these universities despite the threats of closure hanging over them. After two years of legal wrangling, the *Guardian* won the right to publish the watch list, noting that:

> "Secret files obtained under the Freedom of Information Act reveal a catalogue of financial difficulties facing universities over the past five years. They include running out of money, severely under–recruiting students and serious management weaknesses."[219]

A 2009 report on crumbling buildings was also paid for by the HEFCE (a publicly–funded body). Nevertheless, its findings only became public, again after a prolonged legal battle between HEFCE and the *Guardian* newspaper. Clearly, the HEFCE didn't consider this material to be of public interest. The stance adopted by the HEFCE in both situations appeared to be that of repressing any information that might paint UK universities in an unfavourable light. Whether universities were at risk of closure due to financial mismanagement or whether students were living or studying in unfit and possibly dangerous conditions, the reaction was the same – to bury bad news.

The HEFCE's position hadn't changed by 2010 when the *Sunday Times* decided to publish an updated version of the watch list. This attitude, to suppress important information (at the taxpayer's expense), typifies the selfish and self–absorbed nature of our degree-factory universities. This is because the protection of the system and of the perceived success of expansion is always more important than the protection of anything or anybody else. The self–interest of those benefiting from expansion dictates that there must be no doubt that the policy of expansion has been anything other than a total triumph and that universities are a valuable public good. This is simply not the case, though, when we look at the reality of expansion. Many of the additional graduates have taken dud degrees at third–rate universities which will offer them little or no economic advantage during their careers. For too many, studying for a degree will leave them and their families significantly worse off than if they had never applied to university. Expansion has not addressed the UK's skills shortages and it has also ushered in decades of serious financial instability for universities.

THE MONEY FLOWS IN

Following the introduction in 2012 of annual tuition fees up to £9,000 and then increasing every year with inflation, it seems that universities' financial situations have improved dramatically. In the year prior to the £9,000 fees, the UK's 160+ universities and Higher Education institutes had reserves of £14.7 billion, mostly concentrated in the elite universities. By the academic year 2016–17, these reserves had ballooned to £44.27 billion – coincidentally more than the total schools budget for England of £40.22 billion.

At the same time as their reserves rocketed, the universities were hit by a wave of damaging strikes by lecturers angered at proposals to change their pensions to cover an estimated £6 billion deficit in their pension scheme. As the *Times* reported, vice chancellors argued: "that they could not afford to make greater contributions to staff pensions or fund the generous defined benefit structure into the future without risking the financial health of their institutions."[220]

The recent flood of money into universities from the increased fees has resulted in a burst of enthusiasm for increased spending on new buildings – libraries, lecture theatres, laboratories and accommodation blocks. In 2017, universities spent about £4.87 billion on capital projects, up from £3.7 billion in 2012. What remains to be seen is who actually ends up footing the bill for the universities' new-found prosperity and increasing numbers of building projects – students taking ever-greater loans to pay ever-increasing tuition fees or taxpayers landed with the bill for massive, ever-mounting levels of student loan defaults as huge numbers of graduates fail to find the elusive graduate-level jobs (see Chapter 13 *The Student Loans Fiasco*).

CHAPTER NINE

ACADEMICS: RUNNING TO STAND STILL

"Some 84% of the 314 (Higher Education) staff surveyed said they suffered from stress... and 46% had depression. 62% said their work performance suffered.... This led to 25% taking time off work, with 5% quitting their job" Teacher Support Network Group 2014[221]

"62% of UK academics were actively considering moving abroad or into the private sector ... (It also found that) 47% had suffered ill-health because of their job and 55% would not recommend a career in Higher Education to their children."[222] UCU (University and College Union) research 2006

If we ask who has actually benefited from expansion, we can now discount a number of groups. Many students receive, on average, a worse deal in terms of their teaching and learning in spite of the massive rises in tuition fees first in 2006 and then in 2012. Many graduates are less likely to find graduate employment yet face crippling levels of debt. The economy and employers have been provided with graduates in subject areas that they neither want nor need and still face skills shortages in key areas. Taxpayers face shouldering the ever-increasing debt mountain likely to be left unpaid by graduates without graduate salaries. So, if the answer so far is "none of the above", then who does this leave?

The most obvious answer would be universities and their employees. After all, expansion has seen many new universities established and hundreds of thousands of new jobs created within those universities. So surely expansion has at least been a good thing for universities and their employees?

Unfortunately, the evidence does not support this proposition. Expansion has seen the finances of many universities stretched to breaking point until the 2012 tripling in tuition fees and, whilst there is subset of university employees who do seem to have rather enjoyed expansion, they are in an exclusive and well-paid minority. For most academics, expansion has resulted in a deteriorating professional environment, declining relative pay, greater levels of stress and the erosion of academic culture and values. In this, their experiences are simply a mirror image of the student experience post expansion. The same messages have been heard over and over again from academics throughout expansion. They often suffer from stress, struggle to manage impossible workloads and are bullied and pressured by universities into passing undeserving students. Union surveys examining academic stress levels strongly suggest that all of these problems have worsened throughout expansion:

> "The present survey (from 2010) suggests that levels of perceived stress have increased in recent years ... 81% of Higher Education respondents agreed or strongly agreed with the statement 'I find my job stressful', compared with 74% in the 2008 survey."[223]

In addition to this deterioration in working conditions, academic pay has failed to keep pace with that of other professions, with which it was comparable prior to expansion, such as solicitors or accountants. Post expansion, academics are also increasingly likely to be part-time or to be paid on an hourly basis. Expansion has not only made life more difficult for academics, it has also made it much more challenging and less rewarding for graduates who want to become academics. This has created a very real threat to the continuing ability of universities to develop and train their future workforce. In fact, the only group of people within universities for whom expansion appears to have been an unqualified success are vice chancellors. Their pay has rocketed both in absolute terms and relative to anybody else who works within a university. Their perks and conditions are often eye-wateringly impressive and there appears to be minimal connection between this pay and the performance of their universities.

ACADEMIC WORKLOADS

Academic workloads have changed in three ways during expansion. Firstly, they have increased due to the growing numbers of students that academics now teach and assess. The more seriously an academic takes their teaching and assessment, the more stress they can suffer as they try to complete a thankless task. The second problem is that academics now need to cater for a much greater ability range amongst their students. From an academic's perspective, this completely changes the nature of their role. Rather than acting as an expert transmitting information to a potentially receptive and capable audience, the academic is required to think and act more like a secondary–school teacher, pitching material at the pace of the slowest class member:

> "...the numbers of students with language difficulties and the number of students who simply cannot cope with a degree are making teaching more and more frustrating."
> Anonymous lecturer UCU Stress Survey[224]

As some universities will discipline staff when a percentage of their students fail a module, the easiest (and in fact the desired) response is for an academic to dumb down teaching and assessment to the lowest level that ensures passes for all. Students are happy, their parents are happy, the university management is happy, politicians are happy and this means less work for the lecturer. The academics who don't take this route not only make life difficult for themselves in the short term, they also damage their future promotion prospects.

The third workload problem is increased paperwork. This frustration is a constant theme in research into academic stress and runs through much of the evidence submitted to the 2009 House of Commons Select Committee report into universities. Paperwork further reduces an academic's time both to conduct research and to work with students. This often results in academics undertaking unpaid overtime. A 2013 UCU (University and College Union) report, based on labour force statistics, found that lecturers were one of two occupational groups with the highest levels of unpaid overtime: an average of 11.1 hours per week.[225]

Academic workload issues are also distributed unevenly. Those at new universities often face the heaviest workloads, partly as a result of the additional needs of their many students and a lack of government funding to address these needs. These problems were identified early on in New Labour's *Widening Participation* agenda. In 2002, the lecturers' union NAFTHE surveyed 1,000 lecturers in new universities, revealing that they:

> "...are spending much more time on preparation, assessment, administration and the needs of non–traditional students. ... 57% said preparation hours had increased and contact time with students had diminished and 42% now experience 'frequent or severe' stress. More than 60% described work with non–traditional (widening participation) students as now 'significant' or 'very significant.'"[226]

Survey after survey show that academics resent the additional resource and time that this paperwork diverts from their teaching and research in a system in which this has already been squeezed to the minimum. We can see this from individual academics' quotations in the 2008 UCU survey on stress, which talk about:

> "Increased bureaucracy taking up valuable time: ie having to justify everything that is done to leave a 'paper trail.'" [227]

> "The relentless increase in paperwork and administrative procedures and the declining staff student ratio."[228]

"The difficulties come from bureaucratic burdens imposed
by remote administrators, pointless form–filling."[229]

It is also visible in the collective responses of academics in surveys. In
2007, another UCU and ATL (a union for education professionals)
survey into stress found that: "77% of respondents felt that their
workloads had increased over the past three years. Asked what factors
had contributed to this, more than 83% blamed more administrative
duties, while more than 47% cited rising student–to–staff ratios."[230]

In 2008, a UCU survey reported on the impact that this
increased paperwork had on the capacity of academics to work with
and support their students. Despite the backdrop of increasing fees
during the previous decade, the survey found that: "...nearly eight
out of ten said they were spending less or the same amount of time
with students as they did ten years ago. But lecturers say they are
snowed under with paperwork. One in four said they spent more
than 25 hours a week on administration."[231]

Not much had changed a decade later. In 2017, a *Times Higher
Education Supplement* survey of over a 1,000 academics found over
72% complaining that there was "too much administration associated
with teaching at my institution".[232]

BULLYING

"Only 45% of UCU members in Higher Education could
say they were never subjected to bullying at work." UCU
Stress Survey 2011[233]

"At least 1,957 university staff asked for support or advice
due to bullying or harassment during 2007, 2008 and 2009.
The true figure is likely to be a great deal higher since
many universities do not record informal complaints."[234]

Academics are bullied for a variety of reasons – because they refuse to collude in "dumbing down", because they aren't producing the expected research outputs[235], or because they are struggling with paperwork and workloads. The 2008 UCU report provided the following anonymous quotations from academics:

> "I have been bullied and have received counselling for this. I am now on regular medication." [236]

> "Our head of department bullies staff who speak their mind ... Bullying takes the form of higher teaching loads, less resources for research, and unreasonable requests."[237]

> "I have managed to 'keep my head down' and therefore do not suffer from direct bullying or intimidation; I see its effects on others. This is extremely upsetting and frustrating as I feel I am powerless to do anything about it."

In many cases, the bully is also a victim of bullying by their own bosses. Some universities foster and reproduce a culture of bullying across the whole organisation. A 2007 UCU survey of Leeds Metropolitan University found that: "Some 96% of respondents said they felt inhibited about positively criticising policies of Leeds Met and 63% reported witnessing bullying at work. 42% feel intimidated at work, 37% feel their work is belittled and 24% feel they have been humiliated by bullying incidents."[238]

This not only runs contrary to the underlying spirit and culture of academia, but it is also detrimental to the well–being of staff and their ability to teach and inspire students. The growth of bullying as a management technique within UK universities seems to be a direct result of the degree–factory university. It is most visible in new universities, where the majority of expansion has occurred with limited resources. In the 2012 UCU stress survey, 14 out of 15 English universities with the worst stress levels for bullying were new universities.[239]

THE NEXT GENERATION

"Only about a third of postgraduates, who are employed as teachers, feel that they receive appropriate supervision and feedback. In a survey of 350 postgraduates... 63% per cent had received no advice on professional development or training." *Times Higher Education Supplement* 2011[240]

Universities are facing an even bigger problem than a demoralized and unhappy workforce. It isn't clear that they have a sustainable system in place to develop the quantity or quality of future academics that expansion has made necessary. There are many dimensions to this problem, but the underlying issue is a short-term and reactive approach to employee management that has been driven largely by expansion. There are three specific concerns: an increased reliance on international academics within UK universities, the growth in the number of part-time academics within universities and ever-decreasing pay levels for academics. Each of these issues is well-documented and each negatively affects teaching and learning.

1. Dependence on international academics

The UK has been highly successful at attracting academics from around the world to teach in its universities (Figure 1).

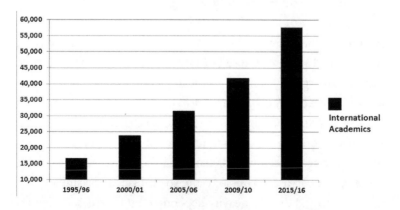

Figure 1 - **The growth of international academics in UK universities**

During the last twenty years statistics show that: "In 1995/96 a total of 16,705 overseas academics were employed (13.2% of the total workforce). By 2015/16 this figure was 57,548 (21.3% of the total workforce)."[241]

This is a massive increase in both the relative and absolute numbers of international academics employed by UK universities. It has happened largely because overseas academics with more experience and a greater track record of publications from many countries, where salaries are lower than in the UK, can often be employed for the same salary as a domestic postgraduate with no experience or publications. Because staff salaries represent by far the largest part of a university's running costs, this is a key area where universities can save money. The increase also reflects the fact that UK universities are not producing sufficient postgraduates in STEM subjects to keep pace with the demand for people to teach and research in these subjects. This was the view of the Universities and Colleges Employers' Association:

> "The influx of overseas academic staff reflects the impact of the Research Assessment Exercise (RAE) as Higher Education Institutes seek to improve their ratings and shortages of qualified, home post–doctoral students in particular subjects to fill teaching posts." [242]

As a result, the subjects where our universities increasingly rely on international academics are STEM subjects and languages, the same subjects that generations of politicians and business leaders have assured us are of central importance to the UK's long–term economic success. A 2007 report by Universities UK (UUK) noted that: "The majority of foreign academics tend to be younger than their UK colleagues and are concentrated in languages, computer science, maths, physics, engineering, technology and social or political studies."[243]

Not only is the UK heavily dependent on overseas academics for STEM subjects, we are also increasingly dependent on recruiting international research students to study these subjects at postgraduate level. The scale of this issue was made clear in the same UUK report, which revealed that in STEM and language subjects: "Non–UK students are particularly prominent at postgraduate level, making up 71 per cent of taught postgraduate enrolments and 48 per cent on research programmes in 2005/06."[244]

This shortage of domestic STEM postgraduates reflects the unbalanced and dysfunctional way in which expansion has occurred in UK universities at the subject level.

2. The rise of the part-time academic

"In 1994/95 there were 102,701 full–time academic staff and 12,020 part–time academic staff. In 2015/16 there were 135,015 full–time academic staff and 66,365 part–time academic staff."[245]

Between 1994 and 2016 the number of academic staff on full–time contracts increased by 31% while those on part–time contracts increased by over **500%** (Figure 2).

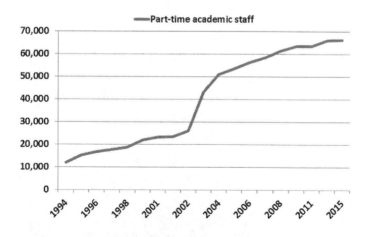

Figure 2 - Part-time academics 1994-2016[246]

This figure cuts to the heart of expansion – it has been done on the cheap, with disregard for the long–term consequences for universities, the quality of the student experience and the quality of graduates. By definition, part–time academics have less time to offer students. Moreover, they have fewer employment rights and reduced job security. All of this makes them both cheaper and much more compliant employees, more vulnerable to pressure by university management who not only have the carrot of a full–time contract, but also the stick of removing contracted hours. Young academics (especially young female academics) and academics from ethnic minorities are disproportionately represented amongst these part–time academics. In 2011, 38% of full–time academic staff were female compared with 55% of part–time academic staff.[247]

This precarious twilight world between proper employment and postgraduate status can continue for many years until an academic can secure a full–time post within a university. This uncertainty favours those with independent means or a family able to support them, further reducing the potential pool from which future academics can emerge.

3. Academic pay

In addition to worsening work conditions and increased barriers to entry, expansion has also seen the rewards associated with academia reduce substantially. In the 1980s, a senior lawyer, a GP and a professor might have expected to earn roughly equivalent salaries. In 2009, in contrast, the average UK professor made £66,000[248], the average GP salary was £110,000[249] and the salary of a circuit judge was £128,296.[250] This makes it even more difficult for universities to attract the brightest and best students to academic careers. Professor Alison Richard, the vice chancellor of Cambridge University, told the House of Commons in 2007:

"... a very bright graduate will not necessarily stay on to do a PhD. It is now very difficult to find a British student studying subjects like engineering and economics at post-graduate level. Competition from overseas universities and from industry offering better salaries and career opportunities entice the best students away."[251]

Not only is academic pay uncompetitive against other professions, it is also uncompetitive compared with academic salaries elsewhere in the world. The USA, Canada and Australia pay their academics more than the UK. Countries investing in their universities, such as China and the various oil–rich Arab states, are also offering significantly higher academic salaries under much more favourable tax regimes.[252]

Whilst many academics might not be primarily driven by economic motivations, they will require an economic settlement which allows them access to certain basics such as a mortgage. The relative decline in academic pay is undermining even this. For example, between 2009 and 2015 academic pay rose by 5.4% against inflation of 17.2%, meaning a real terms decrease of 11.8% in academic pay. As the cost of living increases and salaries remain stagnant, this will only increase the pressure on academics or would–be academics to consider other career avenues.

The problems in academic pay are exacerbated by the collective pay bargaining orchestrated by the academic unions. As a result of this agreement, academics in different subjects receive very similar, if not identical, pay depending on their seniority rather than their performance or the relative value of their subject expertise. It also means that different universities largely pay the same rates to their staff, whether they are working at Derby or Oxford, Cambridge or Cumbria. This means that a professor of engineering receives roughly the same salary as a professor of media studies. This in no way corresponds to the different salaries that these two professors could expect to earn for their respective expertise in the international academic marketplace or the commercial sector. Nor does it correspond to the value the academics provide to their students and taxpayers.

The relative fall in academic salaries, the imposition of a collective pay structure and the need for universities to recruit staff with academic experience and publications have also hampered the efforts of universities to recruit specialist staff for key subjects. In 2009, the House of Commons Select Committee took evidence from professional bodies for medicine and engineering which revealed two concerns. In subjects such as medicine, where the professional rewards far outstrip those of academics, it is impossible for universities to offer salary packages that would attract staff with these skills. If a qualified doctor can earn about twice the salary of an academic, then how many doctors are likely to want to take a pay cut of that magnitude to teach? Given the growing need for medical academics to train increasing numbers of doctors to care for a growing and ageing population, the Medical Council stressed the seriousness of this issue in 2009:

> "There has been a dramatic fall in the academic workforce over the past decade. The number of senior academic trainees and fully qualified academics stands at only 2,937 – a fall of 27% since 2000. In addition, clinical academics are an ageing group ... The decline in the academic workforce has occurred at the same time as an unparalleled increase in the number of medical students and the establishment of new medical schools, especially in England." [253]

The Engineering Council raised the issue of universities prioritizing recruitment of staff with academic papers and journal articles over those with practical real-world experience. This is driven by the universities' need to maximize their research revenue by employing academics with numerous publications. It therefore precludes the recruitment of staff from industry with experience but few publications. Unfortunately, these are the people with exactly the skills needed to teach future generations of engineers how to design bridges and circuit boards for nuclear power stations. The Engineering

Council warned that: "Thus, increasingly, engineering students are being taught by staff who may have little direct experience of engineering practice.... funding constraints militate against universities employing engineering academics who are from industry as they lack the required publications record (for the) Research Assessment Exercise."[254]

VICE CHANCELLORS: PAY AND PERFORMANCE

Expansion has not been doom and gloom for all those who work in universities, however. In fact, there is one group of university employees who seem to have done rather well out of it: "Average vice chancellor pay in 1994/95 was £94,000.[255] In 2015/2016, average vice chancellor pay (including pension contributions) was £274,405."[256]

In 2012, a review of public–sector pay found that the median vice chancellor pay was over 15 times that of staff at the bottom of the university pay scale, and that this ratio was 19:1 within Russell Group universities.[257] In comparison, pay increases for academic staff have lagged dramatically: "In 1995/96 the average academic salary was £25,873, by 2008/09 this had risen to £43,486."[258]

Between 1994 and 2016 vice chancellors' average pay increased by **nearly 300%**. The total inflation rate between 1994 and 2016 was **87%.** So, if vice chancellors' pay had simply kept pace with inflation, their average pay would now be around £175,000. To put this into context, the last two decades of these above–inflation increases cost students and the taxpayer an additional £16 million or so per year. A 2012/13 investigation revealed that Russell Group vice chancellors enjoyed an average **salary rise of more than £22,000** or around **50%** of the average academic salary. This average increase of 8.1% for vice chancellors in 2012/13 contrasted sharply with a 1% average increase for other university employees in the same year. In 2014, Sheffield University awarded its vice chancellor an annual increase of £105,000 (a 39% increase), in the same year the university continued to ignore pleas to pay its staff the living wage of £7.65 per hour.

Universities UK (UUK), the body which represents vice chancellors, has routinely defended these possibly indefensible increases.
In 2012 Nicola Dandridge, their chief executive, said that the salaries
of vice chancellors: "...reflected what it takes to recruit and retain
individuals able to run complex, multimillion–pound organisations,
which are operating in an increasingly competitive, global market".[259]

Unfortunately for this argument, vice chancellor performance
has not always matched pay. For example, in 2014 the *Times Higher
Education Supplement* published research showing that vice chancellors' pay often grew in the face of declining applications to their
universities, noting that: "In one case, a vice–chancellor's total
remuneration package rose by nearly a fifth despite applications, a
key factor in a university's financial health … falling by a quarter".[260]

Similarly, research in 2014 by the Brighton Business School,
which examined vice chancellor pay awards in relation to university
performance indicators (such as improvements in funding awards
and widening participation), found that a "significant proportion"
of these awards bore no relation to performance.[261]

Whereas vice chancellors were traditionally seen as academic
leaders, they now wish to be viewed as Chief Executive Officers
leading dynamic multi–million pound organisations. This heroic
re–imagining has been deployed regularly to defend the trebling of
their average salaries during the last 15 years. Baroness Blackstone's
statement in 2002 is typical: "But clearly, universities will wish the
salaries of their vice–chancellors to reflect the fact that they are
successfully running multimillion–pound businesses".[262]

This analogy is not entirely accurate as universities are still
largely state–funded institutions rather than "multimillion–pound
businesses". Vice chancellors are not competing at risk in a genuinely open marketplace. But rather they are operating an oligopoly
in a walled garden within the public sector that they have lobbied
extensively to remain walled. The number of these "businesses" suffering financial crises and rising concerns over their product quality
might also raise questions about the use of the word "successfully".

Within many universities, the drive away from academic excellence towards corporate managerialism has been led from the very top. It is not simply that vice chancellors have failed to safeguard academic standards; often their reinterpretation of their role has actively fostered the decline of academic culture and values within universities. Professor Geoffrey Alderman expressed it thus:

> "...vice chancellors ... see themselves ... as business managers intent on achieving 'market share'. In this quest, academic standards are viewed as subordinate and, hence, dispensable. In particular, vice chancellors have permitted and indeed encouraged the decline in academic standards in the desperate search for (a) increased income from 'full cost' fee–paying international students, (b) more favourable student retention rates and (c) .. higher positions in various 'rankings' or 'league tables'."[263]

Moreover, given an evident decline in academic standards across the whole Higher Education sector, it might seem difficult to justify an average salary of over £272,000 a year. Even more pertinently, what is the rationale for vice chancellors who leave under a cloud of mismanagement and financial crisis receiving enormous pay–offs, such as the £265,000 handed to a vice chancellor who left their university in crisis in 2010?[264]

The reality is that many of the financial crises in UK universities have been directly linked to executive mismanagement. Often the actions of senior management have precipitated or worsened financial problems. The most obvious example is that of London Metropolitan University, created in 2002 from the merger of two troubled universities, London Guildhall University and the University of North London. In 2009, the university's vice chancellor resigned following a series of accounting errors which left the university £56 million in debt. The chair and other members of the university's board of governors were forced to resign by the Higher Education Funding

Council for England (HEFCE). The university's audit committee also departed. The *Guardian* reported that: "The university is facing up to 550 job cuts among its 2,300 staff, following the revelation that it had been overpaid for students who failed to complete courses. It is understood to be taking a £15m funding cut this year and is in negotiations about how it will pay back a further £38m."[265]

Apart from the scale of the debt, the most notable point was the requirement for HEFCE to force the resignations of senior management. This not only showed a whole system of institutional governance failing to provide checks and balances against mismanagement, it also highlighted an executive unwilling to accept any responsibility for their failures.

The crisis at London Metropolitan might have been the biggest to hit the Higher Education sector to date, but it was not an isolated incident. There have been plenty of other instances where the massive financial rewards offered to vice chancellors have signally failed to attract "individuals able to run complex, multimillion-pound organisations". The 160+ UK universities and Higher Education institutes lose on average at least one vice chancellor a year under a cloud. This does not include a number of other vice chancellors who retired "more quietly" shortly before or after crises hit their universities

Date	University	VC Departure
2015	Sussex	Vice chancellor to step down after disciplinary proceedings against 5 students collapse, requiring compensation and apologies.
2014	Durham	Vice chancellor resigns soon after a vote by the university's senate over whether to reduce his powers.

Date	University	VC Departure
2014	Plymouth	The university suspended the vice chancellor after they spent £95,000 on seven handcrafted chairs for graduation ceremonies.
2013	East of London	Vice chancellors and two pro vice chancellors resign following the closure of the university's Cyprus campus.
2012	Canterbury Christ Church	Vice chancellor resigns suddenly and without explanation from the university.[266][267]
2011	Wales	An undercover investigation showed payment for bogus qualifications. The university declined to comment on the subsequent departure of the vice chancellor.[268]
2011	London School of Economics (LSE)	(Director) Vice chancellor resigns over the LSE's links to Libya.[269]
2011	Abertay Dundee	The vice chancellor disputed that he had retired following suspension. He pursued an employment tribunal claim. The university refused to make public the reason for his suspension.[270]
2010	Gloucestershire	Vice chancellor resigns/retires early following a financial crisis, senior resignations and industrial tribunals.
2009	East of London	Vice chancellor was suspended following allegations of a lack of leadership and vision.[271]
2009	London Metropolitan	Vice chancellor resigned in the wake of accounting mistakes which created a £56m deficit.[272]
2009	Leeds Metropolitan	Vice chancellor resigns avoiding suspension for bullying allegations.[273]

Date	University	VC Departure
2005	Ulster	Vice chancellor resigns following an investigation into allegations of lax financial management, bullying and attending meetings drunk.[274]
2002	University College London	Vice chancellor quits after a letter of no confidence from senior staff.[275]
1999	Lincolnshire and Humberside	Staff called for the resignation of vice chancellor, claiming "gross mismanagement" 18 months after an 80% vote of no confidence.
1998	Thames Valley	Vice chancellor forced out after the QAA reported that the university could no longer be trusted to safeguard the quality of its degrees.[276]
1997	Glasgow Caledonian	Vice chancellor sacked for "gross misconduct".[277]
1996	Swansea Metropolitan	Vice chancellor resigned following revelations about lax academic standards.[278]
1996	Portsmouth University	Vice chancellor resigned following an inquiry into expenses irregularities.[279]
1995	Huddersfield	Vice chancellor left after a 98% vote of no confidence and the removal of elected staff members from the governing body.[280]

Figure 3 - Vice chancellor departures 1995-2015

Many of the senior managers who have left their universities in "difficult circumstances" were amongst the best paid. For example: "In 2007/08 (the London Metropolitan vice chancellor) received a salary of £330,000. The average vice chancellor pay for that year was £194,000" and "in 2009/10 (the Gloucestershire vice chancellor) received a salary of £399,000. The average vice chancellor pay for that year was £213,000."

Neither of these vice chancellors "successfully" ran "multimillion-pound businesses". More accurately, they ran publicly-funded organisations into the ground. The problems of Gloucestershire and London Metropolitan are only the most visible examples which contradict the argument that you have to pay such high salaries to recruit the best possible talent for senior management roles within universities. Whatever the case, it is doubtful that any other public-sector employees have seen anything like this rate of salary increase. The average vice chancellor now earns £100,000 a year more than the prime minister and the **highest vice chancellor salaries are in excess of £500,000** for non-elite universities.

CHAPTER TEN

EMPLOYERS: "WHERE'S THE BEEF?"

Whilst individual universities can do little about the state of the national economy, collectively they have failed to prepare many of their graduates for the post–expansion labour market. Rather than adapting their support and guidance to the new conditions, they have continued to operate on the basis that all graduates will get jobs simply by virtue of having degrees. This issue was mentioned time and time again by the graduates interviewed for this book: *"The system doesn't prepare you for the sheer amount of work that you have to do to get a job after your degree. I really wasn't expecting it to be this hard."* Engineering graduate

Expansion has itself undermined many undergraduates' career preparation as the sheer size and scale of universities now make it difficult, if not impossible, to offer more intensive and focused careers advice formally to all students during their study. Resources spread ever more thinly within universities only exacerbate these problems.

One of the central arguments for expansion has been the alleged need of UK employers for more graduate–level skills. This proposition has looked increasingly threadbare as employers have regularly raised concerns about both the quantity and quality of UK graduates provided by expansion. Already by 2004, the President of the British Chambers of Commerce was calling for more school leavers to start jobs rather than degrees, noting that:

> "The drive to get more and more students into university is having a damaging impact on both business and students. Rather than following the route to university, young people should consider the excellent opportunities available to them through pursuing vocational routes of learning. Business is suffering from an acute skills shortage, which is a barrier to raising productivity and competitiveness."[281]

Since 2000, UK business organisations have produced research outlining four specific issues that have undermined employers' confidence in expansion. These include an oversupply of graduates both generally and in specific subjects; graduates lacking basic skills such as numeracy and literacy; graduates unable to think and act independently; and graduates lacking basic subject knowledge. In 2013, a YouGov survey of 635 employers found that 52% believed that either none or few graduate recruits were actually ready for the work place.[282] Worryingly, many post–expansion graduates appear to **agree** with this assessment. A 2011 survey by Totaljobs. com found that:

> "Half of all recent graduates believe their university educa-
> tion did not adequately equip them for the world of work,
> and a quarter wouldn't recommend Higher Education to
> those currently studying for their A– levels."[283]

If employers and graduates are now raising the same questions about the effectiveness of post–expansion degrees as preparation for the modern workplace, then why aren't universities or indeed the government listening to them?

THE SUPPLY AND DEMAND OF GRADUATES

Rather than meet employers' repeated demands for more STEM graduates, expansion has seen our universities produce a massive surplus of graduates in subjects such as journalism, social work, forensic science and sports science for which there is limited or shrinking demand from employers. In 2012, our universities had three times more sports science students than physicists and three times as many English students as chemistry students. Whilst English teachers can be useful occasionally, it is hard to remember a desperate shortage of them during the last two decades that threatened our economic success and required their numbers to double. In 2012, we also had about 10,000 more students doing design studies than we had studying maths, physics and chemistry combined.

Business organisations have been issuing warnings about UK universities oversupplying graduates in questionable subject areas for a number of years. In 2004, the CBI described the British economy as:

> "...under serious threat as its world–class science base is eroded while it faces strong competition from new, as well as traditional, international rivals. The mismatch is such that some British businesses are recruiting from overseas. Competitors such as China, India, Brazil and parts of Eastern Europe produce hundreds of thousands of scientists and engineers each year."[284]

Employers have also voiced concerns about the quality as well as the quantity of the STEM graduates that our universities produce. Many employers who are looking for STEM graduates have become so concerned about the quality of UK graduates that they now focus on recruiting international graduates instead. In 2008, the Association of Graduate Recruiters (AGR) stated that: "Of the 217 employers surveyed, 25% are now actively marketing their UK vacancies to overseas graduates in order to 'recruit the very best talent that is available.'[285] Underlying these concerns are familiar issues about both the curriculum shrinkage within UK degrees and their failure to stretch the brightest UK graduates to their full potential. In 2008, the Oxford professor of mathematics Marcus De Sautoy described a similar recruitment pattern amongst financial firms in the City of London:

> "The great majority of the mathematicians they rely on are recruited from overseas. Countries such as China and India have realised the crucial role mathematicians play in the success of their economy and are pumping out fantastically competent mathematicians that increasingly

fill the hole left in Britain. The cost to the UK economy since 1990 of not raising homegrown mathematicians totals £9 billion."[286]

Such warnings echo over a decade's worth of research into what UK employers want from university expansion. Specifically, a higher quantity and quality of science, technology, engineering and maths (STEM) graduates. For example, the Confederation of British Industry's 2015 Education and Skills survey found 52% of employers struggling to recruit experienced STEM staff and 42% experiencing similar difficulties in recruiting STEM graduates. In the same survey, 40% of employers complained about the content of STEM qualifications and 34% about the quality of STEM graduates.[287] Problematically, this demand for STEM graduates is only likely to increase in the future. In 2013, the Social Market Foundation produced a report which suggested that an ageing workforce will leave around 100,000 STEM vacancies a year in the labour market of the future. To fill a gap of this size, UK universities would need to produce an additional 40,000 STEM graduates annually.[288] But, in spite of the Great Expansion, it looks like Southern European, Eastern European and Asian universities will have to produce these STEM graduates for us.

This research also points to a growing interest in degree subjects which require graduates to think logically and analyse complex data. Research into this area consistently shows that employers also want graduates who can think independently and creatively and who have learnt how to learn. Finally, they want graduates with ICT skills, strong literacy and numeracy, who are motivated, hard–working and flexible. Instead of meeting these requirements, expansion has:

1. Fuelled growth in soft subjects, such sports science, dance and drama, for which there is little or no demand.

2. Reduced in absolute or relative terms the annual supply of STEM graduates.

3. Created a massive oversupply of graduates in areas where there is low and/or static demand from employers (e.g. law, psychology, photography).

4. Evolved a factory model of Higher Education which discourages the independent and creative thinking employers want in favour of a mechanical approach to learning.

5. Failed to address the problems that many school leavers have in literacy, numeracy or subject knowledge.

As a result, there is a large and growing gap between what universities are supplying and what employers actually need. But the most fundamental issue, and one which has been routinely ignored by policy-makers and universities, is that our labour market simply doesn't need the number of graduates that expansion is providing. Research by the Confederation of British Industry (CBI) in 2008 found that: "There are currently 10.1 million graduates in the UK but only 9 million graduate-level jobs."[289]

Other investigations into the UK labour market have consistently identified skills shortages for employees with vocational qualifications equivalent to A-levels, rather than degrees. In addition to STEM-level graduate skills, what employers really need are school leavers with specific vocational training in areas such as care or retail. This is not just the case for today's labour market, it is likely to be the case for the labour market of the future, too. In 2013, the Telegraph reported on research from the US government which predicted that:

"…just one out of the top nine occupations expected to create the most jobs this decade requires a degree. The picture is truly dire for graduates: only 5 of the top 30 fastest–growing occupations expected to create the most jobs by 2020 require a degree and 10 of the top 30 don't require any kind of qualification. Among the top 10 fastest–growing are retail sales staff; food preparation; customer service reps; labourers and freight, stock, and material movers; lorry and van drivers; and various healthcare aides."[290]

The types of non–university vocational qualifications, which would support careers in these growth areas, do exist. But they have been demoted in the race to get an ever–increasing number of students to university. The *de facto* message of expansion to young people and their parents has been that non–university vocational qualifications are the second–class, or even third–class, citizens of the qualifications world. The most compelling evidence of the influence that this attitude has exerted can be found in surveys of new mothers of whom a staggering 97% now want their babies to attend university.[291]

The scale of the graduate oversupply problem becomes clear when we consider the numbers of graduates now working in non–graduate positions, as the *Guardian* noted in 2016: "Over one in 10 childminders (11.5%, according to the 2014 Labour Force Survey) are graduates. One in six call–centre staff have degrees, as do about one in four of all air cabin crew and theme–park attendants." [292]

One newspaper reader, responsible for recruitment at a call centre, remarked: "*I'm increasingly interviewing graduates with useless degrees*". What is also clear is that, despite experts raising concerns about this for over a decade, their warnings have been roundly ignored by universities and successive governments in their rush to expand the UK's Higher Education sector. For example, back in 2004 labour market academics Professor Keep and Dr Mayhew criticised the 50% target for Higher Education participation as unnecessary and unhelpful, arguing that it:

"... has major implications for the economy, where there remain a substantial number of jobs with vocational requirements below degree level, not least in craft and technical occupations. It is doubtful whether graduate courses (honours or foundation) are an effective or efficient means of meeting such demand."[293]

The problem of an oversupply of graduates at the regional level was raised in 2002 by the think tank Local Futures. In an analysis of the skills profiles of the nine English regions, they found that:

"...the number of high-skilled jobs is failing to keep pace with rising qualifications. Between 1994 and 2000, a period of healthier economic growth, the proportion of workers in the capital who had a degree or equivalent rose by over 22%. The number of jobs in the most graduate-intensive industries rose at little more than a fifth of that rate. The mismatch is repeated around the country.... the graduate labour pool grew by 23% between 94–00, while knowledge-intensive industries raised their share of national employment from 48% to 50%, an increase of less than 5%."[294]

In the same year, the Institute of Directors was equally critical of the impact of expansion on the provision of a skilled workforce for employers: "The current obsession with sending as many young people as possible into Higher Education undermines vocational training by making it appear a second best. This helps no one, least of all the many students who study inappropriate Higher Education courses."[295]

In short, despite the fact that improving the quality of the UK's workforce has supposedly been the *raison d'être* for expansion, in practice both the aims and implementation of the policy have drawn sharp criticism from a broad coalition of its intended beneficiaries.

They have attacked the policy for creating an oversupply of graduates, for trivialising non–university vocational training and, finally and most consistently, for expanding UK Higher Education in a variety of poorly–chosen subject areas. Rather than these criticisms being addressed, they have instead been repeatedly ignored by policy makers and universities bent on a policy of expansion at any cost.

DEGREE CHOICES AND THE JOB MARKET

Leaving aside the swathes of students studying degree subjects for which there is absolutely no employer demand, universities have knowingly created a grossly disproportionate number of places on vocational degree subjects such as law and psychology. Successive governments have ignored this academic mendacity as part of a complicit agreement to drive expansion with little or no regard to the long–term consequences for students. This pattern has been repeated in numerous subjects: for example, the supply of forensic science, physiotherapy and social work graduates all massively outstrip the demands of employers in these areas.

LAW GRADUATES

In 2012, there were around 54,000 full–time undergraduates studying law at UK universities, providing about 17,000 law graduates a year. The annual number of training contracts available in 2011 for trainee solicitors was a mere 5,441. By 2015 this had increased to 5,457, an additional 16 places. In 2011 there were 22,915 entrants to law degrees, by 2015 this figure had risen to 25,755 an additional 2,840 students

The scale of this problem is clear in Figure 1:

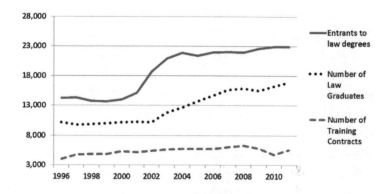

Figure 1 - The oversupply of law students 1996-2011

Whilst some of these graduates might secure other jobs working in the legal sector (paralegals, legal secretaries), many won't even get that opportunity. In fact, there are so many undergraduates studying law, that law students are almost more likely to end up as baristas than barristers. As for being 'called to the bar', the bar many of these law students will be called to won't require any great legal knowledge. An in–depth knowledge of cocktails would probably be more useful.

The professional bodies for solicitors and barristers, the Law Society and the Bar Council, are quite explicit on their websites about *exactly how difficult it is* to obtain a training position in either role. As one law graduate, now working in a call centre for a medical claims company, said "unless you know someone who knows someone, you haven't a chance". Similarly explicit advice about the scarcity of legal positions for graduates is noticeably absent from the web pages of university law departments eager to attract new student fee fodder nor is it mentioned in sundry university comparison websites.

FORENSIC SCIENCE DEGREES

In 2011, the government Forensic Science Service (FSS), which employs the vast majority of the UK's forensic scientists, was listed for closure by the government. Even before this announcement, it was clear that there was a massive gap between the supply of and demand by employers for "CSI" degrees. In 2011, the *Guardian* noted that the FSS: "...employed 1,600 people, not all of them scientists, while LGC Forensics, Britain's largest private provider, employs 500 people. But with more than 8,500 forensics students in the UK, it's little surprise that the FSS website warns applicants that its advertised jobs see responses from 1,000 applicants."[296]

Universities were quite aware of this. But they continued increasing the number of CSI–related courses. The most important thing for them was recruiting enough students to continue to run their degree courses. Considerations about what subjects were actually needed by the UK economy and what degrees would be most useful to graduates didn't seem to factor in to their decisions about these universities' degree portfolios. If a subject was popular, they either set up a course in that area or expanded their existing courses to bursting point. The government, the key employer for many of these graduates, did nothing to stop this folly... because it was assisting expansion.

PHYSIOTHERAPY

The same practice has been evident in physiotherapy, where a massive oversupply eventually led to huge numbers of unemployed graduates. By 2006, the Chartered Society of Physiotherapists stated that the situation was so serious that: "...the latest job figures for England showed that 93% of this year's 2,529 physiotherapy graduates did not have an NHS job to go to."[297] This was despite the fact that: "The society said graduates devoted more than 1,000 hours of free service to the NHS, and their training cost the public purse around £2m each year."[298]

You may remember that these were the same physiotherapy degrees that had proved so popular that a number of universities had resorted to using lottery software to pick applicants during the admissions process.

SOCIAL WORK

In 2011, a British Association of Social Workers' representative posted on the Centre for Workforce Intelligence website, asking for advice on how to support graduates in social work who couldn't find work:

> "The British Association of Social Workers has been contacted by lots of newly qualified social workers (NQSWs) who are really struggling to find work. The situation has been caused by a number of factors, including a doubling of the number of social work students in the last 7 years. If anyone has any ideas of how to help the NQSWs who are not finding work, or information from other professions as to how they are dealing with similar situations it would be greatly appreciated. To quote an unemployed newly qualified social worker *'I have applied for 30 social work posts in children and families local authority work and every time have been told that I was not appointed because I had not completed the first year of newly qualified social work'.*"[299]

To provide an idea of the scale of the problem of oversupply, in 2010/2011 the government funded 78,540 new students on undergraduate courses in psychology, law and social work when there were only around 15,700 training places (Figure 2).[300]

Subject	Starters
Psychology	27,115
Social work	24,610
Law	26,815
Total	78,540
Training positions available	15,700
Projected oversupply of law, social work and psychology graduates	62,840

Figure 2 - New students in vocational subjects for 2010/2011[301]

After graduation **less than 20% of these graduates** would have found a position to train as a lawyer, social worker or psychologist. This situation was problematic in 2010/11. Today, with average graduate debts approaching £60,000, it is beyond shocking that the government and the Student Loans Company continue funding these numbers of students and that our universities continue providing places for them. But, then again, these student numbers continue to support expansion and the students willingly apply for these degrees in the probably mistaken expectation of a professional career.

Even worse, despite knowing about the existing oversupply of law and psychology graduates, many universities still also offer postgraduate conversion courses in these subjects, allowing graduates in different subjects to apply to professional training courses for these areas. These courses are expensive and time–consuming and generally provide most students with little opportunity to actually gain employment in these already massively oversubscribed areas. They do, however, provide useful revenue for universities and employment for academics.

There are around 1,500 students undertaking psychology conversion courses in the UK annually and a typical course might cost around £5,000.[302] In 2011/12, UK universities and colleges provided places for a further 5,301 students on law conversion courses at fees ranging from £6,000–£13,000.[303] These courses are full–time and therefore necessitate a further year of economic inactivity and a further £20,000 or so of debt. That these conversion courses are unlikely to enable most of their students to gain access to these professions is of little significance to universities chasing a lucrative revenue stream. Those running these courses are perfectly aware of this. But they carry on recruiting students – course fee fodder – regardless.

Interestingly, the USA has experienced a similar problem with universities producing a massive oversupply of law graduates to an already saturated and disinterested job market. Disgruntled law graduates have reacted by suing their law schools for "misleading information in their prospectuses" which has saddled them with huge debt and no means of repayment.[304] It isn't difficult to foresee this scenario occurring at some point in the UK in the next few years. If this happens, many university faculties may find themselves with a difficult case to argue.

It would not be impossible to limit places for students on those courses where the government is the key or indeed only employer. There is already an example of this in the recruitment and training of doctors, where the number of places at UK medical schools is capped and limited in agreement between Higher Education Funding Council for England, the Department of Health and the NHS. If this approach works for doctors, then why not apply it to social workers, forensic scientists or psychologists? Similarly, if professional bodies such as Law Society and the Bar Council are absolutely clear about how many new graduates their professions can take each year, it should not be beyond the capabilities of the universities and the Student Loans Company to limit student numbers to something approaching the level of demand in the jobs market. But, of course, this isn't done as it would interfere with the, mostly university–educated, elites' favoured policy of ever more university expansion.

VOCATIONAL DEGREES

Even when universities *do* develop "vocational" degrees, they often fail to provide graduates with the skills necessary to work in the relevant industries. Forensic science and games programming degrees both provide clear illustrations of this issue.

Following the popularity of television shows such as *CSI*, the last decade has seen a dramatic increase in interest from students wanting to become crime scene specialists. There was already an established route into this profession and a static number of potential places for graduates each year through government recruiters. Many universities chose to ignore these basic facts and set up their own CSI–badged degrees to attract applicants. Unfortunately, these degrees were often rushed, badly designed and provided no benefit to students wishing to work in these fields. In 2005, a House of Commons Select Committee investigating the value of these degrees stated that:

> "We heard extensive evidence that a large proportion of the forensic science courses on offer provide poor preparation for a career in forensic science. Clive Wolfendale, Deputy Chief Constable of North Wales Police, called the majority of forensic science degree courses *'a savage waste of young people's time and parents' money'*. He also told us that in a recent selection process they had 50 applicants for three crime scene examiner jobs."[305]

Universities knew this. But they continued increasing the number of CSI–related courses. The only relevant concern for them was cynically recruiting enough students to run their courses.

In 2008, the professional body of games programmers condemned 95% of UK undergraduate degrees in this area as unfit for purpose and unlikely to provide a graduate with a job in the industry:

"Leading figures in the video games industry are unhappy with the 95% of degree courses at UK universities that are unaccredited and fail to equip graduates with the necessary skills to build a career in the industry. Of the 81 universities in the UK offering video gaming–related degrees, only four are accredited."[306]

In 2007, Orla Byrne, vice–president of HR for gaming company Activision, stated that what the industry needed was a greater supply of STEM graduates rather than graduates with variable quality degrees in gaming, noting that a: "…student with a very strong physics or maths degree will make a strong, if not better, contribution than someone (with) a pure gaming degree."[307]

In other words, yet another group of employers was asking universities to increase their output of STEM graduates instead of developing poorly–designed degrees that might sound fashionable and interesting to students, but which offered little in the way of employable skills. Perhaps this is starting to sound familiar?

GRADUATE SKILLS

Research during expansion has consistently shown that employers are also worried about graduates leaving universities with limited skills. One example of this is elite UK graduates failing to secure the best international jobs due to a lack of language skills. In 2011, a policy meeting at the House of Commons heard that UK graduates were unable to compete for top places in multinational organisations and companies for whom a second language was a prerequisite. The most obvious example of this was a failure in applications to the European Union, where only 1.5% of the 51,000 applicants for jobs in 2011 were British, with only *seven* successful applicants.[308]

In a number of interviews undertaken for this book, several graduates mentioned how they were told that they would need to pay the full price for any language tuition that fell beyond their undergraduate degree. As result of this, they could not afford to develop or improve their languages from their existing standard. Prior to expansion, these same language courses were provided either free or at a minimal cost. Despite the fact that today's graduates are expected to pay far more for their actual degrees, the degree–factory university offers *fewer* of the additional extras which would enable graduates to compete more effectively in both the domestic and international job markets.

Additionally, employers are concerned about UK graduates lacking basic skills in literacy and numeracy. Research published by the Chartered Institute of Personnel Development in 2010 asked businesses to comment on how they thought graduates' literacy and numeracy had changed in the previous five years: "Only 6 per cent of employers believe that these skills have improved, whilst 42 per cent and 35 per cent respectively feel that literacy and numeracy have worsened amongst graduates."[309]

These findings were supported by the CBI Education and Skills Survey in 2010, which questioned over 600 senior managers in UK companies. This found that the number of companies investing in remedial literacy and numeracy courses for employees had risen from 15% to 18%. Half of the companies contacted lacked confidence that they would be able to recruit to their graduate–level positions in the medium term.[310] Since 2000, there have been multiple pieces of research highlighting that UK employers are seriously concerned that they cannot find enough graduate recruits of a sufficient quality to meet their recruitment needs.

Expansion has diluted the undergraduate experience for nearly all students. The brightest are not being tested or stretched by their study as they would have been prior to expansion. Moreover, the massive inflation of degree classifications has made it much more difficult for employers to differentiate between the good and the outstanding graduate. In 2012, *Personnel Today* commented on a survey of 182 graduate employers which found that:

"... many employers faced barriers when trying to recruit graduates, with poor-quality applicants cited as the biggest problem. Four-fifths (80%) of those surveyed said they faced difficulties recruiting graduates due to a lack of skills, knowledge or the attitudes of the candidates. The findings are similar to a recent survey from the Association of Graduate Recruiters, which found that one-third of employers had failed to meet their targets on recruitment in 2010–11 because of a lack of candidates with the right skills."

Perhaps the single most worrying symptom of this disconnect between universities and employers is that UK universities are even struggling to provide the requisite calibre of graduate that they would employ themselves. Many of the elite research–intensive universities are increasingly looking for research students (graduates) in STEM subjects from overseas. In other words, **they** are not happy with their own product. A 2011 Higher Education Funding Council for England report noted that:

"...the number of international students studying taught postgraduate STEM courses has almost doubled in eight years. However, for home students the rise was just 1 per cent. In mechanical engineering, international student numbers grew from 22 per cent of the total studying population in 2002–03 to 54 per cent in 2009–10. The numbers of postgraduate research students in STEM courses followed a similar trend. There was a 23 per cent increase in the international student population between 2002–03 and 2009–10, while the number of home students fell by 2 per cent."

In 2009, the Institute of Physics noted in a submission to the House of Commons committee on universities that European universities now regard UK Masters degrees as inferior in content and structure to their own Masters degrees: "Europeans do not consider our Masters programmes to be at a comparable level to their own Education."[311]

Ultimately, if UK universities are not prepared to demonstrate faith in their own outputs, then why should they expect other UK employers to do so? Moreover, as far back as 2001, the Wellcome Trust (the research council responsible for medical research) articulated the fears of its members in a report:

> "Senior scientists yesterday criticised the 'massive dumbing down' of UK degree courses, which they say has made graduates ill-prepared for research. Many university supervisors are turning to students from the rest of the European Union who, they say, are better qualified and better motivated."[312]

The report went on to criticise the research skills and knowledge that UK undergraduates developed during their time at university: "Many UK students are thought to finish their first degree with little or no relevant individual, practical research experience and were felt, therefore, unlikely to be able to complete a substantial piece of high-quality individual research within three years."[313]

All in all, these problems do not constitute a resounding and enthusiastic vote of confidence from either potential employers or the universities themselves in the quality of graduates being produced by British universities following the Great Expansion.

GRADUATE NURSES

One other issue resulting from the rush to get as many people as possible into Uni and on to degree courses has been the move to change some occupations from vocational training-based to becoming degree-based. Nursing is a good example of this. Nursing degrees have been one of the main subject growth areas during expansion.

In 1986, under Project 2000, the NHS started moving nurse training away from hospital-based schools into colleges and universities. The next change was that nursing started to morph from being a (often 18-month) diploma qualification to becoming a 3-year degree. Then in 2009, the Department of Health announced that by 2013 it would require all new entrants into nursing to be graduates. The profession is critical to the nation's health and there is a wealth of statistics with which to compare healthcare during the period when nursing moved away from the practical, hands-on focus of hospital-based schools to a more academic approach first in college diplomas and then to an even more academic university degree. Consequently, nursing provides a useful lens for analysing the supposed benefits brought by more increasingly academically-educated people into the workplace.

The prospect of nursing becoming graduate entry did raise concerns within the NHS that it would restrict the number of people entering into the profession and eventually lead to staff shortages similar to those experienced in the 1990s and 2000s. But the change was strongly supported by the Nursing and Midwifery Council, possibly because they saw this as a way of enhancing the status of nursing.

At first the necessity for nurses to have a degree wasn't too much of a problem as, until 2017, nurses were given bursaries to help cover their tuition and living costs. But in 2017, these bursaries were abolished and student nurses were forced to take out loans just like most other students. The result was an immediate drop of 23% in the number of people applying to study nursing. Given the relatively low earnings profiles of nurses, it is easy to see how the prospect of incurring tens of thousands of pounds of graduate debt could act as a serious disincentive for potential entrants to the profession.

If we believe that college-based diplomas and then university degrees provide more skills, more knowledge and create a more effective workforce as was claimed by the NHS at the time when nursing became a college-based diploma and then a degree subject, we should expect to see some form of improvement in the running of hospitals and particularly in the outcomes for patients from more nurses having college diplomas and then degrees. But there appear to be few such positive changes for patients following the introduction of college- and university-educated nurses. There have been no major news stories from successive governments to highlight dramatic decreases in mortality rates or massive increases in the quality of care within hospitals. It is a reasonable assumption that, if there had been, politicians would have been very quick to claim credit for these successes.

What politicians were less keen to discuss during expansion was the rise in hospital-acquired infections. In his 2009 book *Squandered* David Craig noted that the UK had: "... about 300,000 cases of hospital-acquired infections each year, about 50 times higher than some other European countries."[314]

Two of these infections, MRSA and C Diff are potentially fatal. Statistics showed huge increases in the numbers of patients contracting them and in the number of fatalities resulting from them. Full information on both conditions is limited, but estimates suggest that the number of MRSA cases doubled between 1997 and 2004, when they reached over 7,200 a year. We can see a similar pattern with MRSA fatalities, in 1997 MRSA killed around NHS 250 patients, by 2006, this figure was closer to 1,500. In 2001, the NHS reported fewer than 20,000 cases of C Diff contracted in its hospitals. By 2005/06 this had reached nearly 55,000 cases. In 1999, C Diff fatalities in the NHS were under 1,000 per year; by 2006 they were over 4,500. Moreover, these figures are likely to be underestimates due to the political pressure that was put onto hospitals to under-report both cases and fatalities as the scale of the problem started to be covered by the mainstream media. Several newspapers subsequently reported that deaths, which could be attributed to other causes were, to reduce this media pressure on hospitals.[315]

The main issue in the growth of hospital-acquired infections was a lack of basic cleaning within wards. At one point, the situation was so dire that even someone like Claire Rayner CBE, a former nurse, President of the Patients' Association and prolific writer on health matters, twice caught MRSA in dirty NHS hospitals. She described her experiences in one hospital:

> "The dust in the corner of the ward just got worse and worse. It was disgusting. Bedpans were left at the side of the bed for God knows how long. Nobody tidied up. It was a depressing and dirty place …there was a piece of dressing on the floor which I noticed when I was admitted. It was still there when I was discharged."[316]

The eventual solution was to subject hospitals to a so–called "deep clean".

Some commentators have since suggested that college–educated and university graduate nurses, with an emphasis on theory rather than practical skills, were a contributory factor to declining standards of cleanliness during this period. A former intensive care nurse, Rona Johnson, linked the two areas in the *Daily Mail* in 2009:

> "... many 'graduate' nurses feel they are too superior to clean floors and change beds. As a result, the incidence of lethal hospital infections is going through the roof. Indeed, many patients would be horrified by how today's nurses even ignore essential routines such as regular hand–washing….. Student nurses were removed from the hospitals and trained in lecture halls, rather than wards. Many less glamorous but vital elements of nursing care – such as cleaning dropped off the syllabus and were replaced by empty, jargon–filled theorising about 'holistic care' and 'cultural sensitivities.'"[317]

This may be a controversial view. But what is clear is that the introduction of more academically–educated nurses certainly had

no discernible positive impact in preventing the spread of hospital–acquired infections. The net result of these infections was that
tens of thousands of people acquired serious illnesses, or even died,
rather than being cured as a result of going to hospital.

Other problems within the NHS have included ongoing concerns about the neglect of patients (especially the elderly) on NHS
wards. The most publicized case was at Mid–Staffordshire: "A secret
inquiry held last year found between 400 and 1,200 patients died after
suffering routine neglect by hospital staff between 2005 and 2009."[318]

National surveys have revealed a depressingly similar picture
across the NHS, suggesting that the true number of patients who
suffer neglect is more than 200,000 per year. When patients are
asked for their views on their treatment, their response is often
highly critical. Katherine Murphy, the chief executive of the Patients
Association, had this to say: "... patients should not be left starving
or thirsty, they shouldn't be left in pain and they shouldn't be forced
to urinate or defecate in their bed because the nurse designated
to them says it's easier for them to change the sheets later than to
help them to the toilet now. Yet this is what is happening around
the country every day."[319]

One of the most harrowing accounts of the dirty conditions
and poor patient care in NHS hospitals was given by Midlands
housewife Amanda Steane in her book *Who Cares?* recounting how
her husband eventually committed suicide after being horrifically
disabled as a result of repeated neglect in several badly–managed
and dirty NHS hospitals. In her book she describes seeing patients
unable to eat their food because it had been placed out of reach and
then taken away uneaten, unable to drink water, again because it
was placed out of reach, and lying for hours in soiled beds while
graduate nurses chatted to each other about their social lives, love
lives, their pay rises and other similarly important issues. Again to
quote Claire Rayner: "The food was served by catering staff, instead
of nurses, and we barely got time to eat it before the tray was taken
away." Why this poor care should be the case when many nursing

degree courses boast that they "offer a person-centered approach, offering holistic care for the individual and their family" may remain forever an unsolvable enigma.

There is one further consequence of this upskilling of nurses. Nurses are increasingly taking on jobs, which previously would have been done by doctors. At the same time, care assistants are picking up some of the more menial tasks that used to be done by nurses. It's not always obvious that these changes benefit patients. For example, one of the authors suffered a very minor stroke in April 2018. After a couple of hours in A&E, the author was 'assessed' by a specialist stroke unit nurse, rather than a qualified doctor. The nurse concluded that the author hadn't had a stroke and he was eventually sent home. When the author saw a neurologist five days later, it took the neurologist probably less than two minutes to confirm that the author had in fact suffered a minor stroke – a diagnosis that was confirmed by an MRI scan seven days after the neurologist's assessment. Though by then, the 6-hour window for treating the minor stroke had long since passed. NHS guidance is that all patients suspected of having a stroke should be scanned within one hour of arrival at the hospital, not almost twelve days later. This might indicate either that our supposedly more qualified nurses are being asked to do work that is beyond their competence levels or else that they are so confident in their own knowledge and abilities that they don't ask for help from a more qualified person when they should.

The filthy wards, the rise in hospital-acquired infections and the wrong diagnoses may not be entirely the fault of college-educated and graduate nurses. But neither are they a ringing endorsement of the contribution to the NHS as a result of nurses' increasingly academic qualifications and university degrees. This raises the question as to how successful an academic qualification, such as a college-based diploma or a university degree, can be in imparting a practical, rather than a theoretical, understanding of care for patients. In 2011, the *Telegraph* commentator Christine Odone made exactly this point:

"A senior executive of a care charity told me, off the record, how he rued the day that degrees became compulsory for nurses. The move professionalised what had hitherto been a vocation. Until that point, only those truly dedicated to soothing fevered brows and administering TLC joined the nursing ranks."[320]

The high stakes involved in national healthcare provide a graphic illustration of the effectiveness (or not) of a more academically–educated often graduate work force. With other industries and sectors, it is not so easy to isolate their obvious successes or failures. But it is worth asking the question though: has the mad scramble to hand out university degrees like confetti led to any other examples of workplace problems which have been created or worsened by the shift towards a (usually heavily–indebted) graduate workforce?

CHAPTER ELEVEN

WHAT ABOUT THE ECONOMY?

Whenever arguments are made about how expansion boosts national economic performance, we rarely hear anything about the costs or the disadvantages of expansion. If we were to believe politicians and university leaders, every pound that has ever been spent on Higher Education has been an extraordinarily wise investment.

We have already seen that this is untrue at the individual level. Many graduates will achieve little or no return on their investment and increasing numbers will incur a massive liability and falsely–raised expectations from their degree. The same is true at the national level. Some money spent on Higher Education is well spent. Much though has been wasted on substandard degrees in pointless subjects at third–rate or worse institutions, poor teaching and oppressive bureaucracy.

The current system incentivises universities to accept students who are not likely to benefit in terms of learning, earnings or employment prospects. As a result, it encourages expansion regardless of the cost to graduates, parents or taxpayers. Exactly where the lines between solid investment and squandering are drawn is subjective and should leave room for a genuine public debate. For the last thirty years, however, the very idea of lines or even a debate at all has been largely ignored. Despite this absence, those three decades have still produced plenty of data with which we can now measure the economic contribution of expansion.

Much of the literature on Higher Education spending is published by universities, or by those employed within universities, hardly the most neutral and disinterested voices. This literature generally offers little more than an encomium to the immense economic value of said investment. It seeks to extol rather than explain and offers the critical impartiality that one would expect from any corporate public relations material.

A different perspective was provided in a 2009 report by the Adam Smith Research Trust entitled *The Broken University*. In this report, James Stanfield approached Higher Education spending using the idea of "what is seen" and quantified by the traditional literature and "what is not seen" or the hidden costs of this expenditure:

> "... when a government spends £14.3 billion, those receiving these funds are clearly going to benefit ... Experts are then tasked with attempting to measure how much everyone benefits ... and this is identified as a positive gain. *What is not seen* is that because the government makes no money of its own, for every £1 it spends it must first remove at least £1 from the taxpayer's wallet. Therefore, when the government spends £14.3 billion on Higher Education, taxpayers are forced to spend at least £14.3 billion less in their local community."[321]

This point is never addressed in the publications extolling the value of Higher Education – that government spending can only occur through taxation, and that this taxation inevitably means that the taxpayer has less money to spend. *The Broken University* continues:

> "It is therefore meaningless to claim that £14.3 billion public investment in Higher Education has had 'a direct economic impact on the UK economy' or that its impact has been 'substantial' and 'very important at the macro-economic level', without also acknowledging that removing £14.3 billion from taxpayers' wallets will also have a substantial economic impact."[322]

The Broken University also refutes the idea that government spending on Higher Education would **categorically** generate more economic growth (or benefits) than if this money was spent (or saved) by taxpayers:

"As it is impossible to predict if more economic growth will be generated if the £14.3 billion is spent by the taxpayer in the local community or if it is spent on Higher Education, then there is no evidence to show that there will be any economic benefit from the annual £14.3 billion subsidy to Higher Education."[323]

Moreover, there appear to be no reports looking at what benefit to the economy could have been realised if the £14.3 billion Higher Education spending had been directed at supporting a much smaller (half?) number of students and thus having more financial resources per student enabling improved teaching and lower tuition fees so that better–educated students could graduate with much lower levels of debt than many of today's students. Nor are there any reports analysing the economic benefits if a greater percentage of students studied more useful courses such as STEM subjects, so that more of them found well–paid employment after graduation, rather than UK companies having to recruit from abroad to meet their skills needs. In addition, most reports lauding the value of the annual £14.3 billion spent on Higher Education don't consider the possible benefits to the economy if this money had been spent on other public goods like roads, railways, police officers, power stations, doctors and so on.

Furthermore, government is generally an inefficient conduit for investment, meaning that every pound of government investment will cost the taxpayer significantly more than a pound in tax. Some economists have placed a figure on the difference between how much the government spends versus how much this spending achieves, suggesting that, due to administration costs, waste and incompetence, the government actually realises only around 40 pence worth of services for every pound taken in taxation and spent.

The central point of *The Broken University* is that **university is not free, somebody must pay for it.** And money used for Higher Education is money that could have been used for other purposes.

Those who pay for our universities and those who have their budgets limited as money is diverted to Higher Education are entitled to an honest assessment of the value that Higher Education spending adds to wider society. Unfortunately, the inflexible beliefs of expansion's vested interests about the economic and social benefits of Higher Education act to prevent a rational and balanced analysis of the impact and value of expansion.

THE ECONOMIC IMPACT OF EXPANSION

If we take our cue from *The Broken University* and set aside the bromides of politicians and vice chancellors to measure the actual economic impact of expansion, it would be more accurate to sum it up thus: "Expansion appears to have had no discernible impact on the UK's national economic performance".

For decades now, we have been lectured on how vital university expansion is for our future economic performance. These strictures have repeated the importance of a more productive workforce to compete internationally or spoken about the significance of expansion in enabling the UK's transition to a "high skills" economy. Unfortunately, the reality has not matched the rhetoric. If we examine the period 1978–2011, we can see the following economic trends:

1.   There has been no step change in the growth of the UK's GDP during this period.[324] In other words, the UK's economic growth has continued much as it did prior to expansion

2.   There have been no significant changes to the UK's productivity as measured by our GDP per capita figures[325]

3.   There have been no noticeable increases in average salaries to reflect ever more graduates entering the jobs market

Given that the growth rates of GDP, productivity and average salaries have remained broadly consistent before and during expansion, it is hard to accept the idea that more graduates have created a more efficient and better–paid national workforce. In other words, there is very little evidence of a bang for all of those bucks.**

To illustrate this point, Figure 1 compares the rate of UK GDP growth with the percentage increase in the number of people in Higher Education – the UK Higher Education Initial Participation Rate (HEIPR) – between 1978 and 2011.

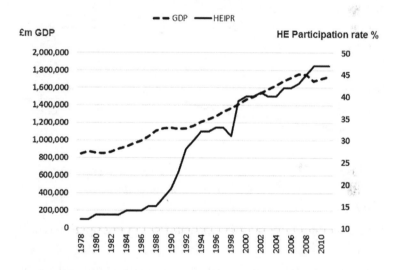

Figure 1 - UK GDP growth against UK HE participation rate

** There is an argument that without expansion there would have been a reduction in GDP growth as the UK struggled to maintain a human capital advantage in the face of increased global competition. This argument runs into difficulties, however, when we consider Western countries (such as Switzerland) which did not adopt expansion and outperformed the UK economically over the same period. It is also requires us to accept on faith that such a reduction a) occurred and b) was neatly redressed by expansion to such an extent that it maintained existing growth rates…

From looking at the chart, there is no obvious link between the dashed line representing GDP and the solid line showing the increase in the Higher education participation rate. The growth rate of GDP seems largely unaffected by the tripling in the numbers of people moving into higher education.

Figure 2 compares the percentage increase in UK productivity (GDP per capita) with the percentage increase in the number of people in Higher Education.

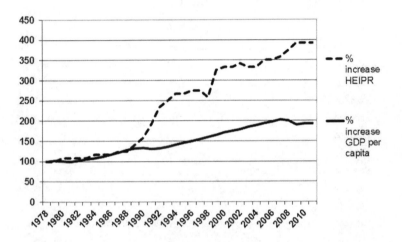

Figure 2 - UK GDP per capita against UK HE participation rate[326]

From 1990 onwards, the dramatic growth in the Higher Education participation rate has in no way been matched by corresponding increases in productivity. Exactly why the UK's productivity growth has remained so flaccid in the face of a huge influx of social science and arts graduates into the economy will probably have to remain one of the great economic mysteries of our time.

Moreover, there have been no significant increases in real average pay across the UK. Figure 3 tracks the rate of increase in UK average pay against the rate of increase in Higher Education participation between 1978 and 2011 (using 1978 as the index year). The increase in the national average wage that has occurred is not remotely proportional to the massive increases in Higher Education participation.

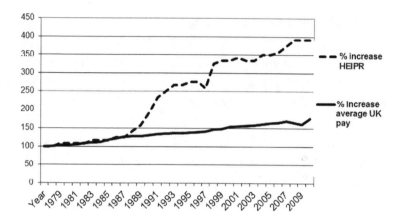

Figure 3 - Increases in average UK pay and UK HE participation 1978 -2011[327]

This makes it difficult to see where the increased tax revenues from graduates will come from, or how the graduate premium has been maintained during expansion. If expansion has increased the number of graduates and the graduate premium has allegedly remained intact, then it follows that there should have been a proportionate increase in real terms average pay. Scotland, for example, has had a significantly higher Higher Education participation rate than the rest of the UK for a long time, and yet this has made no discernible difference to its economic performance. Germany, with a Higher Education participation rate of just over half that of the UK, has consistently outperformed the UK economically.

This point has been made repeatedly by economists studying the link between education and national economic performance. They suggest that there is little hard evidence that an increase in graduate numbers will significantly improve national economic performance. Professor Wolf offered this warning in 2002: "It is no more self-evident that since some education makes some of us rich, more would make more of us richer than it is that 'two aspirin good' means 'five aspirin better.'" [328]

THE ADDITIONAL ECONOMIC COSTS OF EXPANSION

Expansion has brought with it a series of additional costs – liabilities which are never placed against the benefits claimed for an expanded Higher Education system. These include the loss of tax revenues from students who could be working, the hidden cost of family support, the escalating cost of student drop-outs and the massive growth in the amount of bad student debt. Here we'll just look at the cost of drop-outs. The astonishing growth of student bad debt will be covered in Chapter 13 *The Student Loans Fiasco*.

THE COST OF STUDENT DROP-OUTS

In 2012, the non-completion rate for undergraduate students in UK universities was a worrying 22%.[329] By 2015 this figure had improved marginally to 19.8%. But it still meant that about 1 in 5 students were leaving universities with debt but no degree. More importantly, as the *Daily Mail* noted, these average figures masked huge variation in rates at different universities: "The University of East London has lost 46.2 per cent of its degree students, Bolton University 45.1 per cent..... The University of the Highlands and Islands in Scotland has lost 51.4 per cent. In contrast, Cambridge lost just 2.8 per cent, Oxford 4.2 per cent."[330]

Figure 4 illustrates the UK universities with the five best and worst completion rates in 2012. There is a massive gap between these.

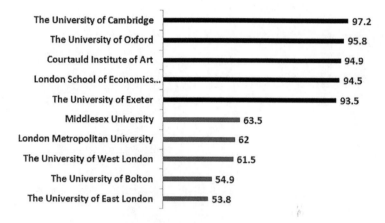

Figure 4 - Degree completion rates in England in 2012[331]

Drop-outs create serious cost implications for the individual students, universities and the taxpayer. For the individual, they receive no degree and often no academic credit, but significant debt. If we concentrate on full-time undergraduates, a 20% non-completion rate across nearly 1.21 million full-time domestic students equates to 240,000 students dropping out each year. Expansion is now creating 240,000 young people a year with debt and little to show for it. This is not the social mobility promised by expansion – it is regressive, wasteful and stupid.

Drop-outs also create additional expense through the wastage they cause within universities. In 2001, Professor Mantz Yorke estimated the cost of drop-outs to UK universities at about £200 million annually. For some peculiar reason, the Higher Education system has not seen fit to commission more recent research into this important subject.[332] More worryingly, rather than universities with high drop-out rates being criticised, fined or even closed down by funding bodies, they remain able to recruit roughly the same number of students, year after year, regardless of the cost to students and taxpayers.

CHAPTER TWELVE

SCHOOLS: SUPPLYING COURSE FEE FODDER?

> "Almost half of academics (48 per cent) and nearly as many administrators and professional staff (43 per cent) do not think that students are well prepared for university study by their schooling, while just 28 per cent of academics and 38 per cent of administrators believe that students have a good grounding for higher study." *Times Higher Education Supplement* Teaching Survey 2017[333]

A key factor in the decline of standards within universities has been the inability of schools to produce sufficient numbers of the quality of applicants required by expansion. This situation is not entirely the fault of schools. The New Labour pledge to ensure that 50% of young people attended university by 2010 put immense pressure on schools (and the education system as a whole) to produce a completely unrealistic step change in the number of university applicants. This pressure ultimately contributed towards a culture of "teaching to the test", so that as many school leavers as possible meet the minimum entry requirements for university, rather than the minimum academic quality needed to actually benefit from Higher Education.

It was at this point where the spirit of the *Robbins' Principle* was broken. Consequently, we have a vicious cycle in which university expansion places pressure on schools to produce more course fee fodder to fill up universities. This leads to schools focusing on quantity of qualifications at the expense of quality of learning and to universities receiving increasing numbers of school leavers who are unable to work at undergraduate level. In response, universities then reduce their own standards in teaching and assessment, creating a downward spiral.

Defining the quality of school leavers is, of course, subjective and it is particularly difficult making comparisons between different generations of students. Despite this, it is possible to consider several key areas such as qualifications, subject knowledge, study skills, literacy, numeracy and motivation to illustrate how and why many schools are failing universities and school leavers alike. In each of these areas, there is plenty of evidence from academics, counsellors and even students to suggest that many school leavers are finding themselves unprepared for and often overwhelmed by the demands of Higher Education.

STUDY SKILLS

"One of the things that one notices in student essays is how much damage has been done by the imposition of artificial structures for essay-writing. They've been drilled into writing a particular way, making particular kinds of arguments in a particular order and not writing their own ideas or responding to questions in a fresh and original way." Robert Tombs, Professor of History, Cambridge University[334]

"... undergraduates when they arrive, don't seem to know how to write essays. People who are undoubtedly extremely bright are grappling with difficulties in that area which once upon a time would have been inconceivable."[335] David Abulafia, Professor of Mediterranean history, Cambridge University[336]

As the quotes above suggest, UK universities, including Oxbridge, face serious difficulties in teaching the current generation of students. Even bright and capable students with excellent exam results are struggling to cope when they leave an increasingly spoon-fed and modularised environment within schools. The above quotations are from academics at a prestigious university, working with the brightest undergraduates. If students with A grades may need remedial classes in essay–writing and basic skills, what is this likely to mean for those undergraduates arriving at university with two E grades?

The shift from A–levels to university has traditionally been challenging for undergraduates. This difficulty derives from the differences between directed and self–directed study. Whilst GCSEs and A–levels have set syllabuses and close monitoring by teachers, degrees have longer and more nebulous reading lists and little or no specific direction from an academic. Undergraduates are supposed to develop into fully–independent learners during the course of a degree. They are not necessarily supposed to arrive as independent learners at induction. But they are expected to have the ability to think critically, to discuss complex and abstract ideas and to respond effectively, both verbally and orally.

Increasingly, academics are complaining that many school leavers have few of these skills. It is not that they are any less intelligent, rather that they have not been trained to think or write independently or critically. Often undergraduates arrive with an expectation that they will be spoon–fed answers rather than having to work them out for themselves. The consequence is a widening gap between A–levels and degrees. This leaves universities with the choice of failing large cohorts of students or finding some way to bridge this gap. In 2009, the Select Committee report noted: "Many universities find themselves having to offer classes in essay–writing because students are unable to write critically."[337] The Select Committee commented that this problem was not only being identified by academics, but also by the students: "One study showed that the majority of first–year university undergraduates felt that A–levels had not prepared them for university."[338]

This realisation must be particularly difficult for students who have achieved high grades at A–levels but then found the move to degree–level study much harder than anticipated. This is likely to be a significant factor behind the growing levels of student stress reported at Oxbridge. In 2010, Professor Guy Claxton, an expert on learning, noted that 15–20% of Cambridge students were being referred to academic counsellors. In the same year, a total of 1,200 students were referred at Oxford. He claimed that:

> "... these high–achieving youngsters are becoming more and more vulnerable because they are being spoon–fed more and more efficiently by their teachers to get them through their exams. There is more modularisation, more packaging and learning is more chopped up."[339]

Multiple submissions to the 2009 Select Committee described a generation of undergraduates with good qualifications who were struggling with undergraduate study. Professor Roger Brown mentioned: "...more students than previously who were 'not well prepared for degree–level entry, and this is true even for students with good A–level results.'"[340]

In 2009, the think tank Reform argued that A–level exams were producing a generation of "Satnav" students, unable to think independently and direct their own learning: "The 5.5m A–level papers sat each year contain 'nonsense questions' that have been stripped of the intellectual integrity they had 60 years ago and fail to prepare students for university."[341]

This criticism of school exams highlights the fact that the general lack of preparation for undergraduate study is the result of a systemic failure within the wider education system. Political pressure to meet targets distorts the aims and objectives of universities, schools and exam boards alike. When targets are placed ahead of quality, the result is that increasing numbers of young people leave schools without having learnt how to learn.

In 2012, Cambridge Assessment, an arm of the university's qualifications group, conducted research over an 18–month period with 633 academics. They asked them about the support they provided to new undergraduates, finding that:

"... more than half of lecturers think that undergraduates are unprepared for degree–level study. Three fifths (60%) said that their universities are providing extra 'support' classes, usually focusing on writing and independent learning. Nearly three quarters (72%) said that they have changed their teaching styles for students who are not ready for university study."[342]

In 2012, the Economic and Social Research Council contacted 1,600 students studying mathematics, science, engineering and medicine. Their report highlighted that in many schools maths teaching was almost exclusively focused on passing qualifications, with minimal time spent preparing students for studying maths at university. The result was that: "... many students suffered a 'culture shock' at university after failing to get the level of assistance they were used to at school or college. Professor Geoffrey Wake, who co–authored the study, said the demands placed on students taking degree courses 'came as a bit of a shock for many students.'"[343]

LITERACY AND NUMERACY

Schools failing to develop self–study skills and spending too much time "teaching to the test" are problematic issues. But they might be regarded as some of the expected difficulties involved in a massive university expansion over a relatively short timescale. These types of problem highlight the issues involved in trying to scale up a system designed for the smaller, more academically–able cohort of students in the 1980s to the much larger, less able cohort of students today. In this it is possible to have some sympathy for schools – after all, finding nearly 50% of potential undergraduates from each and every year group was never going to be easy.

What was certainly not expected from schools, however, was a growing inability to provide university applicants who meet the minimum requirements of school leavers in the developed world, namely that they have basic numeracy and literacy skills. Unfortunately, the evidence suggests that during expansion many schools have failed to equip their leavers with these prerequisites (despite doubtless encouraging them to apply to university). As the *Telegraph* noted in 2012, the net result of this was that:

> "Some six–in–10 academics are providing 'additional support classes' for first years..... universities stage basic lessons in writing skills amid complaints that too many school–leavers struggle to structure an essay, spell properly or use correct grammar. Many institutions also provided additional tuition in basic numeracy."[344]

Thirty years ago, it was unimaginable that universities would run remedial courses in grammar, punctuation, essay–writing and basic numeracy. But this is now a widespread phenomenon. These remedial courses cut even further into the resources available for degree–level study. This, in turn, creates pressure on universities to reduce the actual content covered during a degree. The unseen victims of this are the bright and talented undergraduates who have received decrementally less academic substance during expansion.

It is also striking that these problems in literary and numeracy occur right across our universities, despite students having achieved top grades and regardless of subject. In 2007, Richard Pike, chief executive of the Royal Society of Chemistry, commented:

> "Most universities have to offer remedial maths courses for new science undergraduates because they are giving up the subject after GCSE. Many chemistry students have not opened a maths textbook for two years because A–level maths is regarded as too difficult by students and schools."[345]

In 2006, a Nuffield Review report, based on research with 250 academics at 16 universities (including Oxbridge), identified similar concerns with tutors complaining that many school leavers lacked: "...a good grip of grammar and had a 'fear of numbers'. They believe the relentless burden of school exams is leading to an attitude among students that 'if it's not assessed then it's not important.'"[346]

STUDENTS LACKING MOTIVATION

Even more challenging for universities post expansion is the reality that many school leavers arrive without the motivation to study. Given the importance Higher Education places on independent learning, this is perhaps the greatest failure of expansion. In 2009, the Institution of Engineering and Technology argued that: "...the 'teach to test' regime in schools is leading to an increase in students with problems of poor motivation and attitude to learning."[347]

This is a problem of institutionalisation amongst many school leavers. Like today's undergraduates, they are the products of a bureaucratic factory system which values targets rather than learning. A lack of motivation is even harder for universities to tackle than an inability to think independently or an absence of basic numeracy or literacy. Whilst the latter could be taught, how does an academic even begin to motivate a lecture hall of students with little interest in their subject?

Students don't simply adopt a mechanised approach to learning upon arriving at university. Rather, they have generally learned it through thirteen years of the school system. All of these issues – remedial literacy and numeracy classes, disengaged students and rising class sizes suggest that expansion has slowly started to turn universities into comprehensives, a *de facto* extension of the compulsory education system. Or, as PM Wetherill, Emeritus Professor of French, University of Manchester, stated in a letter to the *Guardian*:

"For a long time now, university departments have been invaded every year by ill–prepared students who don't

realise that learning a foreign language is a hard slog which
involves boring things such as gender, conjugation, when
to use the subjunctive and how to put a sentence together.
Far too many of them have been led by their teachers at
school into thinking that anything goes."[348]

THE DECLINE OF KEY SUBJECTS WITHIN SCHOOLS

Schools are also failing to deliver sufficient numbers of students
with the qualifications necessary to study for degrees in subjects of
strategic importance, such as STEM and modern languages. This is
reflected in the decline or stasis in the number of students studying
these degrees during expansion.

This failure is also visible in the closures and mergers of a
number of STEM and modern language schools and departments
across UK universities. There is little universities can do to resolve
this issue. Student subject choices at A–level and GCSE have been
heavily influenced by government policy. This has encouraged state
schools to widen participation and support expansion by focusing
on delivering quantity rather than quality to universities. As is so
often the case with expansion–related policy, this drive has generated
a series of unintended consequences. It has, for example, provided
a perverse incentive for schools not to offer what are perceived to
be hard subjects to pass or get high grades in, for example STEM
subjects and modern languages. The system therefore encourages
schools to ensure that their students achieve the best possible exam
results, regardless of subject or indeed an individual pupil's interests
or aptitude.

This creates a powerful influence to push schools towards the
easiest possible subjects at GCSEs and A–levels, towards watered–
down vocational qualifications and the easiest possible exam boards.
It also incentivises schools to shy away from pushing their brightest
and best students to take hard or difficult subjects as this might
drag the average grades of the school down. It means that "difficult"

subjects such as German, economics and physics are often avoided by schools and students. The final Select Committee report in 2009 noted that the:

> "....Royal Society and the Institute of Physics stated some subjects at A–level were more difficult than others and it was easier to achieve top grades in subjects like media studies and psychology than it was when taking subjects like maths, physics and chemistry."[349]

This shift in subjects has created a vicious cycle. As student numbers in hard subjects decline, so do staff numbers. As fewer students within schools take these hard subjects, it becomes more difficult for schools to justify the existence of departments and teachers who only look after a minority of the schools' students. Eventually whole subjects can disappear from schools and with them departments. In 2009, Elizabeth Truss, Deputy Director of the think tank Reform, noted that: "Mathematics teachers are already in short supply, only 76 per cent of those teaching maths (in schools) have a maths qualification."[350]

This reflects a wider problem of a shortage of STEM and language teachers within schools. Schools, like universities, provide one of the worst–paying employment destinations for graduates with degrees in these subjects. Given the overall shortage of STEM graduates within the economy, it is also reasonable to assume that those STEM graduates who do decide to teach in their subject are unlikely to be the brightest or the best from their cohort.

Government policy has had further indirect impacts on subject choices at schools. The long–term decline in students applying for language degrees was partly created by the government's decision, in 2002, to allow students to drop languages as a compulsory subject at the age of 14.[351] Again, this was a decision driven by a desire to improve overall pass rates and in turn to boost the available cohort described by the Robbins Report as *"qualified by attainment"* to apply to university. It had a dramatic effect on the number of modern language GCSEs awarded (Figure 1).

Subject	2000	2016
French	347,007	144,892
German	133,659	50,271

Figure 1 - Decline in modern language GCSEs

We can see a similar pattern in A–levels. Figure 2 shows that the numbers of students taking these subjects fell by two thirds between 1993 and 2016.

Subject	1993	2016
French	29,886	9,672
German	10,857	3,842

Figure 2 - Decline in modern language A-levels[352]

Figure 3 shows reductions in students taking A–levels in "difficult" subjects such as economics and physics. It is worth emphasising that these declines occurred during a demographic increase within schools.

Subject	1993	2016
Economics	36,248	29,385
Physics	38,168	35,344

Figure 3 - Decline in economics and physics A-levels[353]

Whilst figures for students taking A–level chemistry and biology have increased during expansion in absolute terms, they have done so at a very modest rate and their current improvement masked serious declines in the 2000s in chemistry. In 1993, physics A–levels represented 5.2% of all A–levels taken. In 2016 this had fallen to 4.2%. For biology these figures fell from 7.5% to 6.5% and for chemistry from 6.2% to 5.6%.

Despite growing numbers of pupils during expansion, schools failed to significantly increase the numbers of students taking STEM subjects at A–levels. This failure is highlighted by a corresponding growth in soft subjects such as media, film and TV studies, expressive arts, psychology and sports studies. Many of these subjects doubled or even tripled their A–level enrolments during expansion (Figure 4)

Subject	1993	2016
Sports Studies	7,686	16,896
Psychology	22,111	59,469
Media, Film and TV Studies	7,056	28,140
Arts and Design	34,751	43,242

Figure 4 - A-level subjects on the increase[354]

Not only has the school system failed to provide an adequate subject mix across all university applicants, it has also failed to provide an equal distribution of subject choices to all students.

A further concern is that there are increasing socio–economic and geographic dimensions to the subject choices being offered to students for their GCSEs and A–levels. The decline in GCSE languages is most visible within the state sector and is particularly concentrated amongst students from the poorest families. In 2010, a survey of 668 secondary schools by CiLT, the national centre for languages found that: "Languages (are) least popular in comprehensives: in 60% of them, three–quarters of pupils are not taking a language at 14."[355]

The same phenomenon is also apparent in science subjects. In 2015, the Royal Society for Arts, Manufactures and Commerce (RSA) published research showing that in North East Lincolnshire 50% of local schools did not offer triple science GCSEs, whereas in Sussex every school did. The RSA report warned of growing numbers of "subject deserts" in local authorities and noted that this was disproportionately affecting young people within poorer neighbourhoods.[356]

This means that students from poorer backgrounds are often provided with limited subject choices by their schools, but are still being spurred on to apply to university where these subject choices may constrain them to less prestigious universities and less than useful degrees. For this they will still accrue maximum debt but receive little or no increase in earnings. It is tricky to reconcile this with the ongoing governmental quest of delivering "social mobility" and "social justice" through the expansion of Higher Education.

CURRICULUM SHRINKAGE

> "A–levels were a good proxy for first year university entry; A–levels do not fulfil that need now" Professor Roger Brown, former vice chancellor of Southampton Solent University [357]

Previous evidence has suggested that many degrees now cover less material than would have been the case prior to expansion. There are many reasons for this phenomenon including a declining number of contact hours, larger class sizes and broader ability range amongst undergraduates. Another crucial factor in this shrinkage is that the curriculum of GCSEs and A–levels has also reduced significantly. The most alarming evidence for this comes from elite UK universities. In 2002, the Director of Imperial College, Sir Richard Sykes, noted that: "Imperial has had to turn most of its science courses into four–year degrees. That's a big change because the standard of the A–level has fallen so much over 10 years that we have to bring them up to speed before they can get on with their courses."[358]

Geoff Parks, the director of admissions at the University of Cambridge, made a similar point about his university's undergraduates in 2005, stating that: "Cambridge had admitted 142 fewer under-graduates this year than last because of an increase in four–year degrees, which are now common in engineering and the sciences, the result of pupils knowing less than they used to."[359]

In 2003, research by the campaign groups *Save British Science* and the *Deans of Science* described a mismatch between:

> "...what students were learning in schools and what they were expected to know once they arrived at university... (58%) of science course leaders polled claimed less than half their intake had strong enough mathematical knowl-edge, while 47% claimed their students did not have basic practical skills. The problem was worse on physical science courses, where 70% reported that less than half their intake had sufficient knowledge of maths."[360]

Dave Robb, a senior academic at Imperial College, reiterated the same concern six years later. He added that this situation was not just worrying for the UK's economy, it was also potentially hazard-ous for people who depended on the knowledge of these graduates in the future:

> "We need students coming into our university who are really confident with their basic mathematical and physi-cal principles. Engineers have got to get things right. You can't say, 'this looks about right'. You have got to believe in those calculations. There are people's lives at stake. If you get the calculations wrong, engineers can kill."[361]

The difference in subject knowledge between today's students and those of previous generations was made apparent by comparing the results from a long–running induction test run by York University's electronics department. The test had been created to identify any subject areas in which new students might struggle, so that they could receive additional support from the department. The results of the test over time were depressing, if predictable: "If today's A–grade students had sat the test 15 years ago, they would have come bottom of the class. The report showed that the average test score dropped by almost half over the 15–year period – from 78% in 1985 to 42% in 2000."[362]

Similar evidence was provided by a variety of bodies to the 2009 House of Commons Select Committee on universities. The submission from the Engineering Council painted an analogous picture to that of York University but across a wider canvas: "At least 60 departments of mathematics, physics and engineering give diagnostic tests to new undergraduates. They reveal 'strong evidence' of a steady decline over the decade up to 1999 in basic maths skills and the level of mathematical preparation."[363]

So, in addition to equipping their students with remedial classes for literacy and numeracy, many undergraduate degrees now spend a huge amount of time in the first year providing essential subject knowledge for students and developing an understanding that would have previously occurred during A–levels. In 2004, York University revealed that it spent 40% of its first–term lectures on maths revision. Ken Todd a lecturer at the university outlined the issue: "Ten years ago we had one person teaching maths; today we have a team of six – plus support staff – who are all needed to get the students up to speed. Today's students are weak – they simply don't read and write maths as well as they should."[364]

This solution can also have potentially expensive and distressing consequences. The sudden introduction of complex mathematical material during these remedial sessions leaves some students unable to cope. If they had made this discovery during A–levels, then they could have made their university applications accordingly. Discovering this at university leaves them to choose between strug-gling though material that might be beyond them or dropping out, accruing student debt without academic credit. This problem was outlined by the Institute of Physics in 2009: "In physics, engineering and some other sciences, one of the most frequent reasons for non-completion is the lack of preparation for the mathematical content of the course. The physics in A-level physics is not described mathematically but it most certainly is at university."[365]

Despite repeated warnings about the declining content of A-levels in STEM subject areas, the government and exam boards don't seem to be listening. In 2009, the think tank Reform and a group of 64 maths professors were so concerned about the introduction of a new A-level called the "use of mathematics" that they took the unprecedented step of publicly criticising the qualification, arguing that: "The content of the qualification is not of A-level standard and does not provide sufficient preparation for studying at university... (it) may cannibalise A-level mathematics as schools and students seek the 'easier' option."[366]

The course still went into operation in September 2011. Given the concerns raised by these professors about the standard of this new A-level, it seemed reasonable that they should also refuse to accept it for students seeking admission to their degree courses. However, such an approach was clearly unacceptable to a number of influential figures within the school system. Mick Brookes, the General Secretary of the National Association of Headteachers, described this reaction as "intellectual snobbery", arguing that the professors: "....should get down from their ivory towers. They should be out in the world where young people live and exist and they should be appreciative that young people have great skills in the use of technology and we have to latch on to that. We cannot continue teaching an outdated 19th-century curriculum."[367]

Critics were therefore unhappy if universities rejected certain qualifications within their internal admissions processes. They were also unhappy if academics raised public concerns about any qualifications and/or stated explicitly that they would not accept students with them onto their courses. This appears to leave the preferred option being for these academics to say nothing and to accept any qualification for any course. This raises the question as to who, other than admissions tutors (professors and academics), is really in a position to understand whether or not a qualification will equip a student for study on their course?

Are politicians, teachers or union representatives able to speak with authority on how useful a qualification will or won't be for a student applying for a particular undergraduate degree? Alternatively, will these teachers, politicians and union representatives be on hand to provide the additional teaching, funding and resource to help the student if the qualification hasn't prepared them for a specific course? Most universities and professors are keen to receive applications from the widest possible range of applicants. But if they choose to exclude certain qualifications, then the most logical explanation for this is that they don't want to take on students who will struggle with their courses, divert (very) limited time and resources and who will have a higher likelihood of failing or dropping out.

Perhaps the single most compelling piece of evidence as to the systemic nature of curriculum shrinkage within schools was provided inadvertently in 2011. The *Telegraph* reported (and videoed) the comments of a senior examiner for Edexcel, one of the UK's main examination boards, during a meeting with teachers:

> "Ms W*****, the chief examiner for Edexcel GCSE Geography, said that teachers should pick her company's exam because *'you don't have to teach a lot'*. Ms W***** also expressed her disbelief that the geography exam had been cleared by the official regulator. *'There's so little [in the exam] we don't know how we got it through [the exam regulator]'*. She claimed it was *'a lot smaller [than other boards] and that's why a lot of people came to us'*."[368]

Essentially, Edexcel's sales pitch to schools and teachers could risk being seen as promising that they could achieve good exam results with less teaching and/or with less able pupils. This would, in turn, mean less knowledge for students and future problems for UK universities in dealing with this reduction. The pitch might appear to have been made in the belief that it would appeal to schools. In other words, that promising low content and minimal teaching would secure sales of their qualifications.

This approach could indicate that some exam boards may not be competing with each other on the quality of their qualifications, but on their ease. The implication is that each exam board tries to game the system and get qualifications passed with the minimum content possible. This view was supported by Jon Coles, an ex–director general at the Department for Education. In 2012, he described how:

> "... major exam boards were attempting to win business from schools by promoting GCSEs and A–levels as 'more accessible' than their rivals. ... setting tests that 'barely meet' the minimum requirements expected of exam papers and then haggling with the qualifications watchdog to get them approved."[369]

The above suggests that there have been too many sections of the compulsory education system (including teaching unions, exam boards and schools), which have complicitly opted for the easiest of solutions, dumbing down, when addressing the problems expansion has created. Though, any sympathy that we might feel for schools being asked to perform a mammoth and perhaps impossible task without the necessary resources, should be considered against the damage that such complicity has caused to academic standards throughout the education system. It should also be set against the fact that schools, which have engaged in this type of behaviour, have ultimately benefited themselves to the disadvantage of both their students and the taxpayer.

There is, of course, a final party not yet mentioned, which bears ultimate responsibility for the dumbing down of school syllabuses and assessments: the UK government. Their involvement in this farrago has been exemplified by the issue of grade inflation at GCSE and A–levels.

GRADE INFLATION

"Nearly **45,000** people achieved AAA at A–level nationally in 2010. The number of A grades at A–level has grown by over 68% in 10 years."[370]

Until 2012, every year A–level and GCSE results improved upon the previous years' results. We can see this pattern in all subjects between 1988 and 2011:

GCSE grades – In 1988, 41.9% of papers received grades A to C. By 2011, this figure was 69.8%. In 1994, the A* grade was introduced, with 2.8% of papers achieving this grade. By 2011, 7.8% of papers achieved A*s.

A–level grades – In 1988, 77% of exam papers received grades A to E. By 2011, this figure was 98%. In 2010, the A* grade was introduced to offer greater differentiation.[371]

The A–level pass rate had, in fact, remained fairly constant at around 70% from their introduction in the 1960s until 1980.[372] The subsequent rise happily coincided with a burst of Higher Education expansion in what was then the polytechnic sector. The greatest level of grade inflation has occurred in the top grades for both GCSEs and A–levels. A much larger group of students are now achieving the top grades in both exams:

"In 1988, 21.2% of GCSE grades were A or B. By 2011, A*, A and B grades comprised 44.9% of total awards."[373]

"In 1993, 30.5% of A–level grades were A or B. By 2012
A*, A and B grades comprised 52.6% of total awards."[374]

This phenomenon has created a now familiar series of unintended
consequences. How, for example, can university admissions tutors
choose between a glut of students who all have perfect sets of A*
grades at GCSE and A grades at A–level? This problem was already
evident in 2002, when the *Guardian* reported that:

"Certain courses will typically attract between 25 and 30
applicants for every one place. About half of these will be
predicted to achieve three As, predictions that are very
likely to be met given that slightly more than 20% of all
candidates in A–level exams now gain an A grade."[375]

It is for this reason that the A* grade was introduced to GCSEs in
1994 and in A–levels in 2010. Grade inflation has increased at such
pace, however, that the GCSE A* grade is now simply the *de facto*
A grade and an A is simply a former B. By 2005, problems were
already occurring in Oxbridge admissions: "Oxford and Cambridge
together rejected more than 10,000 applicants last year who went
on to achieve straight As at A–level."[376]

By 2008, the situation had worsened. The *Telegraph* reported
that Oxbridge had rejected 12,000 "straight A" applicants that year:
"Oxford was set to turn away 5,000 while Cambridge rejected 7,000."[377]

The A* grade at A–level also poses new difficulties, however,
given the disproportionate success of private–school pupils at gaining
A* grades in comparison to state–school students. Research in 2010 by
the Independent Schools Council outlined the scale of this problem:
"Half the A–levels taken by pupils at independent schools were graded
A or A* this year... Across state and private schools as a whole, 8%
of A–level entries were graded A*, with 27% getting an A or A*."[378]

For the elite universities, the A* grade poses a dilemma. Here
is a tool to help them sort through the vast swathes of triple–A

candidates. But it is one that will probably result in an increase in privately-educated students, putting the universities yet again on a collision course with politicians worried about any threat to the idea of universities having an important role in promoting "social justice". Closer inspection of A* grades revealed how significant this advantage was in some subjects. In 2011, the *Times Higher Education Supplement* reported: "In mathematics, more than 4,000 A* grades were awarded to private-school pupils last year, compared with fewer than 3,500 for the whole state sector. This was despite the fact that just 15 per cent of A-level candidates were privately-educated."[379]

Given the pressures of grade inflation, universities have had no choice but to use the new A* grade. By 2011, 15 universities had courses for which they required the grade. The *Telegraph* reported: "Last year Cambridge and Imperial College, London, were among five institutions to ... require the A* grade. Ten more have included it in offers this year... (this) list includes less-established institutions such as Brighton and Reading."[380]

That this requirement has spread so fast to non-Russell Group universities shows the extent of the problems caused by exam grade inflation.

GRADE INFLATION AND FALLING STANDARDS

There is no definitive answer as to whether grade inflation corresponds to falling educational standards. Politicians, students and teachers' unions all argue vociferously that this is not the case. The basic pattern is problematic though – yearly improvements across all subjects at GCSE and A-levels do not suggest random fluctuations or even organic improvement. As with degree grade inflation, the pattern of improvement was constant over more than three decades. There is evidence suggesting that the boundaries set to achieve different grades for GCSE and A-level have been shifted during the years of grade inflation. A number of officials at various exam boards have gone public with their concerns. In 2001, the think tank Civitas reported that:

> "Jeffrey Robinson, a senior examiner in GCSE maths for the OCR Exam board, claimed that pupils achieving As and Bs would have received C and D grades ten years earlier. The pass mark for a C grade had fallen from **65% in 1989 to 48% in 2001**."[381]

When today's A–level students have their performance in standard tests compared against students of previous years, they also perform notably worse. In comparative research at Durham University, academics found: "... that over the course of the study, students went on to get A–level results on average two grades higher than those who got comparable test scores 20 years earlier."[382]

One of the academics involved, Professor Robert Coe, noted that because it did not deal with the content of A–level exams, it did not prove that A–levels were getting easier. He did also state, though, that: "It's pretty clear the ability levels corresponding to the same grades (at A–level) are going down each year."[383] These findings tally with the declining performance of students on university induction tests. They also triangulate with the evidence presented earlier in this chapter, which suggests that many undergraduates now lack subject knowledge, basic skills and the ability to think independently, despite achieving "good" GCSEs and A–levels.

Expansion is fuelled by, and in turn distorts, the wider educational system. If the goal of increasing participation at universities must be pursued at any cost, this licences any number of behaviours within schools and universities that are the antithesis of a learning society. Watered–down content, grade inflation, teaching to the test... all are implicitly acceptable if they promote expansion.

Despite the problems described above, it should be noted that recent signs within the school system have been more encouraging. For example, the last few years have finally seen GCSE and A–level grade inflation go into a small reverse following a shift in government policy. In addition, concerns over grade inflation have also seen many schools choose alternative qualifications over GCSEs and A–levels for their students, a shift that should (in theory) increase pressure on domestic exam boards to ensure the quality of their curricula. However, the uptake of these qualifications has been much more prevalent within private schools, again raising the spectre of a qualifications apartheid between those pupils who have access to the best qualifications and those who do not.

UNFAIR ACCESS?

"Almost a quarter of England's sixth forms and colleges have failed to produce any pupils with the top A–level grades sought by leading universities. Some 594 (23.4%) of the 2,540 schools teaching A–levels had no pupils with the two As and a B in the subjects recommended for top degree courses." *BBC News* 2013[384]

One of the most controversial aspects of expansion has been the relative failure of students from state schools to obtain places at elite universities. This failure is even more marked for students from lower socio–economic backgrounds, creating difficulties for the argument that expansion is providing social mobility and social justice. The best jobs and the best graduate returns are generally reserved for students who attend the best universities. The result is that our elite universities have faced mounting political attacks from all parties for failing to provide what has been called "fair access".

But is this really a "failure" of universities? Or is it that UK *schools* are failing to provide an adequate number of candidates who are aware of and willing to apply to these elite universities? The answer depends on your point of view. Should universities simply select on the basis of the best candidates that apply, or should they *contextualise* candidates' applications on the basis of their backgrounds taking into account the advantages privately–schooled applicants might have enjoyed over their state–educated counterparts?

Before rushing to answer, it is often ignored that many of the UK's elite universities are already going to considerable lengths to level this playing field themselves. Following several well–reported supposed 'scandals' of elite universities turning down state–school students with excellent A–level results, the Liberal Democrat MP Evan Harris presented evidence to the House of Commons that Oxford was already favouring state–school pupils in its admissions: "...statistics showed that while the great majority of all entrants gained three A grades at A–level, 23% of comprehensive pupils were admitted with slightly lower grades, compared with 17.2% from independent schools."[385]

The same approach was visible in 2008, when Cambridge University dropped its requirement that applicants should have a foreign language GCSE. This decision was taken solely to facilitate applications from state–school students, with the university stating that: "… having a formal entry requirement that at least half of all GCSE students are unable to meet 'was not acceptable in the context of Cambridge's commitment to widening participation and access'."[386]

In 2012, the *Guardian* newspaper sat in on Cambridge's admissions process. Based upon their reporting, it was quite clear that the university's admissions tutors were already trying extremely hard to contextualise applications:

> "The phrase 'a good school' comes up repeatedly in the tutors' discussions. It is used most frequently about private and grammar schools, but also some comprehensive schools, and has a double meaning. 'A good school' is a high–performing one .... when a candidate comes from 'a good school' they are also cut less slack."[387]

The reality is that the admissions processes of elite universities like Cambridge already discriminate in favour of students from underachieving schools. This is not even a new phenomenon – it was a major reason for Oxford and Cambridge dropping their entrance exams during the 1990's, as these were perceived to discriminate against state–school applicants.[388] Broadly speaking, it would be reasonable to characterise most elite UK universities as highly supportive of various governments' desire to achieve more proportionate access for state–school pupils. Individually and collectively, the majority of the people working within the UK's elite universities strongly support the concept of social justice and the belief that a university education can help to promote this.

Ultimately, those who desire to see social justice delivered through universities want them to override their academic selection criteria with social justice criteria. They wish to ensure that there is a greater equality of outcome for entrants to elite universities from different social groups, regardless of performances at interview, their predicted grades in exams or their readiness to undertake a specific degree. This attitude ignores the contextualisation that already occurs and the experience of admissions tutors. It also ignores the role that schools play by not supplying enough credible candidates for Oxbridge and the Russell Group universities.

The media narrative about fair access generally starts by complaining that, whilst private schools only educate 7% of the UK's children, they account for around 45% of the intake to Oxbridge. On the surface this is startling. But the picture looks very different when we look more closely at the actual applications made to Oxbridge. In 2011, Oxford University received around 37% of its domestic applications from privately–schooled students and 63% from state–schooled students.[389] The proportions in domestic applications to Cambridge University were very similar with around 33% from privately–schooled students and 67% from state–schooled students.[390] Private–school students have an advantage over their state–school counterparts in gaining entry, but it is not a huge one. The real advantage they enjoy is that **proportionally more of them apply to these universities in the first place**. If state schools increased the overall volume of applicants to Oxbridge and other elite universities in proportion to their size, this would dramatically close the gap in admissions with private-school students.

The Sutton Trust charity has a strong interest in education and has produced a number of reports during the last ten years looking at the background of entrants to the UK's elite universities. The findings of these reports are stark – the gap in performance between the state-school and private-school sector is huge. Even when state-school students achieve better grades than their privately-educated counterparts, they still do markedly worse in gaining entrance to top universities. According to the Sutton Trust: "A student in a state school is as likely to go on to a leading university as a student from the independent sector who gets two grades lower at A-level." [391]

The Sutton Trust identified two key factors for this gap. These were the relative aspirations of these young people and the quality of advice they received from their schools. There can be little doubt that the levels of aspiration and of advice received by pupils at the UK's top independent schools will provide them with a significant advantage in gaining admission to an elite university. Not only will they have a peer group who are often selected on ability through entrance exams, they will also have a large number of teachers who attended the best UK universities and who can provide expert advice and guidance on application forms and interview technique.

Whilst the dice are loaded against state-school students, the actions of some state-school teachers disadvantage them even further. In 2008, the Sutton Trust discovered that:

> "...only 54 per cent of teachers in state schools said they would recommend their brightest students to apply to Oxbridge. Fifty-six per cent of the 500 teachers surveyed wrongly thought it cost more to study at Oxbridge."[392]

In 2009, the Sutton Trust found that a common theme amongst teachers in state schools was advising bright students that they would not fit in socially at Oxbridge and should therefore not bother applying. Speaking to the *Times Higher Education Supplement* Sir Peter Lampl, the founder of the Trust, stated that: "Many highly able pupils from non–privileged backgrounds wrongly perceive the most prestigious universities as 'not for the likes of us', and often lack the support and guidance to overcome this misconception."[393]

Unfortunately, it appears that this problem is getting worse. In 2012, follow–up research by the Sutton Trust suggested that 54% of state school teachers would **not** advise their academically–gifted students to apply to Oxbridge.[394] The survey also showed that, of the 730 teachers surveyed, many had very inaccurate ideas about the numbers of state–school students educated by the universities and the cost to students. It would be interesting to know how many of these teachers regularly read angry opinion pieces in the *Guardian* about elite universities discriminating against state–school pupils and a lack of "fair access" for state–school pupils.

This problem was visible in figures released by the Department of Education in 2009. These showed that nearly 1,400 schools and colleges, which teach A–levels, failed to send any pupils to either Oxford or Cambridge Universities. Moreover, 330 schools and colleges did not send a single student to a Russell Group university. This problem was experienced directly by one of the graduates interviewed for this book. They were studying at a state school and were clearly academically outstanding, achieving all A or A* grades at GCSE and regularly coming top or very near to top in all subjects. They took five A–levels during the sixth form and decided to apply to Cambridge to study economics. Unfortunately, their teachers were not supportive of this decision, with one suggesting that the student was "aiming too high" in wanting a place at Cambridge. The school provided little assistance in university interview practice, with a single practice interview given by a teacher who had no experience of what sort of questions might be asked or what the university would be looking for. They also provided no guidance on which college to apply to at Cambridge.

The student's teachers, personal tutor and head of sixth form failed to alert the headmaster (himself a Cambridge graduate) that a student was applying to Cambridge.

In addition, the school also entered all of the maths students for AS–level module examinations in January when there had been considerable teacher absence and it was openly acknowledged the students were not sufficiently prepared. Rather than waiting and allowing the students to sit the exams in June, the school decided that the students would benefit from the January exam practice. This student specifically objected to this and was told that if she didn't sit the examination she would be entered anyway and awarded zero. The school did, however, insist that the results of these examinations would not be published. Despite this, it became apparent during the student's Cambridge interview that the results had been published.

Because of the university's experiences with students dropping out due to their inability to cope with the level of maths required to study an economics degree, this inevitably set back the student's prospects and undermined them in the interview. With little interview practice, a poorly written reference (which it transpired had not been proof–read and contained half–finished sentences), the forced use of external examinations as "exam practice" and no encouragement or support, the student was not offered a place. Cambridge colleges send written feedback to schools in relation to every interviewee. This student's school failed to relay this feedback to the student and failed to discuss the experience with them following the interview. One teacher did however smugly say that the student had "shot herself in the foot", but then refused to explain why. Having achieved 5 A–levels at A grade, with an array of 100% results, the interviewee went on to take a first class degree in economics at a Russell Group university.

Their school was considered to be a good school within the local area. Nonetheless, it had not sent any students to Oxbridge since it had been a boys' grammar school some decades earlier and many of the teachers had little inclination to help the interviewee.

In fact, some of them displayed exactly the sort of reverse snobbery identified in Sutton Trust reports, going out of their way to discourage the student from applying. Several years later the student still felt angry and let down, not only for the total lack of help, but also for the way in which the school actually handicapped their application.

This failure of advice and guidance is partly created by the relative lack of state–school teachers who have themselves attended Oxbridge and, to a lesser extent, the Russell Group universities. It might be difficult to significantly adjust the number of teachers in the state school sector who have attended Oxbridge or the Russell Group in the short term. It is professionally inexcusable, however, that every secondary school teacher responsible for university applications cannot provide accurate and unbiased information to their students about admissions to elite universities. Information about entry processes, criteria and intakes is freely available on the internet and should take any teacher about a day to find and digest. This clearly has not happened in many state schools. As the Sutton Trust pointed out in 2012:

> "...state school teachers hugely underestimate the propor-
> tion of state school students at Oxbridge. When asked what
> proportion of state school students were at Oxbridge 14%
> of teachers said they didn't know. Of the 86% of teachers
> who gave an answer only 7% thought it was over 50% and
> almost two thirds thought it was less than 30%. The actual
> number admitted to Oxbridge is 57%."[395]

If more state–school students were given accurate advice by their teachers about Oxbridge and the Russell Group universities, more would apply to these universities. If more state–school teachers actively encouraged and supported students to apply to these universities, again, more of their students would apply. If state schools accounted for 80% rather than 63% of applications to Oxford University, then their percentage of places would rise significantly.

The issue of low applications from state schools to elite universities appears, in no small part, to be cultural with many state schools wanting to avoid failure rather than achieve success. This mindset is not necessarily the fault of individual schools and teachers; instead it is another manifestation of a target culture within the education system. This culture would rather see all students pass mediocre qualifications with poor exam boards and is in evidence when teachers dissuade their students from applying to elite universities. It would prefer all students to be accepted at poor or middle–of–the–road universities – with poor job prospects after graduation – than applying to and maybe failing to get into the best universities. This culture is not only about fulfilling targets and avoiding failure, it is also about minimising or avoiding competition and anything that might be construed as elitism. It is a mindset that strives for equality of outcome rather than opportunity and it is a mindset that leads to mediocrity or worse.

CHAPTER THIRTEEN

THE STUDENT LOANS FIASCO

They say that nothing is ever so bad that government can't make it worse. And that's certainly true of government efforts to 'improve' and 'modernise' and 'transform' how we pay for our universities. UK governments, of all political parties, are no strangers to wasting prodigious amounts of our money. The NHS computer system was supposed to cost us about £2.4 billion. It was scrapped after about £4 billion or £5 billion was spent. Actually nobody really knows how much money was wasted. The London Olympics were coincidentally also supposed to cost taxpayers a mere £2.4 billion. They actually cost us over £9 billion and made some insiders very rich indeed. Then there are destroyers that won't destroy much as they often don't work, aircraft carriers with no aircraft, spy planes that couldn't spy, the Millennium Dome which lay empty for years, supposedly 'smart' motorways that are anything but smart and many more similar exercises in profligate, public-sector ineptitude. But these many billions are just small change compared to the massive bill taxpayers could be landed with due to the student loans fiasco.

Each year students borrow about £10 billion to £12 billion – a figure that has been increasing as tuition costs have risen. Coincidentally, the current Foreign Aid budget of over £13 billion a year would cover the cost of student tuition fees and maintenance loans in their entirety. As much of our foreign aid is wasted through incompetence, bureaucracy and corruption, diverting some or all of our foreign aid to help pay for our university system might appear a reasonable alternative to the prospect of future UK generations being saddled with massive, unrepayable debt. Unfortunately, the foreign aid budget is something of a virtue–signalling comfort blanket for the UK's political class and their fellow–travellers in the media, who can afford both to pay for their own children's education and to be extremely generous with other people's money. Thus it is hard to imagine them voluntarily relinquishing something so morally and ethically valuable (to them) for something as trivial and practical as our Higher Education system and graduate debt.

So, the big question is: how much of this massive amount of money being loaned to students will actually be repaid and how much will be dumped back onto taxpayers? The House of Commons committee which scrutinised recent Higher Education reforms noted:

> "A large number of variables can affect the likelihood of loans being repaid, including the initial size of loans (larger loans are less likely to be repaid); the proportions of male and female graduates and their earning profiles (recent trends show once employed, male graduates tend to earn more than female graduates and so are more likely to repay in full); and the behaviour of the economy, including inflation, interest rates and earnings growth."[396]

All in all, not terrifically enlightening and certainly not answering the question of how much would actually be repaid by students and how much would have to be picked up by Britain's ever gullible taxpayers.

THE STUDENT LOAN BOOK AND GRADUATE REPAYMENT

Students who drop out of university, graduates unable to secure employment, graduates employed in non-graduate jobs and graduates who decide to disappear off to work abroad are all unlikely to repay their loans. In each case, this debt is likely to become bad debt – a cost to be borne ultimately by the taxpayer. Unsurprisingly, the scale of this problem has not been fully articulated to the public during expansion. In 2008, a parliamentary question raised by the Liberal Democrats revealed that:

> "A third of students who started university since fees were introduced in 1998 are earning too little to make

repayments on their loans. Nearly 400,000 graduates have not made repayments on their loans up to seven years after they graduated because they are not earning above the £15,000 threshold."[397]

It should be noted that this was the situation before tuition fees increased from around £3,000 a year to £9,000 or more a year and when the threshold for starting repayments was only £15,000 a year compared to the new, more challenging level of £25,000 a year introduced in April 2018. With much higher tuition fees and a much higher threshold before repayments start, the bad debt situation described above will be quite limited compared to what we can expect in the future. In fact, the long-term cost of bad debt is something which should concern UK taxpayers as the overall size of the UK student loan book (the sums owed by graduates) is increasing dramatically. In 2015, the government estimated that the student loan book at the end of the 2014-15 financial year had reached £73.5 billion.[398] Though another government publication a year later put the figure at just below £70 billion. (Figure 1).

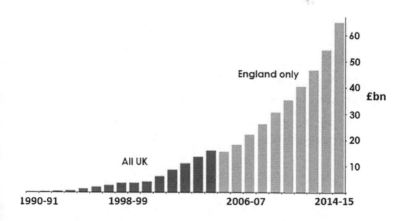

Figure 1 - The UK student loan book £ Billions 1990-2015[399]

From 2016 onwards, the (possibly misnamed) Office for Budget Responsibility (OBR) estimated that the Student Loans Company would lend more than £12.7 billion a year.[400] Within a couple of years the student loan book will be around twice what we spend on defence every year. The Government projected that the cash value of publicly-owned student debt in **England alone** would have increased to £100 billion at the end of the financial year 2016–17, £500 billion in the mid-2030s and £1,000 billion – one trillion pounds – in the late 2040s. As these are official estimates, we can safely assume that they are likely to be somewhat optimistic in outlook.

The problem for the repayment of this ever-growing debt mountain is that many graduates will not hit the repayment threshold even in the event of them finding work quickly. Moreover, when graduates do start making loan repayments, the majority will never repay in full – partly because their wages remain too low for them to do so, partly because of the size of their loans and partly because of the crushing burden of compound interest.

Figure 2 is taken from Student Loans Company repayment data in 2016. It shows that between 2010 and 2014, around 40% UK and EU graduates were not making payments on their loans (for a variety of reasons). It is worth re-emphasising that these repayment figures were against a repayment threshold of £15,000 per year till 2012 and then £21,000 a year rather than the £25,000 threshold for graduates from 2018 onwards. We should expect the "unable to repay" section of the chart to expand significantly for the 2015–2019 repayment figures and then to grow again impressively for the 2020–2024 period.

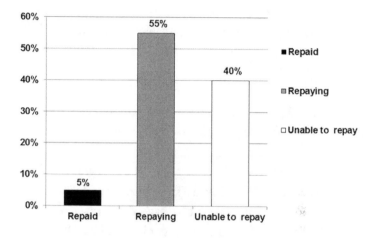

Figure 2 - Graduate repayment of student loans 2010-2014[401]

Between 2001 and 2006, the percentage of graduates unable to make repayments hovered between 26% and 32%, before rising to 53% by 2012. The figure for 2014 graduates means that, two years after graduation, the majority of graduates (53%) were not in a position to start paying back their student loans as their earnings fell below the repayment threshold. This is not a track record to inspire confidence in the sustainability of the new loans system. Whilst the coalition government responsible for the system acknowledged this difficulty, incredibly it maintained that the system was unlikely to generate any additional cost for the taxpayer. But, as most of today's politicians will be comfortably and lucratively retired by the time the taxpaying public realises the immense amount of student bad debt for which they will become liable, we should perhaps not be surprised at current politicians' insouciance?

At the time of the funding reforms, a number of independent commentators rejected the government's forecast as overly optimistic and their objections appear to have been borne out since. For example, in 2012, the Institute of Fiscal Studies warned that:

"…. the government's analysis over–estimates the number of graduates at the top of the distribution who would earn enough to face the full 3% real interest rate while they are making repayments."[402]

Clearly, if graduates don't earn enough, their loans will not be repaid. The government has already reluctantly admitted that many graduates will not repay their loans.[403]

To give an idea how difficult it would be for a graduate to repay their loans in full, we can look at a simplified example. We'll assume there is no inflation and take a graduate who earns £25,000 a year in their first ten years in their post–graduation job, £35,000 a year in their second ten years of working and a more impressive £50,000 a year in their third decade of work. This graduate would have to repay their loan at a rate of 9% of all income above the threshold of £25,000 (at the time of writing).

We'll further assume that the graduate borrows £9,000 a year for tuition fees and that their parents are earning almost £40,000 a year so they're able to borrow around £7,000 a year for living expenses. By the end of their course, the graduate would owe £48,000 plus interest giving a total of about £51,000.

During their first ten years working, the graduate wouldn't have to repay anything because repayments only start once a person is earning over £25,000 a year. Moreover, no further interest would be added to their loan during these ten years as interest only starts accruing once the graduate earns over the £25,000–a–year threshold.

During their second decade in work, while earning £35,000 a year, the graduate would repay 9% on £10,000 a year (their salary of £35,000 minus the £25,000 threshold). That's £900 a year. However, each year their debt would accrue interest at 1.5% – about £750 a year on average (this would be slightly higher at the start of the second ten years in work and slightly lower towards the end). So, the graduate would only succeed in reducing their outstanding loan by their payments of £900 per year minus £750 per year interest which gives £150 a year. By the end of this decade, the total owed would be around £49,500. Even after their ten years of repayments, this graduate would still owe slightly more than the £48,000 they had initially borrowed.

Then, during their third decade in work, the graduate would repay 9% of £25,000 a year (their salary of £50,000 minus the £25,000 threshold). That's £2,250 per year. But over these third ten years in work, the graduate would be accruing interest at 3% – over £1,250 on average a year. During this third decade in work, the graduate would reduce their loan by less than £10,000 (£2,250 a year payments minus interest of over £1,250 a year equals less than £1,000 a year for ten years).

So, even though this fairly well–paid graduate would have been repaying their loan for twenty of their first thirty years in work and have repaid a total of £31,500, they would still owe over £39,500. After thirty years, the rest of the loan – over £39,500 – would be written off. Many graduates will come nowhere near these earning levels. The Institute for Fiscal Studies (IFS) estimated that around 83% of graduates would fail to repay their loans in full within the thirty years repayment window.

The way the student loans system works creates two very distinct groups of graduates. There are the 17% (using the IFS figures) of graduates who will go on to be high earners and be able to pay off their loans in full. For these graduates – lawyers, doctors, engineers, bankers, business executives etc – the student loan resembles any other form of loan in that there is a strong incentive to pay it off as quickly as possible to avoid the debilitating burden of compound interest. If a graduate believes they will be earning comfortably over £60,000 within twenty years of their graduation, and hasn't taken any career breaks, for example, to have children, then they should probably investigate whether it would be worth paying off their loan as rapidly as they can.

However, there are the 83% of graduates (again using the IFS figures) who will fail to pay off the total of their loans plus interest.

For these 83% of graduates – nurses, teachers, social workers, most arts graduates – the loans system works like a 'graduate tax' rather than a loan. This is because the amount they have to pay each year will only be linked to their earnings, not the size of their debt. As with any tax, they should pay as little as they legally can. Anyway, by the time graduates have reached the point of thirty years after graduation, their student debt almost magically 'disappears' whether they owe £10, £10,000 or £50,000. Some of these students in the 83% may feel a psychological pressure to try to pay down their loans as it may make them feel they are reducing their debts. But to do this would be financially illiterate. This would just be throwing money down the drain. After all, most people don't go to HMRC and offer to pay more income tax than they actually owe. Similarly, their parents or grandparents may think 'if I give say £10,000 to help reduce a graduate's student debt, this will make it easier for them to get a mortgage'. Again this would be wrong. A gift of £10,000 to help pay a deposit on a home would no doubt be very helpful. But for most of the 83%, £10,000 to reduce their student loan debts would be money torn up and chucked in the bin. So, for 83% of students (and their parents and grandparents) there is an almost perverse incentive to pay off as little of their student loans as they legally can. That's wonderful for these 83% of students. They should relax about the size of their student debts and have a party. It's not quite so wonderful for the taxpayers who are going to have to pick up the tab for the tens of billions of pounds of unpaid loans.

For years there has been dispute as to how large a liability the taxpayer will face. Worryingly for taxpayers, in 2012 the investment company Skandia seemed to corroborate the above figures when it estimated that:

> "....unless a student starts earning £50,000 per year imme-
> diately after graduation, it's likely that a significant amount
> of this debt will be written off by the government. In 30

years' time the UK government is likely to be sitting on huge liabilities as it is forced to potentially write–off debt of between £30,649 and £64,935 for each full–time student who graduates."[404]

In 2012, three million people in the UK (10% of the workforce) earned above £50,000 and the number of new graduates who did so was negligible.[405]

The net impact of graduates who are unable to repay their loans is covered by the term 'the Resource Accounting and Budgeting (RAB) Charge'. This is effectively bad debt that will have to be taken from other areas of government spending like the NHS, defence or social care, though not, of course, from our ever more generous foreign aid budget. Prior to the introduction of the new funding system with the £9,000 per year plus inflation ceiling on tuition fees in 2012, the government expected an RAB Charge of 26.5%, meaning that "...for every £1,000 in loans, approximately £735 would be expected to be repaid with the remaining £265 being 'lost'."[406] In May 2011, the Higher Education minister David Willetts wrote an article for the *Times Higher Education Supplement* noting: "We estimate that about 30 per cent of these loans will not be repaid – close to the estimate reached using slightly different methodology by the Institute for Fiscal Studies."[407]

This estimate contrasted sharply with a government publication examining graduate earnings later that year, which suggested an RAB Charge of 37%.[408] In other words that £370 out of each £1,000 spent on loans would have to be written off. In 2011, the university think tank Higher Education Policy Institute (HEPI) argued that when the RAB charge reached above 47%, the new system with its £9,000+ per year fees would be more expensive than the old system with its £3,000 per year fees. They stated: "Our view is that a RAB cost of 50 per cent or higher is quite possible for a three–year programme **for students paying a £9,000 fee and taking out maintenance loans of £4,000 per annum**."[409]

But the RAB charge could indeed be higher than 50%. Many experts have also questioned the government's assumption about the long–term resilience of graduate earnings. In 2012, the Intergenerational Foundation think tank produced a report called *False Accounting* which noted that:

> "... the viability of the loan scheme depends on making predictions about the general shape of the economy and graduates within it for the next three to four decades. Current indications about the graduate premium suggest it will be eroded further except in a small group of professions."[410]

This brings us on to another great unknown: how many graduates will emigrate to avoid repayment? A 2012 Home Office report into emigration found that nearly 50% of those leaving were either professionals or company managers and very likely graduates:

> "...a 'large and increasing' number of executives, scientists, academics and doctors have chosen to leave Britain in the last 20 years. Around 149,000 British citizens emigrated last year, and 4.7 million now live overseas."[411]

Even if we adopted a low estimate of 25% of emigrants being graduates, this would require the Student Loans Company to obtain payments from around 37,000 graduates who emigrate each year, or face writing off *at least* £1.8 billion of debt annually. The graduates who emigrate are also likely to be those with the highest earning potential, the very graduates upon whose repayments the financial sustainability of the loans system is based. Professor Robin Lane Fox, an Oxford academic, observed:

> "I live daily with the debtors at ground level. When consulted, more than half of them say they will emigrate

rather than repay. Otherwise, they are condemned to
a *nine* per cent rate of surcharge on their income tax for
the next 30 years."[412]

Higher Education Statistics Agency figures in 2011 showed a significant increase in the number of UK graduates from elite universities
moving overseas six months after graduation: "Almost one-in-10
British graduates from institutions such as Cambridge, Durham,
Exeter and Oxford who found jobs in 2011 were working overseas.
It emerged that 5,175 students were working overseas, an increase
of 27 per cent."[413]

Does the Student Loans Company (SLC) have a robust system in
place to ensure that this debt is recovered? The SLC is already experiencing great difficulties collecting repayments from EU graduates.
Student loan schemes in New Zealand and South Africa have faced
the same problem and struggled to find a workable solution. These
schemes operate on a much smaller scale, however. This is without
mentioning the ongoing organisational troubles of the Student Loans
Company itself. The suspension and eventual dismissal of their
Chief Executive in 2017 was followed by a public spat with senior
Whitehall figures about the organisation's fitness for purpose. As
the *Guardian* noted in 2017, this was the third Chief Executive to
leave the organisation under a cloud since 2010.[414]

The company has also been involved in widespread allegations
of fake debt collection notices being sent to students and escalating
levels of complaints about poor customer service. In 2016, 86,000
graduates were overcharged by the company's systems after repaying
their loans.[415] There have also been regular reports of bullying and
alarming rates of staff sicknesses – 16 days on average annually –
within the company.[416] This compares rather unfavourably with 8.5
days per year in the public sector as a whole and just 5.2 days in
the private sector. Any of these individual issues should give pause
for thought; taken together they raise serious questions about the
competence of this organisation to deliver such a Herculean task.

The inherent problems of the student loan book are apparent to the private sector if not the government. In 2008, the New Labour government passed a bill allowing it to sell the student loan book off to the private sector. Despite many attempts, it took until early 2017 for a government to announce the sale of a mere £4 billion of student loans for graduates from 2002 to 2006. Perhaps what this delayed sale illustrates is that the private sector understands that a student loan book is only as valuable as the qualifications it underwrites. After all, if their degrees don't provide graduates with well-paid jobs, there will be insufficient graduate earnings with which to pay the graduate loans. A poor degree choice is not only a bad investment for the graduate, it is also a bad investment for whomsoever lends them money to study. All of the above raises the interesting question as to exactly how the government valued the loan book to enable its sale. Given its extended gestation, a cynic might be forgiven for wondering about the small print of this deal and what it will eventually mean for Britain's long-suffering taxpayers.

The government has changed its estimates of the level of non-repayment of student loans from 30% to 37% to 47% and back to 20% over six years. These constant changes should start worrying taxpayers who are going to have to pick up the bill for the student loans fiasco. After all, it is no more possible to procure substantive repayments from a cohort of forensic science graduates-cum-baristas than it is to wring blood from a very reluctant and uncooperative stone. This all leaves a worrying open question: who is going to pay for the £100+ billion student loans outstanding by the time this book is published?

THE SOCIAL IMPACT OF STUDENT DEBT

"You can't not live on credit'; 'living within your means: credit's part of it – what you can get... loans, credit, debts"
Jo, Politics and Philosophy (undergraduate)"[417]

One major social change that the student loans fiasco has contributed to is a shift in young people's attitude towards debt. In the first instance, the vast majority of students now have no choice about taking out loans to cover their tuition fees and living costs. They have no other way of paying. Throughout their degree they are also likely to run up overdrafts and take on credit cards. All of this is slowly but surely desensitising students and graduates towards debt. As long ago as 2002, when university tuition fees were much lower than today, a survey by Kensington Mortgages found that student debt was regarded by many young people as the starting point for money problems later in life:

> "About 63% of 18 to 30–year–olds who have money problems claim they were caused by student debts, while 28% of people who regularly miss debt repayments also blame their time as a student for their situation. Across all age groups, 14% of people who are in debt say their troubles started when they were trying to survive on a shoestring while studying at university."[418]

Whilst some in the university sector have protested about the rises in student fees, in practice most universities have simply pushed up their fees as high as they dare and banked the cheques. It would be a rare sight for any university to advise a prospective student not to take a degree with them as the degree will cost more than it's worth to the student.

With the phasing–out of the student grant and the introduction of student loans from 1990, the creation of top–up fees in 2006 and the trebling of fees in 2012, universities have actively encouraged and facilitated this accrual of debt. After all, they have ever–increasing numbers of courses to fill with university course tuition–fees fodder.

This normalisation of debt has been based on the idea that a degree is a solid investment in the young person's future. Students and potential students have been assured time and time again that this will ensure future dividends through a much higher earning capacity. However, the evidence suggests that for the majority of students – both those taking vocational courses, for which there is a limited jobs market, and those taking dumbed–down, soft degrees from third–rate institutions for which there is virtually no jobs market – this is simply not the case. Despite this, neither governments nor universities have suggested any possible downsides or small print to this debt for graduates, their parents, or indeed, for taxpayers. Unfortunately, these downsides are now becoming quite evident. A reduced disposable income can mean that the rites–of–passage experiences which young adults expect: being able to move away from home; running a car; buying a house; getting married and starting a family are now being delayed or prevented altogether. Individually, this can be demoralising and depressing. At the national level, it is effectively placing barriers between a generation of heavily–indebted graduates and life as independent and self–sufficient adults. These are not additional or lifestyle extras, these are the basic expectations of adult life. Rising levels of graduate student debt are putting these fundamentals ever further out of the reach of graduates. As the levels of graduate debt increase, so we should expect the severity and frequency of debt–related problems to increase.

HOUSING

Perhaps the most obvious example of the social impact that this debt is having can be seen in the growing problems faced by grad-uate first-time home–buyers. Even as long ago as 2006, before the economic crash and increased fees, research by Scottish Widows found 53% of graduates under 40 unable to access the property market. The report noted that:

> "Home ownership is such an 'unrealistic dream' that one in ten say they cannot ever imagine buying, and almost

half of them think it could be between two and ten years
before they buy their first home. Even among those graduates who have succeeded in getting on to the property
ladder, almost two–thirds had to rely on buying with a
partner and 68% said they would not be able to buy them
out if they were to split up. Almost a third say they cannot
save for a deposit."[419]

Another report in 2006, published by the Thomas Charles Debt
Consultancy, supported this pessimistic outlook amongst graduates. When they examined graduate home ownership from 2001
they found that: "Only one in ten people who have left university
since 2001 currently own their own home, with 58% saying they
have been unable to purchase somewhere because of their debts."[420]

Despite the government's assertions to the contrary, the evidence suggests that the increase in student fees and maintenance
loans has seriously exacerbated this problem. Research in 2015 by
the Higher Education Commission warned that: "Thousands of
middle–class professionals face missing out on mortgages because
of 'onerous' debts generated by the new university tuition fees and
the ... implications of such high levels of graduate debt at a time of
stagnating wages and rising house prices"[421]

The study continued to raise concerns over the problems
created by: "... financial rules requiring mortgage lenders to track
monthly outgoings – including loan repayments, gym membership
and socialising – when assessing mortgage applications."[422]

The problems caused by monthly loan repayments were underlined in 2012, by research from the Royal Bank of Scotland. This
showed that repayments, on an average graduate salary and after
essential bills, accounted for 7% of the disposable income that a
first–time buyer needs to save for a deposit. The same research also
showed the problems that these loans create in paying a mortgage
once a house has been purchased. Without student loans, a buyer
with a 90% first–time buyer mortgage on a graduate income would

spend 40% of this income on their mortgage, with student loans this increases to **44% on average and 60% in London**. [423]

Large numbers of graduates are finding it not only hard to buy a house but simply to move out from the family home. In 2011, research by Mintel found that 27% of these "boomerang" graduates were living with their parents.[424] The latest figures from the ONS show a record 3.2 million 20–34 year–olds still living in the family home, a 28% increase from 1997. [425] At the same, time the average age of first–time buyers in the UK had risen to 37 in 2014 – up from 23 in the 1960s and 30 in 1974.[426]

For many graduates, the return home is bound to be a sobering experience, losing the financial freedom and independence of undergraduate study. It will be the first time that reality really starts to intrude on the narrative they have been sold. Rather than providing a *Brideshead Revisited* key to the adult world, graduate debt and its monthly repayments are more likely to delay the transition into independence for most graduates. As the Higher Education Commission put it in 2013: "We are deeply concerned the Government may have created a loan payment system where, for example, a teacher is unable to secure a mortgage at the age of 35 because of the high level of monthly loan repayment."[427]

But, as well over 200 of our MPs own one or more buy–to–let properties, any increase in the number of graduates forced to rent, rather than buy, their homes would only be a benefit to our well–paid, well–pensioned, generously–expensed parliamentarians.

PART THREE
WHAT NOW?

CHAPTER FOURTEEN

THE COMING CRISIS

Given the number of supposedly highly–intelligent, and certainly highly–paid, people running our often degree–factory universities, it seems surprising that they appear to be oblivious of the crisis into which they are so enthusiastically and lucratively leading our Higher Education sector. Expansion has been good for these people with their big salaries, generous expense accounts, often free housing, maybe a knighthood, gong or two or perhaps even a peerage and many other perks. But they have created an ever–inflating bubble. As history has so often shown, at some point all bubbles burst – and the bigger the bubble, the greater the damage done when boom turns to bust.

The Great Expansion was a massive and costly bet on an under-graduate degree being the optimal launching pad for nearly every bright and ambitious young person in the UK. But by expanding the wrong universities, by lowering entry requirements to fill up their courses almost regardless of students' abilities, by offering easy rather than useful degrees, by oversupplying the jobs market with graduates who have no hope of ever having a career relevant to their degree and by saddling many of these graduates with unrepayable levels of debt, our universities have sown the seeds for their own inevitable nemesis.

Moreover, as university fees have increased and student debt has risen, so have students' expectations of what they should receive for these fees. Universities are facing greater scrutiny about their teaching, assessment and what graduates of specific courses might reasonably expect in career opportunities and additional earnings from their degrees. Students have become paying consumers and they are increasingly finding out that what they have bought – their degrees – have not met the marketing claims made by their univer-sities. Universities should expect reprisals from students who feel their consumer rights have been infringed, possibly in the form of organised protests, social media campaigns and legal actions.

This is already happening in America where law graduates, unable to find legal employment, are suing universities for advertising under a false prospectus.[428] And in 2018 a student, who achieved a First at Anglia Ruskin University, launched a legal action against the university accusing it of giving her a useless Mickey–Mouse degree. Given the massive oversupply of graduates in vocational subjects such as law, psychology and social work, it is not far–fetched to anticipate many more such actions being taken against UK universities during the next decade, particularly as ever more students find out how skilfully they were tricked into mortgaging their futures for often third–rate degrees from often third–rate institutions.

However, the main threat to our universities resulting from their mismanagement of the Great Expansion will probably come from an inability to recruit sufficient students to provide enough money to keep the university bubble inflated. Student numbers will fall for three main reasons:

1. There will be a declining number of school leavers to feed into our degree factories due to falling birth rates

2. It will become more difficult for universities, especially those at the lower end of the academic scale, to recruit students as people increasingly realise that many degrees incur huge costs without giving corresponding benefits

3. Increasing international competition for the best students will reduce the number of both international and domestic students applying to UK universities

Student fees remain by some distance the largest income stream for most UK universities. The smaller and less established a university, the greater is their reliance upon this income. Maintaining the current level of student fee income will prove more difficult as demand for places in UK universities inevitably declines.

1. Demographic changes

Changing domestic and international demographics are both likely to reduce the demand for UK Higher Education in the short to medium term. The UK is currently experiencing a substantial domestic demographic dip in people aged 18–20, a decline which is projected to continue until 2020 (Figure 1).

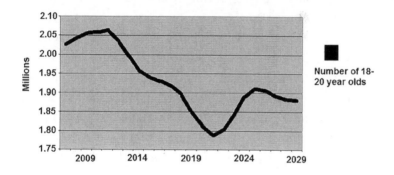

Figure 1 – Number of 18-20 year-olds 2006 -2029[429]

From a peak of 2.07 million young people in 2010, by 2020 there will be 1.79 million; a difference of about 280,000. As the Higher Education Policy Institute noted: "After 2010, this age group (18–20 year olds) will decline significantly for the following decade – by more than 13 per cent between 2010 and 2020."[430]

This decline is mirrored across the developed world, including the European Union. It is also evident in China, where the 'one family one child' policy has dramatically reduced the country's age cohort.[431] This is an especial concern for UK universities as China is their biggest single supplier of international students (and their full market fees).

In the UK, demographics in favour of university student recruitment will start to slowly improve between 2020 and 2025 but then once again worsen from 2026 to 2030. However by then, if not before, universities will be hit by another threat to their income and financial health – increasing questions over the value of many university degrees.

2. Declining return on investment

A second key risk for demand is the increasing body of evidence that the costs of many UK degrees now outweigh the benefits. Growing awareness of the extent to which graduate premiums are dependent on an applicant's choice of university and subject could present a major recruitment challenge for new universities and degrees in 'softer' subjects like media studies and journalism. In addition, the cost of studying in the UK is a growing cause for concern. Our tuition fees for international students are now amongst the most expensive in the world, regularly outpacing inflation.[432] If we take into account international flights and the high cost of living within the UK, then the total cost of a degree is becoming prohibitive: *"... people are realising that there are other places in the world that offer a better education for lower cost, especially East Asia, such as Malaysia and India."* Finance and management graduate.

This cost both reduces the potential pool of applicants and increases the exposure of our universities to global currency fluctuations. In the era of Brexit and Eurozone instability, the dependence on international student fees could prove an Achilles heel for the UK Higher Education system over the next decade.

3. Increasing international competition

This issue could be compounded by international universities becoming less expensive. In 2011, the *Guardian* noted an increase in the number of European courses taught in English and UK students studying overseas: "...more than 2,400 courses available in English in the non–English–speaking parts of Europe, the trend will extend beyond the Netherlands ...but last year a record number, 22,000, were studying for degrees abroad."[433]

The rise in domestic fees has even reduced the relative cost of more expensive overseas universities, such as the Ivy League in America. In 2016, the UK sent 11,600 students to US universities, up from 8,861 in 2010.[434] Moreover, the generous nature of the bursary system in the major US universities allows them to offer their degrees free of charge to bright students who could not otherwise afford them. This potential to graduate from a world–class university with no graduate debt could create a future UK brain drain, preventing the UK universities from recruiting some of the very brightest domestic students.[435]

The increasing number of UK students choosing to study in the US is emblematic of a wider problem facing all universities. Student recruitment (whether domestic or international) has become much more competitive in recent years and this trend is only likely to increase in the future. UK universities are facing growing international competition for students, not only from existing competitors such as the USA and Australia, but also from countries investing massively in their own Higher Education infrastructure. Large student exporters, such as China, are now actively seeking to retain their own domestic students whilst increasing their numbers of international students. In 2010, Professor Richard Levin, president of Yale University, noted that:

"China and India ... seek to expand the capacity of their systems of Higher Education ... and aspire simultaneously to create a limited number of world–class universities. China has doubled the number of its Higher Education institutions in the last decade from 1,022 to 2,263."[436]

The competition to recruit international students is often driven by coordinated national policies aimed at increasing a country's share of the global Higher Education market. Universities UK made this point in 2009: "Many countries including Germany, France,

Singapore and China are all investing in strategies to attract and retain international students."[437]

The scale of some of these countries' ambitions should concern UK universities in the coming years. In 2011, the *Telegraph* noted the Chinese Ministry of Education had: "... promised to double the number of foreigners attending university in China to 150,000 by 2020, making it the largest provider of education to foreign students in Asia."[438]

RECRUITING AND RETAINING ACADEMIC STAFF

Attracting students in sufficient numbers is only one of the challenges brought by increased global competition. A second lies in recruiting and retaining the best staff. This will be made more difficult in the next decade through a combination of demography, finances and globalisation. UK universities will find it more difficult to recruit staff due to an ageing academic workforce across the developed world, a relative decline in the attractiveness of UK Higher Education to the best academics (who tend to be globally mobile) and increased global competition for academics.

1. Ageing academics
A key demographic issue for western universities is the number of 'baby-boomer' academics currently in employment. Over the next decade, universities will face their retirement on a massive scale. A Universities UK report warned of this in 2007: "The proportion of full-time academic staff aged over 55 has risen from 10.8 per cent to 17.1 per cent of the total workforce between 1995/96 and 2005/06."[439]

This had risen to 19% by 2016. Moreover, by 2014, 30.9% of UK academic staff were aged 51 or over. The UK's situation will be compounded by competitors such as Canada, Australia and America also needing to replace their own "greying professoriate" in order to sustain their universities. In 2011, the *Sydney Morning Herald* wrote that: "....up to 40 per cent of academics and lecturers are expected to retire over the next decade, with no one to replace them."[440] A similar pattern is evident in America, where Universities UK commented: "Over 30 per cent of academic staff are reported as being aged 55 or over. Fewer than 10 per cent are under 35 years old." [441]

An examination of UK–based academic recruitment sites already shows multiple adverts from universities in these competitor countries. One of the reasons these countries advertise heavily for academics in the UK is that our universities generally pay much less than their peers in Canada, Australia or America.

2. A worsening offer to academics

Expansion has seen the average pay of UK academics decline relative to other professionals. This has coincided with a rising cost of living and a relative decline in spending on public services. The pay for UK academics is not only significantly lower than its major competitors (the USA, Canada and Australia), it is also falling behind that of countries building their Higher Education systems. For example, in 2010 Chinese universities in Hong Kong were offering salaries of £200,000, double the top end of the professorial pay scale at a Russell Group university at the time.[442] Similarly, high salaries coupled with low tax regimes are now routinely available in many of the Gulf State countries, who are also investing heavily in Higher Education.

The UK Higher Education offer to academics is also dependent on its research funding. For mobile academics, access to large–scale research funds will often be critical to their employment decisions. The next decade will see research funding in the UK fall in relative terms, whilst the budgets of many competitor countries will rise. In 2010, Ralph Cicerone, President of the US National Academy of Sciences predicted: "Swingeing cuts in university and research budgets will force the most talented British scientists to find jobs in the US, Singapore and other countries that are continuing to invest in science throughout the global recession."[443]

These factors will make UK universities less attractive to mobile academics and talented graduates considering an academic career.

3. Increased competition for academics

Many wealthy countries are investing heavily in their Higher Education systems to catapult their universities up international league tables. Other established Higher Education systems are undergoing ambitious mergers to concentrate academic resources and capital to protect or advance their league table positions. Saudi Arabia, for example, has been investing around $10 billion dollars in the King Abdullah University of Science and Technology. Established in 2009, the university's aim is to be comparable to the top ten science and technology universities in the world by 2020.[444]

The same ambition underlines Sweden's plans to merge three universities, creating a new giant institution, which they hope will be better able to compete globally: "…the Karolinska Institute, Stockholm University and the KTH Royal Institute of Technology – have announced that they are in merger talks. This super–university would be the largest in Northern Europe and have a budget of more than £841 million."[445]

What is happening in Sweden is also being proposed in Finland and Denmark, who want to protect their global league table standings, and in France and Germany, who wish to improve their positions in the same tables.[446] Investment on this scale will massively intensify the pressure to recruit the best academics, making it harder for UK universities to compete successfully in this arena.

This represents a major threat, especially to those UK universities which fall outside the very top tier of UK universities. A number of Russell Group universities (Warwick, Nottingham) have traditionally punched well above their funding weight, regularly appearing in global Top 100 league tables. This reputational advantage has greatly assisted them in attracting talented staff, international students and international research funding. With the heightened level of global competition in future and without any additional funding to counterbalance it, these universities may find it difficult to retain this status and the benefits it confers. Unfortunately for these universities, it is difficult to see how any additional funds could be raised in the medium term or, indeed, whether the current level of funding will itself prove sustainable.

A NARRATIVE OF DECLINE?

"The vice–chancellor of Cambridge… has warned that the UK is in danger of losing its standing as a world leader for university education within a decade." *Guardian* (2007)[447]

Between 2004 and 2011 the UK had eleven universities in the Shanghai Top 100 global university *league table*. Of these, six dropped significantly, three remained constant and two improved their rankings."[448] By 2016, the UK only had eight universities in the Top 100. Whilst the actual academic value of these rankings is open to question, they have significant reputational value, both for individual universities and UK Higher Education as a whole. This decline contributes to a wider narrative of decline for UK Higher Education, something that has started to gain purchase in the academic media. In 2012, when British universities performed relatively poorly on the *Times Higher Education Supplement* international league table, Phil Baty, the editor warned that:

"Outside the golden triangle of London, Oxford and Cambridge, England's world–class universities face a collapse into global mediocrity, while investment in top research universities in Asia is starting to pay off."[449]

This perception can eventually create its own reality. Once a narrative of decline emerges, it will be difficult for UK universities to reverse it, either individually or collectively. As more countries seek to compete and establish one or more of their universities in the Top 100, the cost of maintaining a university in this position will inevitably rise. In 2007, the OECD was already signalling this:

> "Rankings are used as a policy instrument. Many govern-
> ments want one 'world–class university'. A world–class
> university is a \$1bn–\$1.5bn–a–year operation, plus \$500m
> with medical school. This would require many HEIs
> increasing funding by 40%."[450]

If a story such as this takes hold, it becomes difficult to counter.
With their resources spread ever more thinly over an excessively
large student contingent of variable quality, how can UK universities show the wider world that they are not in decline without
fuelling this narrative? The long–term danger from a perceived or
real decline is that, if the UK loses its prestige, it will find it difficult
to recover. Whilst the ancient UK universities are likely to always
retain their brand and cachet, it will be much more difficult for
the second, third and fourth tiers of UK institutions to regain this
ground once it is ceded.

A gradual slide down the international league tables by UK
universities has the potential to become a recurring bad news story.
Closures, mergers and high–profile student lawsuits could have
a similar effect, casting the whole of the UK Higher Education
system in a negative light over the next decade or two. The public
(specifically the tax–paying public) might understand and even
accept declining league–table performance in a more competitive
international environment. However, they may struggle to accept
a decline if they see this decline accompanied by ever–increasing
university fees and ever–increasing student debt.

Any difficulties UK universities face in recruiting students
and staff will translate into financial problems. Universities which
struggle to recruit students, especially international students, will
face dwindling fee income. This will reduce their ability to pay
academics, especially the "star" academic names who act as a draw
to domestic and international students. Universities which cannot
attract the best academics will also be less able to attract research
funding. Academics with a strong publications record improve a

university's chances of winning both domestic and international research funding.

Each of these issues – declining student numbers, university funding problems, dropping down league tables and difficulties in recruiting academic talent will represent a major challenge for individual UK universities over the next decade. The collective challenge they may all face is the possible interaction of these issues with the economic and social problems occasioned by increasing graduate debt, an escalating concern over bad graduate debt, a loss of public confidence in the value of degrees and a growing unease at the effect of the modern university environment on the attitudes and values of our young people.

Once universities slip into a self–reinforcing negative spiral, it will be difficult to halt their decline. The last decade has seen long–running scandals in the political and banking spheres which have massively eroded public trust in their respective institutions. Given the possible interaction of the problems outlined above, it is not hard to imagine the UK's universities engulfed in a similar crisis at some point in the next decade. In the worst case scenario for universities, they might find that they had far fewer friends and far more public scrutiny than they might currently imagine possible.

Interestingly, 2017 has provided a small foretaste of this with well–publicised attacks on aspects of the Higher Education system by senior political figures such as Andrew Adonis (one of the architects of tuition fees) and Nick Timothy (Theresa May's former chief of staff). Both men raised questions about the ballooning pay of vice chancellors and the sustainability of the student loans system. Nick Timothy's views were particularly trenchant:

"Certain degree subjects offer no return on investment, while studies show there are entire universities where average graduate earnings 10 years after study are less than those of non–graduates. We have created an unsustainable and ultimately pointless Ponzi scheme, and young

people know it. With average debts of £50,000, graduates
in England are the most indebted in the developed world.
Even if they do not pay off the full amount, graduates face
dramatic increases in marginal tax rates as their earnings
increase." [451]

Universities also had to field criticism in 2017 from a more unex-
pected quarter: the Advertising Standards Authority. Requiring six
universities to withdraw marketing material that contained misleading or inaccurate claims about their performance in academic league
tables and student satisfaction surveys, Guy Parker, the Authority's
Chief Executive, announced to universities that:

"If you're making claims about your national or global
ranking, student satisfaction or graduate prospects, make
sure you practice what you teach: play by the advertising
rules, in particular by backing up your claims with good
evidence. Going to university involves a big financial
commitment and misleading would–be students is not
only unfair, it can also lead them to make choices that
aren't right for them." [452]

Universities are not used to public debate framed in these terms and
their leaders and senior management are particularly ill–prepared for
this type of enquiry. For many of them, it is highly doubtful that they
have even considered fundamental questions about their institutions
and the system they inhabit. If a degree offers less learning in return
for massive debt and limited graduate–level job opportunities, if
one in every two people has a degree, if debt repayment wipes out
the graduate premium for all but the best–paid graduates, if universities are increasingly to become "safe spaces" protected from free
speech, controversy or independent thought, then what exactly is
the point of a degree? If this is the future, then what is the point of
being a graduate or indeed of many of our universities? Even more

pertinently, what has been the point of expansion? These are all questions that university leaders and politicians might find themselves being asked with increasing frequency over the next decade.

CHAPTER FIFTEEN

SORTING OUT THE MESS

After decades of the Great Uni Expansion, it's clear that whatever was promised – a highly–educated workforce, increased social mobility, a more productive economy – none of these have been delivered. Moreover, if our universities are in denial about their own condition, then they cannot be trusted to find and implement solutions to the problems their Great Expansion has created. So, the only people who can sort out the mess must be those outside the university system – government, students, parents and taxpayers – in other words the funders, the users and the customers of universities.

The negative results of the mismanagement of the Great Expansion can be summarised:

1. Graduates
a.   A general and cynical oversupply of graduates.
b.   A shortage of STEM graduates.
c.   An astonishing oversupply of graduates in soft subjects.
d.   A large oversupply of graduates in vocational subjects.

2. Funding
a.   Most graduates will not repay their loans.
b.   Taxpayers face an enormous liability for unpaid loans.
c.   Student numbers are likely to peak and then decline.
d.   If student numbers decline, some UK universities will face a substantial funding gap threatening many with bankruptcy.

3. Falling standards
a.   Many students unable to cope with the academic demands of Higher Education.
b.   A significant decline in the teaching resource per student.

c.   A reduction in the average quality of domestic and international students.
d.   Devaluation of degrees.
e.   A degree–factory system of Higher Education which does not
provide graduates with the skills wanted by employers.

Many of these problems are the result of successive governments
applying a one–size–fits–all model to the UK Higher Education
system and universities wilfully abusing politicians' short–sight-
edness and incompetence to boost their own growth, finances,
power and status.

BACK TO THE FUTURE?

The most obvious solution to the appalling mismanagement, massive
financial waste and cynical betrayal of students during the Great
Expansion might be to go back to where it all went wrong – the
obsession of our elites and academic bosses with the one–size–fits–all,
'Uni–or–bust' mentality. The damage that this mentality has caused
is now obvious to any impartial observer. The respected US academic
Martin Trow, who spent his life researching Higher Education,
described the ham–fisted efforts of successive UK governments
as producing: "...a pattern of policy that resembled a somewhat
unskilled automobile driver who parks by ear."[453]

The results of this "parking by ear" are stark. Thirty years ago,
our Higher Education was far from perfect, but it did offer a genuine
diversity of choice to students, including Oxbridge, a strong tier of
research universities, an array of polytechnics and specialist technical
colleges and the Open University. Each of these offered different
approaches to Higher Education, high quality in–depth teaching at
Oxbridge and the research universities, vocational training at the
polytechnics and technical colleges and a flexible route back into
academia for mature students through the Open University. This
diversity more closely mirrored the actual needs of the country,

rather than the ideological mirages (castles in the air?) that have driven the Great Expansion.

Whilst Oxbridge has retained its identity, most other institutions have converged towards the same homogenous offering for undergraduates. This has generally meant a greater percentage of classroom–based degrees, diluted content and three–year degrees offered full–time to school leavers. This factory model has made it much easier for universities to design and manage their courses, at the expense of quality, relevance, usefulness and differentiation.

In response to a globalised world in which change and increasing complexity are perhaps the only constants, the Great Expansion has delivered fewer and fewer choices about when, where, what and how to study. Expansion has seen many of our universities becoming like bog–standard comprehensives that now charge boarding–school fees.

Nothing has underlined this failure as effectively as the savage decline of the Open University. A highly innovative success story for UK Higher Education, in alternate reality the Open University could have been the institution to manage and deliver any expansion (or contraction) of Higher Education that our economy and society required.

So how do we sort out this mess? Describing any solution in detail would be folly. But we should look instead for principles that would support both a greater flexibility in how students study and a broader range of the types of Higher Education offered to them. This is not rocket science. But to make our Higher Education system fit for purpose again, will require some hard truths and some difficult choices. Better that though, than what is currently on offer to future generations, unpayable debt for often worthless degrees.

We could start by re–branding at least 20 to 30 institutions back to being polytechnics restricted to offering only one– and two–year practical courses that are aimed at equipping graduates with skills that professions genuinely require. Nursing, in particular, is one subject that could and should be moved away from the fixation with a three–year university degree. Journalism is another.

As one journalist remarked *"It now takes three years at a university to learn what we learnt on a 40-week diploma course at the poly"*. In addition, these polytechnics and technical colleges could stop wasting students' time and students' and taxpayers' money on useless degrees for which there is demonstrably no jobs market. Instead they could help turn out some of the professions that the British economy actually needs and will always need – literate and numerate bricklayers, plumbers, carpenters, roofers and skilled employees for the healthcare and retail sectors.

Of course, this can never happen. Politicians can never admit that they got it wrong – especially after politicians from all parties have all been religiously pursuing the same misguided policies for so many years. As for the vice chancellors and academic staff at any soon-to-be polys and technical colleges, they would bitterly resist any such re-branding of their failing but exploitative institutions, any reduction in their perceived status and any threats to their university-level salaries.

That leaves our universities with a choice. Either universities could work together to manage the inevitable shrinkage of our bloated Higher Education sector or universities will be forced to downsize due to a series of financial crises caused by falling student numbers as would-be students wise up to the Great University Con and universities' income falls. Given the greed, self-interest and managerial incompetence of many university bosses, one can imagine that they'll either go crawling to politicians for more support and more taxpayer money or, if that fails, choose the latter option in the hope that they and their institution will survive the coming bloodbath while their competitors go under.

However, were universities to constructively approach and actively manage the inevitable bursting of their expansion bubble, here are some actions they could consider.

TIME TO GO ON A DIET?

The most obvious first step in fixing our universities is to gradually reduce the number of students by say 5% a year for at least the next five years. This would have several benefits such as improving the average quality of the student population and increasing the number of teacher contact hours with students, both of which could be used to improve the quality of teaching and the value of degrees being awarded.

There are several ways this could be achieved:

1. Setting a minimum grade tariff to access loans.
2. Not funding courses with low graduate premiums.
3. Restricting the funding for vocational courses to reduce oversupply.

It is currently possible for a student to enter university with one grade E at A–level. This student is likely to go to a new university, to struggle academically and to receive a poor degree or drop out. If they graduate, they are more likely to be unemployed or have a non–graduate job. Consequently, they are less likely to repay their loans. But should any student, who cannot better one grade E at A–level, automatically be entitled to £50,000 or more of loans? This current "open door" policy has been a contributory factor to falling standards. Ultimately, university is not for everybody and, if an applicant cannot demonstrate a minimum level of attainment and ability, why should there be an automatic expectation of funding? Especially if much of that funding will eventually have to be picked up by the taxpayer.

Or, rather than excluding school leavers with low grades from Higher Education altogether, one solution might be to restrict students with grades below a set tariff to part–time study, providing funding for one 30–credit module initially at the Open University. Passing each module would provide access to further funding on an incremental but increasing basis. This would still allow everybody who wants to access Higher Education to do so, whilst acting as a screening mechanism for those students with the least chance of achieving a graduate premium and thus minimising bad debt for students and taxpayers alike.

Deciding where to draw the line for undergraduate funding is a difficult question. It might need to vary according to the specific grades produced each year. The percentage of grades awarded differs considerably between subjects. It is harder, for example, for a student to achieve top grades in STEM subjects than Arts subjects at A–level. Persisting with **no line**, however, will benefit nobody apart from those universities whose main contribution to the national economy appears to be transforming the coffee–shop barista, call–centre operative and gym assistant into a graduate career.

A further approach would be to limit the loans available for vocational degrees such as psychology, social work and law. In some of these areas, the government is the majority employer of graduates. If the departments involved estimated the number of new recruits required in psychology or social work, then the Student Loans Company could provide loans for this number of students only.

Professional bodies, such as the Law Society, could provide similar estimates. So, if the Law Society identified 5,500 training contracts available in 2011,[454] then the government should have funded this number plus say 25% (allowing for wastage and expansion) in 2012. This would have meant 6,875 graduates, rather than the 24,000 graduates funded in 2010/2011. A similar approach already works successfully with the training of doctors. Why not apply it to all of the vocational degrees where there is oversupply?

Moreover, if the same logic was applied to shortage areas, such as STEM subjects, the government could offer incentives, such as reduced or no fees, rather than caps, for universities to recruit and students to apply. This approach has been used for decades to ensure an adequate supply of teachers. Why not apply it more generally to graduates in key subjects as a whole?

Student headcount could also be reduced by withdrawing or restricting funding for courses and universities with high drop-out rates and low levels of graduate-level employment and salaries. The Student Loans Company and HMRC already possess data which show the universities and courses with high loan non-repayment rates. Allowances could be made for universities with large numbers of part-time or mature students, where higher than average drop-out rates are to be expected. Where universities or courses are shown to have much higher loan non-repayment rates than comparable universities or courses, a few pertinent questions could be asked. These questions might include whether a university or course provides additional value which validates the taxpayer footing the bill for higher non-repayments? Does the university provide a flexible and successful route back into Higher Education for mature students? Does a university particularly benefit students from disadvantaged backgrounds? Or does the university serve a more remote region in the UK, which would otherwise not have access to Higher Education?

If the answer to these questions is a clear and resounding "NO" and the non-repayment level has been consistently far above expectations, then taxpayer funding should be withdrawn. This would prevent many students from taking out loans if they have little or no chance of repaying them and if their courses do not also provide some obvious additional social, economic or cultural value.

Alternatively, one could always cut to the chase and cut all funding to those universities with non-repayment in the bottom 25% of universities (allowing current cohorts to graduate). This would result in a quarter of universities closing or reverting back to being polytechnics or technical colleges. But the simple fact is that these are the universities which provide graduate debt without graduate jobs. They are the universities offering degrees in sports science, forensic studies, gender studies and drama. They are the universities which are cynically recruiting tens of thousands of students in the full knowledge that these students will get debts without the corresponding career opportunities to ever repay those debts.

Whatever the method, some closures would help those universities which remain open to start thinking about providing greater value for the money they receive from their students and the taxpayer. Schools, hospitals, prisons and private companies all close, why should universities be exempt from a normal institutional lifecycle?

DROP THE "UNI OR BUST" MINDSET

Perhaps the most disastrous error of the Great Expansion was that it was based on the clearly erroneous idea that university is the best possible solution for each and every school leaver of average or better ability. This has been compounded by an almost obsessional fixation on a three-year full-time degree as the default option for study. We urgently need to break away from this restrictive view of what Higher Education should look like and widen the choices offered to school leavers beyond a traditional university degree. This partly reflects the changing nature of the students whom universities will need to recruit over the coming years. It is also because flexible and part-time learning would help students and society to mitigate or avoid many of the harmful effects of the Great Expansion.

A part-time degree completed over five or six years will make minimal difference to the eventual age of a graduate in an era of rising retirement ages. It also offers many economic benefits to graduates. Research by Skandia suggests part-time study over five years, rather than full-time over three, enables graduates to earn £31,000 more in their working lifetimes.[455]

In addition, consider the cost of an Open University degree: "Our fee for a standard 30-credit module is £1,393, and for a standard 60-credit module it's £2,786. Most of our students study 60 credits per year over six years for an honours degree."[456] This means total tuition fees of £16,716, rather than the £27,750 which is now typical for full-time undergraduates.

A student studying part-time whilst working and possibly living at home could graduate with considerably less debt even before taking into account their additional earnings, cost of living savings and the reduction of compound interest on student debt. More students studying part-time would result in more students living at home. This would either eliminate or reduce the cost of rent, whilst reducing the demand for rented accommodation in the buy-to-let sector. This would be bad news for buy-to-let landlords and foreign speculators enthusiastically building student accommodation, but good news for communities and first-time buyers – many of whom will be graduates. It would also reduce student debt and many of the wider social problems it creates.

Moreover, if taxpayers' money can be spent on a degree, why not spend it on high value apprenticeships? Training young people represents a significant cost to companies. Government could fund willing companies, with the resources and capacity to offer a vocational training programme, through the Student Loans Company (or, better, tax breaks). This would substantially reduce the cost to employers of offering apprenticeships, thereby making the UK more attractive for employers, whilst helping to reduce the prestige gap between the academic and non-university vocational routes. It should also be possible to direct this funding at sectors where the UK actually has labour shortages, killing two birds with one well-placed stone.

BETTER INFORMATION

"In the City, they call it a "false market". This occurs when erroneous information, often deliberately circulated, becomes the basis for investors' decisions. The result is illogical choices." Jeff Randall, *Telegraph* (2012)[457]

The Great Expansion has created a false market in the admissions process to UK universities, with a distinct lack of accurate information about the outcomes from different degrees. This means many students apply to degrees without any genuine understanding of the long–term benefits and drawbacks they will entail. Instead, they are told the graduate premium is about £100,000 and assured in vague but emphatic terms that university remains a sound (and indeed a necessary) investment in their future.

Given the rising cost of a degree, such vagueness is no longer acceptable. It is especially unacceptable because the government already has the data to provide reliable information on the average returns from all universities and degrees. University comparison websites currently provide limited and misleading information on the costs and benefits of individual degrees, enthusiastically overstating the latter while carefully understating the former. As a result, they have ultimately benefited universities rather than students. Whilst these websites offer information about teaching and learning, they do not provide comparisons over time or against averages for the sector. Crucially, they also fail to show what type of jobs graduates find themselves working in, e.g. whether law graduates are working in law firms or, more likely, call centres.

At the moment, few universities provide clear information for this over a useful time period (say, five to seven years). Universities should be required to provide a clear and unambiguous breakdown of what percentage of their graduates are working in the relevant professions three years after graduation. This information should be highlighted on the university's web pages for each degree and provided to comparison sites. If students could access accurate information about the real average returns from individual degrees and the chances of gaining a job, for example, as a solicitor, from a specific degree, this would dramatically impact on applications. If such information also allowed ranking and comparison between multiple courses and universities, it would shift the balance of power in applications towards the student.

Moreover, one would assume that the provision of accurate information would considerably reduce the demand for soft sub-jects where the returns were found to be minimal or even negative.

It would also address the oversupply of lawyers, psychologists and social workers. Who would apply to a degree course which offered no realistic chance of a job in that profession? However it would also, possibly drastically, reduce the overall number of students applying to university – hence probably universities' reluctance to provide this information to prospective students?

The raw data needed to produce this information is already available in the records of the Student Loans Company (SLC). The SLC has repayment data from each and every student who has taken out a loan in the last 20 years, including the course and university they attended and their salary over the period of repayment. In a 2011 report, Tim Leunig, the Chief Economist of the think tank CentreForum, articulated the full value of this:

> "... there will be sufficient data for us to have a very good sense of the typical income and repayment patterns of graduates who have done different courses, at different universities. It is therefore possible for government to construct a table which records the likely loss to the government for each course at each university, with different levels of fees."[458]

This data is based upon loans made by taxpayers. These loans are made to students by an organisation which is funded by the taxpayer. If the data is anonymised there is no good reason why it should not be made publicly accessible for each and every potential student, parent and taxpayer to access. This information would then be supported by similarly anonymised data from a variety of professional bodies and say, the social networking platform LinkedIn, to establish which degrees lead to professional careers and which do not. Applied correctly, this information could lead to degrees, departments and even whole institutions closing. Universities would be vociferously opposed to this data being made public for exactly that reason. Unfortunately, post expansion a large number of UK universities provide degrees which simply don't benefit graduates, taxpayers or society as a whole. There is no good reason why this situation should be allowed to continue at the expense of either students and their families or taxpayers.

CUTTING TUITION FEES

It's been clear for many years that the numbers of graduates far exceed any job opportunities. Moreover, all the data indicates that this is leading to stagnation and even a decline in graduate salaries for the minority of graduates fortunate enough to even get graduate-level jobs. Furthermore, it's becoming obvious to everyone, except of course government ministers, that less than half of all student loans will ever be repaid. In fact, with constantly rising tuition fees and accommodation costs, it's likely that the level of student loan default will be well in excess of 60%. This is leading to an absurd situation whereby each year students borrow over £12 billion of which we can already estimate that at least £7 billion will have to be written off. So, if the current tuition fees system continues, millions of graduates will spend the first thirty years of their working lives struggling with debts we already know most of them will never be able to repay. This will prevent many from buying their own homes, getting married and starting families. And the financial grief these graduates will experience is quite pointless and even counter-productive. This is truly the Mathematics of the Madhouse.

The universities, naturally, are delighted with the current situation. Following the 2012 rise in tuition fees, huge amounts of money are pouring into their coffers allowing them to go on a spending spree on new buildings and other vanity projects. In fact, what we're witnessing may be a university real-estate bubble. Moreover, no doubt vice chancellors will see their universities' new-found wealth – what they'd probably call the "profitability" of their "multimillion-pound businesses" – as an excellent excuse for their remuneration committees to give them generous salary increases. But, if the university expansion bubble bursts, then we're going to see a significant drop in student numbers and, as always happens during a real–estate bubble, many of the new buildings, being so enthusiastically put up by universities, will turn into 'ghost campuses' – great facilities but with not enough students around to fully use them.

There is therefore a strong case for stopping this lunacy. Instead of tuition fees increasing each year in line with inflation, they should be cut. Maybe they should be halved or, better still, set back at the pre–2006 £3,000–a–year level. In the short term, the government might have to chuck a couple of billion pounds the universities' way to make up for the lost tuition fees income – the £13 billion+ foreign aid budget could easily cope with losing a couple of billion for a few years. For students, a cut in their debts from £50,000 to £60,000 down to nearer £35,000 would lead to an increase in the repayment percentage (by reducing the crushing burden of compound interest) and less damaging effects on their life chances. Moreover, a drop in universities' income might discourage them from splurging their current cash surpluses on projects which will turn out to have been unnecessary once student numbers begin to fall.

In economics, there's a theory called the 'Laffer Curve'. This proposes that there's a certain point at which increasing tax rates leads to decreased tax revenues largely because tax increases lead to changed behaviours – the higher tax rates rise, the greater are the incentives for people to avoid tax. Moreover, it also suggests that lowering tax rates can actually lead to increasing tax revenues. By ramping up tuition fees to extortionate levels, the government has moved into that part of the Laffer Curve where increases in fees will lead to reduced repayments – partly due to the pernicious effects of compound interest. Faced with mountainous debts, many students will move abroad or just give up on any attempt to repay their loans. Were the size of these debts to be reduced by introducing signifi-cantly lower tuition fees, then it's possible (and even probable) that repayment levels would rise.

GREATER CHOICE FOR STUDENTS

Further improvements could be made by extending the range of options for *how* and *where* study can occur. This could be driven by the Student Loans Company allowing more flexibility in the allocation of its loans. There are two obvious and immediate changes that could improve the range of choices available to students, reduce costs for taxpayers and bridge the gap between industry and academia.

1. Funding overseas study

> "(UK) Undergraduates will rack up more debts studying in their own country than almost any other nation overseas, even when the cost of flights are added... only Australia, the United States and Canada were more expensive."[459]
> *Telegraph*, 2012

Funding overseas study already happens when UK undergraduates spend a year at international universities as part of a four–year degree based at a UK university.[460] Unfortunately, this represents the limit to which the Student Loans Company is prepared to fund UK students to study overseas. Any UK student wishing to study overseas is obliged to fund themselves, which begs the question why?

As the fees for some international universities are much lower than in the UK, and the cost of living in many of these countries is also much lower, studying abroad could save everybody money. UK graduates studying abroad might not only develop useful language skills but also international relationships and networks with important economies, such as China, India or Brazil. The taxpayer would benefit from reduced fees, students from increased choice and UK universities from increased competition, although they might not see it that way (which is, of course, their prerogative).

For example, international students wishing to study at Peking University in China, now one of the world's top 50 universities, face fees of around £3,800 per year, alongside much cheaper living costs than the UK.[461] A Chinese website offering guidance to international students suggests that living and accommodation costs per year of academic study equate to around £3,130.[462] This suggests that for £7,000 a year, a UK student could cover their tuition and accommodation costs at a top global university, learn valuable language skills and gain valuable life experience. Alternatively, they could take on much more debt to study at a UK university ranked much lower in the world to study for a degree which will offer them little, if any, graduate premium or other enrichment.

2. Recognising mature students' experience

A major issue facing mature students before they apply to a university is the assumption that they should start studying from the same point as an 18-year-old. If, for example, a 38-year-old marketing manager, with no degree but 20 years of experience has to sit through the same *Introduction to Marketing* class as a school leaver, then this is clearly inefficient for the university and dispiriting for the mature and experienced student.

One way of addressing this is a process known as the Accreditation of Prior Experiential Learning (APEL). APEL allows a mature student the opportunity to sit down and discuss their work experience with an academic who will estimate how much academic credit and at what level this experience may be worth. This process has existed in its modern form for the last forty years and happens in the universities of all OECD countries in one form or another. In France, for example, it is enshrined in law. In the case of our marketing manager, this credit might make it possible for him to complete a part-time degree in two years.

Unfortunately, there are a limited number of universities in the UK that currently offer APEL. This is mostly a reflection of the fact that the government provides no funding for APEL and the process is not eligible for student loans. If this situation was changed, it could have a significant impact on UK universities' ability to attract both mature students and customers from the business world.

WELCOMING PRIVATE PROVIDERS

> "Higher Education should be treated like any other service sector of the economy, with new competitors free to enter without first having to seek special permission from a government agency."[463] The Adam Smith Institute (2009)

One of the key arguments which have been deployed against opening the UK Higher Education system more widely to the private sector is that it will reduce standards and that quality will decline. Given the fact that public universities have utterly failed to maintain standards in learning, teaching and assessment during expansion, such an argument has become totally laughable. The current system has seen massive grade inflation, increased class sizes, reduced curricula, widespread plagiarism, systemic evidence of dumbing down, First degrees obtainable with an average score of 53% and exams being passed with marks of just 14%. Exactly which academic standards are being protected by the status quo?

By its very nature, Higher Education is not a market for companies desiring quick returns. Unlike UK universities, global private providers of Higher Education, such as Laureate and the Apollo Group, did not expand by providing a poor-quality service and worthless, over-priced, dumbed-down degrees to their students. The UK Higher Education system currently has one of the smallest private sectors of any developed country. Our Higher Education system would be more diverse, stronger and more competitive in the long term if it is opened up to private providers. The possibility of falling standards being driven by allowing more private universities into our Higher Education system is not a genuine worry. Rather, it is a plea from a special interest group

(UK universities) for preferential treatment at the expense of their customers (students) and funders (taxpayers). Though one can hardly imagine the outrage and horror of *Guardian* readers were some of our worst-performing universities to be closed and then sold off to private companies.

IMPROVING FAIR ACCESS

One of the most contentious issues within UK Higher Education is the extent to which students from state schools, particularly from disadvantaged backgrounds, gain entrance to elite universities. Much of the criticism directed at these universities has been ill-informed. This has seriously undermined the work that they undertake to widen access amongst disadvantaged students. National rows about elitism have simply reinforced inaccurate perceptions about the better universities amongst potential applicants and teachers.

In 2012, Oxford and Cambridge universities received 63% and 67% of their applicants from state schools, despite these schools educating 93% of the school-age population. If access issues are to be addressed, then these figures need to be raised dramatically. This is not only the responsibility of these universities. It is also the responsibility of any state schools who fail to encourage their students to apply to these universities.

All secondary school teachers should acquire a basic understanding of the university system, including facts and figures about Oxbridge and Russell Group entry, as part of their teacher training. Each state school could be mandated to send *at least* four applications to Oxbridge every year. Schools which have no history of making any successful applications should be required to identify a pool of at least 12 potential candidates in the third form or earlier (allowing them to choose their GCSEs and A-levels accordingly). These schools should be sent information packs by the Department of Education explaining the statistics for competition for each and every degree and college at Oxbridge, and a list of desirable and undesirable qualifications for these courses. These schools would receive additional guidance from Oxbridge interview coaching companies in writing references and targeting applications to different courses and colleges. Guidance could include visits during the sixth form to coach students in interview technique and provide additional reading to assist them at interview.

Simply increasing the number of state-school applications to Oxbridge by 8,000 per year would have a much greater impact on state-school entrance rates than any number of bombastic politicians' speeches or singularly ill-informed broadsheet articles.

TIME FOR CHANGE?

The Great University Expansion has been driven by a combination of faulty assumptions, cynicism, self-interest, greed, wilful ignorance and disastrous mismanagement amongst the people who direct, fund and deliver Higher Education in the UK.

The expansionists want us to believe that all universities, all degrees and all students are equal and that expansion can help to transform our economy from low skills to high skills by unlocking the rich academic potential which runs throughout British society. They also want us to see a university education as an engine for social mobility, regional regeneration and as the gateway to a wiser, healthier civic society.

The twin ideas of university as a public good and that everybody who wants to go to "Uni" should be able to do so have become articles of faith for universities, politicians and the chattering classes. Because of this, the last three decades have seen us sucked up into a "degree bubble", in a similar fashion to previous stock-market and housing bubbles. The main victims of this Higher Education bubble will be future generations – the graduates we offer no choice but a degree and a lifetime of debt. For them and us, expansion and its corresponding debt mountain represent an intra-generational gamble on a horrifying scale.

Whatever the outcome of this wager, there has been a profound lack of thought about the long–term social, cultural and economic ramifications of expansion to date. But if we examine the results of expansion, we find little evidence to support the nature and scale of this bet on expansion. Rather, there is plenty of evidence of negative returns for individuals, society and the economy from an expanded Higher Education system that is flawed in concept, design and operation.

Instead of economic success delivered by a highly–educated population, expansion has given us a mushrooming student debt mountain, falling standards, industrial–scale plagiarism and universities in regular financial crises. This direction of travel is not sustainable for our universities, society or economy. A complex world requires a diversity of solutions and, at the moment, we only seem to have one – a post–school system which has been reduced to an unimaginative mono–vision, literally "Uni or bust".

It's time to stop this intra–generational horror story!

It's time to burst the Great Uni Expansion bubble!

Endnotes

1 Institute of Education Website 15th October 2010 http://www.ioe.ac.uk/45855.html

2 BBC Website, 19th November 2013 http://www.bbc.co.uk/newsbeat/24947191

3 HESA Website

4 ONS Social Trends 1992

5 HESA Website and Office of National Statistics "Social Trends 22"

6 HESA Website

7 T*elegraph,* 12th August, 2011 http://www.telegraph.co.uk/education/universityeducation/8695990/Students–face–leaving–university–with–60k–debts.html

8 The Robbins Report http://www.educationengland.org.uk/documents/robbins/robbins02.html

9 Ibid

10 Dearing Report (1997) www.leeds.ac.uk/educol/ncihe/

11 HEPI (2011) "Higher Education Supply And Demand To 2020" www.hepi.ac.uk/files/2010%20demand%20report%20summary.pdf

12 *Times*, 31 March 2018

13 Ibid

14 Office of the Independent Adjudicator website http://www.oiahe.org.uk/media/115360/oia–annual–report–2016.pdf

15 BBC Website http://www.bbc.co.uk/news/education–27640303

16 Office of the Independent Adjudicator website http://oiahe.org.uk/media/88444/press–notice–annual–report–2012.pdf

17 HEPI (2009) "Student's academic experiences" http://www.hepi.ac.uk/478-1616/HEPI-publishes-updated-research-on-students%E2%80%99-academic-experience.html

18 HoC Select Committee (2009) Students and Universities Report http://www.publications.parliament.uk/pa/cm200809/cmselect/cmdius/170/17007.htm

19 BIS (2011) "The Returns to Higher Education Qualifications" http://www.bis.gov.uk/assets/biscore/higher-education/docs/r/11-973-returns-to-higher-education-qualifications.pdf

20 *Channel 4 News* Fact Check 12th October 2010 http://blogs.channel4.com/factcheck/how-progressive-is-lord-brownes-tuition-fees-system/4360

21 HESA Website

22 Ibid

23 Ibid

24 *Guardian,* 24th January 2016 http://www.theguardian.com/world/2016/jan/24/safe-spaces-universities-no-platform-free-speech-rhodes

25 HESA Website

26 UCAS website http://www.ucas.ac.uk/about_us/media_enquiries/media_releases/2010/210110

27 *Guardian*, 28th October, 2008 http://www.guardian.co.uk/education/2008/oct/28/education-adivce Sutton Trust

28 *THES*, 3rd April, 2014 https://www.timeshighereducation.com/news/more-data-can-lead-to-poor-student-choices-hefce-learns/2012410.article

29 Academic FOI Website http://www.academicfoi.com/aboutus.htm

30 *THES*, 5th July 2012 https://www.timeshighereducation.com/news/marketing-spend-up-but-applications-fail-to-follow-suit/2012107.article

31 *THES*, 5th July 2012 http://www.timeshighereducation.co.uk/story.asp?storycode=420468

32 House of Commons Innovation, Universities, Science and Skills Committee Students and Universities (2009) Report http://www.publications.parliament.uk/pa/cm200809/cmselect/cmdius/170/17005.htm

33 House of Commons Innovation, Universities, Science and Skills Committee Students and Universities (2009) Report http://www.publications.parliament.uk/pa/cm200809/cmselect/cmdius/170/17005.htm

34 *THES*, 16th January, 2014 https://www.timeshighereducation.com/news/rosy-prospectuses-misleading-students/2010522.article

35 BBC, 15th November 2018 http://www.bbc.co.uk/news/education-41984465

36 House of Commons Business, Innovation and Skills Committee Government reform of Higher Education Twelfth Report of Session 2010–12

37 Gov UK Website https://www.gov.uk/national-minimum-wage-rates

38 *THES*, 12th March, 2015 https://www.timeshighereducation.com/features/is-employability-data-being-manipulated/2018930.article

39 *THES*, 3rd July 2014 https://www.timeshighereducation.com/news/how-deep-in-the-red-debt-estimates-miss-the-mark/2014289.article

40 Clearing House for Postgraduate Courses in Clinical Psychology http://www.leeds.ac.uk/chpccp/BasicNumbers.html

41 *Guardian*, 27th April, 2004 http://www.guardian.co.uk/education/2004/apr/27/highereducation.accesstouniversity

42 *THES* 12th March 2013 http://www.timeshighereducation. co.uk/news/many–graduates–would–have–preferred–apprentice– ships/2002517.article

43 *Guardian* ,14th September 2010, http://www.guardian.co.uk/ education/2010/sep/14/university–places–failure

44 House of Commons Innovation, Universities, Science and Skills Committee, Students and Universities (2009) Evidence UCAS http:// www.publications.parliament.uk/pa/cm200809/cmselect/cmdi– us/170/170we98.htm

45 Push website, 18th August, 2010 http://www.push.co.uk/this–month/ in–the–news/results–day–2011/Flunk–rate–and–clearing.htm

46 Push website, 18th August, 2010 http://www.push.co.uk/this–month/ in–the–news/results–day–2011/Flunk–rate–and–clearing.htm

47 *Guardian*, 20th October, 2009 http://www.theguardian.com/ education/2009/oct/20/university–experience–changes–students

48 *Guardian*, 22nd May 2013 http://www.theguardian.com/ commentisfree/2013/may/22/university–student–britain–mental–health

49 BBC Website 30th September 2015 http://www.bbc.co.uk/news/ education–34354405

50 *Telegraph*, 16th September 2012 http://www.telegraph.co.uk/educa– tion/9545232/Students–win–degree–places–with–as–little–as–two–E– grades–at–A–level.html

51 *Guardian*, 20th August, 2006 http://www.guardian.co.uk/commentis– free/2006/aug/20/comment.highereducation

52 *Telegraph*, 24th August 2012 http://www.telegraph.co.uk/education/ universityeducation/9497191/Universities–admitting–foreign–stu– dents–with–poor–English.html

53 *Telegraph*, 20th September, 2012, http://www.telegraph.co.uk/education/universityeducation/9556080/Universities–using–foreign–students–as–cash–cows.html

54 *Telegraph*, 24th August 2012 http://www.telegraph.co.uk/education/universityeducation/9497191/Universities–admitting–foreign–students–with–poor–English.html

55 House of Commons Innovation, Universities, Science and Skills Committee, Students and Universities (2009) Evidence UCAS Evidence Nigel Dyer http://www.publications.parliament.uk/pa/cm200809/cmselect/cmdius/170/170we70.htm

56 BBC Website, 17th June, 2008 http://news.bbc.co.uk/1/hi/health/7358528.stm

57 *Guardian*, 19th September, 2007 User Comment http://www.guardian.co.uk/education/mortarboard/2007/sep/19/isukeducationdoingwellor 15

58 *Telegraph*, http://www.telegraph.co.uk/education/universityeducation/9556080/Universities–using–foreign–students–as–cash–cows.html

59 *Guardian*, 23rd November, 2005 http://www.guardian.co.uk/money/2005/nov/23/highereducation.tuitionfees UUK

60 *Guardian*, 18th September, 2009 http://www.guardian.co.uk/money/2009/sep/18/freshers–week–commercialism–university

61 *THES*, 1st July 2014 https://www.timeshighereducation.com/news/students–relying–on–payday–loans–to–make–ends–meet/2013925.article

62 Natwest (2009) Student Living Index 2009 http://www.natwest.com/global/media/y2009/m–5.ashx

63 *Daily Mail*, 29th September, 2009 http://www.dailymail.co.uk/news/article–1216816/Fresher–students–hotels–rooms–left–campus.html

64 *THES,* 1st September 2011 www.timeshighereducation.co.uk/story.asp?storyCode=417287

65 *Independent,* 27th August, 2011 http://www.independent.co.uk/news/education/education-news/who-said-universitys-like-a-holiday-camp-beds-crisis-sees-students-sent-to-pontins-2344681.html

66 *THES,* 10th February, 2011 http://www.timeshighereducation.co.uk/story.asp?storycode=415154

67 NUS (2012) "Accommodation Costs Survey" http://www.nus.org.uk/en/news/news/student-accommodation-costs-double-in-ten-years-nus-survey-shows/

68 NUS (2016) "Accommodation Costs Survey" http://nus-digital.s3-eu-west-1.amazonaws.com/document/documents/20637/e1416d1aae50226cf42ab902273d89c4/Unipol_NUS_AccommodationCostsSurvey2015.pdf?AWSAccess-KeyId=AKIAJKEA56ZWKFU6MHNQ&Expires=1457827158&Signature=JsBxlPU%2B19YKU%2BLFfYjV0CO60hQ%3D

69 *Guardian,* 15th August, 2015 http://www.theguardian.com/education/2015/aug/15/soaring-student-rents-college-accommodation-crisis

70 *Guardian,* 15th August, 2015 http://www.theguardian.com/education/2015/aug/15/soaring-student-rents-college-accommodation-crisis

71 *Guardian,* 15th August, 2015 http://www.theguardian.com/education/2015/aug/15/students-luxury-accommodation-debts

72 http://www.themoneystop.co.uk/102007/biba-students-should-take-out-contents-insurance.html

73 The Baroness Deech of Cumnor Speech, 28 March 2012, "The Universities: Under Regulation" http://www.gresham.ac.uk/lectures-and-events/the-universities-under-regulation

74 *Independent*, 18th November, 2008 http://www.independent.co.uk/student/news/are-students-safe-1023989.html

75 *Guardian*, 25th September 2000 http://www.theguardian.com/uk/2000/sep/25/highereducation.education

76 Ibid

77 *Guardian*, 13th July, 2008 http://www.guardian.co.uk/uk/2008/jul/13/ukcrime.highereducation

78 Mancunion Website http://mancunion.com/2014/02/24/manchester-ranked-worst-for-student-crime/

79 South Yorkshire Police Website, http://www.southyorks.police.uk/news-syp/reduction-violent-crime-against-students http://www.biba.org.uk/MediaCenterContentDetails.aspx?ContentID=500

80 British Insurers Brokers Association, 12th September, 2005 http://www.biba.org.uk/MediaCenterContentDetails.aspx?ContentID=500

81 *Guardian*, 13th July, 2008 http://www.guardian.co.uk/uk/2008/jul/13/ukcrime.highereducation

82 Generally attributed to WH Auden, but actually appeared in different forms in various publications from about 1900 onwards

83 Adam Smith, *"The Wealth of Nations"* Book 5 Chapter 1, Part 3

84 Lord Byron *"Thoughts Suggested By a College Examination"*, "http://www.gradesaver.com/lord-byrons-poems/e-text/early-poems-thoughts-suggested-by-a-college-examination

85 *THES*, 11th August 2011 2012 www.timeshighereducation.co.uk/story.asp?storycode=417059

86 BBC Website 15th May 2013 http://www.bbc.co.uk/news/education-22484419

87 *THES*, 4th May, 2007 http://www.timeshighereducation.co.uk/story.asp?storyCode=208813&sectioncode=26

88 OECD Website, 2011 https://www.oecd.org/edu/skills–beyond–school/48631144.pdf

89 *THES,* 31ˢᵗ March 2011 http://www.timeshighereducation.co.uk/story.asp?sectioncode=26&storycode=415645&c=1

90 *Guardian*, 31ˢᵗ October, 2006 http://www.guardian.co.uk/education/2006/oct/31/universityteaching.highereducation1

91 *THES*, 4ᵗʰ May 2007 http://www.timeshighereducation.co.uk/story.asp?storycode=208813

92 UCU Website, 27ᵗʰ May 2008 http://www.ucu.org.uk/index.cfm?articleid=3316

93 Bruce Charlton's Miscellany 9th May 2008 http://charltonteaching.blogspot.co.uk/2008/05/class–sizes–in–uk–universities.html

94 House of Commons Innovation, Universities, Science and Skills Committee, Students and Universities (2009) Report http://www.publications.parliament.uk/pa/cm200809/cmselect/cmdius/170/17007.htm

95 Ibid

96 House of Commons Innovation, Universities, Science and Skills Committee, Students and Universities (2009) Evidence UCAS E–Consultation summary http://www.publications.parliament.uk/pa/cm200809/cmselect/cmdius/170/170we06.htm

97 HEPI (2007) *"The Academic Experience of students in English universities"* www.hepi.ac.uk/files/27Academicexperienceofstudents.doc

98 Ibid

99 HEPI (2007) "Professor *Gibbs' commentary"* www.hepi.ac.uk/files/33–Gibbs–commentary.doc

100 *THES,* 1ˢᵗ August 2013 http://www.timeshighereducation.co.uk/news/student–workloads–compared–and–contrasted/2006151.article

101 HEPI (2007) "Professor *Gibbs' commentary*" www.hepi.ac.uk/files/33-Gibbs-commentary.doc

102 Ibid

103 Ibid

104 *Guardian*, 25th September 2007 http://www.guardian.co.uk/education/2007/sep/25/students.highereducation HEPI

105 *THES*, 24th August, 2006 http://www.timeshighereducation.co.uk/story.asp?sectioncode=26&storycode=204943

106 Which University? *"A Degree of Value"* 2014 http://www.wonkhe.com/wp-content/uploads/2014/11/Which-A-degree-of-value-Nov-2014.pdf

107 *THES*, 8th March 2012 www.timeshighereducation.co.uk/story.asp?storycode=419279

108 HESA Website

109 *Telegraph*, 1st January, 2011 http://www.telegraph.co.uk/education/universityeducation/8235115/Dumbing-down-of-university-grades-revealed.html

110 HESA Website

111 House of Commons Innovation, Universities, Science and Skills Committee Students and Universities (2009) Evidence Professor Yorke http://www.publications.parliament.uk/pa/cm200809/cmselect/cmdius/170/170ii.pdf

112 Civitas (2005) "Education: Better results and declining standards? Online Briefing" http://www.civitas.org.uk/pdf/educationBriefing-Dec05.pdf

113 *Guardian*, 6th July, 2008 http://www.guardian.co.uk/education/2008/jul/06/highereducation.uk

114 *Telegraph*, 1ˢᵗ January, 2011 http://www.telegraph.co.uk/education/universityeducation/8235115/Dumbing–down–of–university–grades–revealed.html

115 *Telegraph*, 16ᵗʰ March, 2004 http://www.telegraph.co.uk/education/educationnews/3336381/Dumbing–down–fear–as–leading–universi–ties–award–more–firsts.html

116 Civitas (2005) *"Education: Better results and declining standards?"* Online Briefing http://www.civitas.org.uk/pdf/educationBriefingDec05.pdf

117 BBC Website, 24ᵗʰ June, 2008 http://news.bbc.co.uk/1/hi/education/7469396.stm

118 Quality Assurance Agency Annual Report

119 HoC Select Committee (2009) Students and Universities Report http://www.publications.parliament.uk/pa/cm200809/cmselect/cmdius/170/17007.htm

120 *Guardian*, 1ˢᵗ October 2009 http://www.guardian.co.uk/education/2009/oct/01/universities–need–revamp–higher–education–report

121 *THES*, 7ᵗʰ April, 2009 http://www.timeshighereducation.co.uk/story.asp?sectioncode=26&storycode=406105&c=1

122 *Guardian*, 8ᵗʰ August, 2004 http://www.guardian.co.uk/uk/2004/aug/08/highereducation.education

123 House of Commons Innovation, Universities, Science and Skills Committee Students and Universities (2009) Evidence Geoffrey Alderman http://www.publications.parliament.uk/pa/cm200809/cmselect/cmdius/170/170we24.htm

124 *Guardian*, 22ⁿᵈ May, 2007 http://www.guardian.co.uk/education/2007/may/22/highereducation.universityfunding

125 *Guardian*, 19ᵗʰ December 2002 http://www.guardian.co.uk/education/2002/dec/19/highereducation.uk1

126 *THES*, (2008) "Lecturers survey" http://www.timeshighereduca-tion.co.uk/Journals/THE/THE/23_October_2008/attachments/35_OCT2308_Layout%201.pdf

127 *THES*, 19th November, 2004 http://www.timeshighereducation.co.uk/story.asp?storycode=192485

128 House of Commons Innovation, Universities, Science and Skills Committee Students and Universities (2009) Report Students and Universities http://www.parliament.the-stationery-office.co.uk/pa/cm200809/cmselect/cmdius/170/17008.htm

129 House of Commons Innovation, Universities, Science and Skills Committee Students and Universities (2009) Evidence Sue Evans Manchester MET http://www.publications.parliament.uk/pa/cm200809/cmselect/cmdius/170/170i.pdf

130 *Guardian*, 26th February, 2010 http://www.guardian.co.uk/commentisfree/2010/feb/26/universities-exam-marking-ruling

131 House of Commons Innovation, Universities, Science and Skills Committee Students and Universities (2009) Report Students and Universities http://www.publications.parliament.uk/pa/cm200809/cmselect/cmdius/170/17005.htm

132 Ibid

133 House of Commons Innovation, Universities, Science and Skills Committee Students and Universities (2009) Evidence Richard Royle http://www.publications.parliament.uk/pa/cm200809/cmselect/cmdius/170/170we13.htm

134 House of Commons Innovation, Universities, Science and Skills Committee Students and Universities (2009) Evidence Walter Cairns http://www.publications.parliament.uk/pa/cm200809/cmselect/cmdius/170/170we136.htm

135 *THES*, 6th August, 2004 http://www.timeshighereducation.co.uk/story.asp?storyCode=190494&sectioncode=26

136 *Guardian*, 13th August, 2004 http://www.guardian.co.uk/education/2004/aug/13/highereducation.administration

137 *Guardian*, 18th June, 2008 http://www.guardian.co.uk/education/mortarboard/2008/jun/18/positivemarkingmakesmedesp

138 House of Commons Innovation, Universities, Science and Skills Committee Students and Universities (2009) Report Students and Universities http://www.publications.parliament.uk/pa/cm200809/cmselect/cmdius/170/17005.htm

139 *THES*, 10th September 2009 http://www.timeshighereducation.co.uk/story.asp?storycode=408081

140 *Guardian*, 10th September 2009 http://www.guardian.co.uk/education/2009/sep/10/higher–education–universityfunding

141 House of Commons Innovation, Universities, Science and Skills Committee Students and Universities (2009) Evidence Susan Evans http://www.publications.parliament.uk/pa/cm200809/cmselect/cmdius/170/170ii.pdf

142 T*elegraph,* 28th April, 2011 http://www.telegraph.co.uk/education/universityeducation/8479173/St–Andrews–launches–investigation–into–Syrian–studies–centre.html

143 University of Nottingham website, 23rd March, 2001 http://www.nottingham.ac.uk/business/ICCSR/aboutus.php?c=25

144 HEFCE (2009) *"Review of Moderns Languages provision in higher education in England"* http://www.hefce.ac.uk/media/hefce1/pubs/hefce/2009/0941/09_41.pdf

145 Ibid

146 *Guardian*, 20th May, 2002 http://www.guardian.co.uk/uk/2002/may/20/highereducation.education1

147 *Guardian*, 22nd May, 2002 http://www.guardian.co.uk/uk/2002/may/22/highereducation.education 14

148 *Telegraph,* 22nd February 2005 http:// www.telegraph.co.uk/news/uknews/1484084/ Over-10000-Oxbridge-rejects-went-on-to-gain-straight-As.html

149 House of Commons Innovation, Universities, Science and Skills Select Committee (2009) Universities and Students Evidence Nigel Dyer http://www.publications.parliament.uk/pa/cm200809/cmselect/cmdi-us/170/170ii.pdf

150 *Telegraph,* 10th Feb 2012 http://www.telegraph.co.uk/education/ educationnews/9072505/University-maths-too-difficult-for-British-students.html

151 Ibid

152 House of Commons Innovation, Universities, Science and Skills Committee Students and Universities (2009) Evidence NUS http://www. publications.parliament.uk/pa/cm200809/cmselect/cmdius/170/170ii.pdf

153 *Guardian,* 31st October, 2008 http://www.guardian.co.uk/educa-tion/2008/oct/31/facebook-cheating-plagiarism-cambridge-varsity-wikipedia Varsity

154 *THES,* 16th March, 2006 http://www.timeshighereducation.co.uk/ story.asp?storycode=201951

155 *Telegraph,* 14th March, 2006 http://www.telegraph.co.uk/news/ uknews/1512950/Internet-plagiarism-is-rife-at-Oxford.html

156 *Guardian,* 10th September, 2006 http://www.guardian.co.uk/technol-ogy/2006/sep/10/news.students

157 *Guardian,* 15th June, 2015 http://www.theguardian.com/educa-tion/2015/jun/15/cheating-rife-in-uk-education-system-dispatches-investigation-shows

158 *Guardian,* 29th July, 2006 http://www.guardian.co.uk/uk/2006/ jul/29/highereducation.education 16

159 *Guardian*, 17th February, 2005 http://www.guardian.co.uk/uk/2005/feb/17/highereducation.students

160 *THES*, 16th February, 2017 https://www.timeshighereducation.com/features/the–teaching–survey–2017–results–and–analysis#survey–answer

161 Ibid

162 *Telegraph*, 26th June, 2012 http://www.telegraph.co.uk/education/universityeducation/9357875/How–foreign–students–with–lower–grades–jump–the–university–queue.html

163 Ibid

164 Ibid

165 *Telegraph,* 15th August 2012 http://www.telegraph.co.uk/education/universityeducation/9475564/Foreign–students–favoured–in–two–tier–university–clearing.html

166 *Telegraph*, 27th November, 2011 http://www.telegraph.co.uk/education/universityeducation/8918975/LSE–to–be–criticised–over–1.5m–Libya–donation.html

167 *THES,* 18th February 2014 https://www.timeshighereducation.com/news/oft–warns–universities–over–student–debt–rules/2011432.article

168 *Guardian,* 29th August 2013 http://www.theguardian.com/education/2013/aug/09/should–universities–charge–for–graduation

169 Money Solve Website http://www.moneysolve.co.uk/employment/graduate–unemployment–2011

170 *Telegraph,* 7th November 2012 http://www.telegraph.co.uk/education/universityeducation/9658977/Recession–hit–graduates–doubt–the–value–of–their–degrees.html

171 Institute for Employment Studies *"What do Graduates do Next"* (1997) http://www.employment–studies.co.uk/system/files/resources/files/343.pdf

172 ONS website 19th November 2013 http://www.theguardian.com/business/2013/nov/19http://www.ons.gov.uk/employmentandlabourmarket/peopleinwork/employmentandemployeetypes/articles/graduatesintheuklabourmarket/2013-11-19/half-recent-uk-graduates-stuck-jobs-ons

173 1994 Group (2008) *"Graduate employment and earnings: Are universities meeting student expectations?"* http://www.1994group.ac.uk/documents/public/081118_GEEresearchReport.pdf

174 ONS website 19th November 2013 http://www.theguardian.com/business/2013/nov/19http://www.ons.gov.uk/employmentandlabourmarket/peopleinwork/employmentandemployeetypes/articles/graduatesintheuklabourmarket/2013-11-19/half-recent-uk-graduates-stuck-jobs-ons

175 Sutton Trust Website, 1st May, 2008 http://www.suttontrust.com/news/news/universities-earning-powers/

176 De Vries, R. (2014).*"Earning By Degrees: differences in the career outcomes of UK Graduates"*, Sutton Trust.

177 *THES*, 10th July 2014 https://www.timeshighereducation.com/news/graduate-employment-rates-rise/2014452.article

178 Council of Professors and Heads of Computing (2012) *"CS Graduate Unemployment Report 2012"* http://www.cphc.ac.uk/docs/reports/cs_graduate_unemployment_report.pdf

179 The Complete University Guide website http://www.thecompleteuniversityguide.co.uk/careers/graduate-salaries-and-the-professional-premium/graduate-starting-salary/

180 1994 Group (2008) "Graduate employment and earnings: Are universities meeting student expectations?" http://www.1994group.ac.uk/documents/public/081118_GEEresearchReport.pdf

181 HECSU (2010) *What do graduates do?* "http://www.hecsu.ac.uk/assets/assets/documents/lmi/WDGD_Nov_2010.pdf

182 Local Government Association Website, 1st October 2012 http://www.local.gov.uk/web/guest/media-releases/-/journal_content/56/10171/3717248/NEWS-TEMPLATE

183 ONS Website Graduates in the Labour Market 2013, http://www.ons.gov.uk/employmentandlabourmarket/peopleinwork/employmentandemployeetypes/articles/graduatesintheuklabourmarket/2013-11-19

184 *Guardian*, 10th January, 2009 http://www.guardian.co.uk/education/2009/jan/10/graduate-employment-crisis-rescue-package

185 T*elegraph*, 26 Jun 2012 http://www.telegraph.co.uk/education/educationnews/9356477/Willetts-employers-pick-graduates-from-just-six-universities.html

186 Demos (2010) "A report into the attitudes and aspirations of this year's graduates" www.endsleigh.co.uk/Student/.../Demos_Report_2010_screen.pdf

187 Intergenerational Foundation website "The Graduate premium: manna, myth of plain mis-selling" http://www.if.org.uk/research-posts/the-graduate-premium-manna-myth-or-plain-mis-selling/

188 *Telegraph*, 4th July 2012 http://www.telegraph.co.uk/education/educationnews/9373058/Top-jobs-restricted-to-graduates-with-first-class-degrees.html

189 BBC website, 10th July 2013 http://www.bbc.co.uk/news/education-23247176

190 *THES*, 8th July, 2010 http://www.timeshighereducation.co.uk/story.asp?storycode=412382

191 Gov.Uk website, 9th June 2015 https://www.gov.uk/government/collections/graduate-labour-market-quarterly-statistics

192 HESA Website

193 The Complete University Guide Website http://www.thecompleteuniversityguide.co.uk/careers/graduate-salaries-and-the-professional-premium/graduate-starting-salary/

194 Intergenerational Foundation website "The Graduate premium: manna, myth of plain mis-selling" http://www.if.org.uk/research-posts/the-graduate-premium-manna-myth-or-plain-mis-selling/

195 Andrew Robinson and Simon Tormey (2004) "New Labour's neo-liberal Gleichschaltung: the case of higher education" http://www.commoner.org.uk/07robinson&tormey.pdf

196 BIS (2011) *"The Returns to Higher Education Qualifications"* http://www.bis.gov.uk/assets/biscore/higher-education/docs/r/11-973-returns-to-higher-education-qualifications.pdf

197 *Telegraph*, 12th August, 2011 http://www.telegraph.co.uk/education/universityeducation/8695990/Students-face-leaving-university-with-60k-debts.html

198 HESA website

199 *Telegraph,* 29th May 2015, http://www.telegraph.co.uk/education/educationnews/11639807/Number-of-foreign-students-at-top-universities-doubled-in-less-than-a-decade-research-finds.html

200 HEPI (2004) "Government, Funding Council and Universities: How Should They Relate?" http://www.hepi.ac.uk/files/7GovernmentFundingCouncilandUniversities1.pdf

201 Ibid

202 Oxblogster, 4th December, 2006 http://oxblogster.blogspot.co.uk/2006/12/practice-makes-perfect.html

203 UCU Website, 20th November, 2006 http://www.ucu.org.uk/index.cfm?articleid=2154

204 Tony Dickson (2008) "UK universities and the state: a Faustian bargain?" Institute of Economic Affairs http://www.iea.org.uk/sites/default/files/publications/files/upldbook31pdf.pdf

205 *Guardian*, 16th May, 2001 http://www.guardian.co.uk/uk/2001/may/16/highereducation.administration

206 HESA website

207 *Guardian*, 15th February 2010 http://www.guardian.co.uk/education/2010/feb/15/universities–crumbling–secret–database–guardian

208 *Guardian*, 13th June, 2002 http://www.guardian.co.uk/uk/2002/jun/13/highereducation.education

209 UCU website, 16th July, 2009 http://www.ucu.org.uk/index.cfm?articleid=4083

210 *Guardian*, 21st May, 2002 http://www.guardian.co.uk/uk/2002/may/21/politics.highereducation 20

211 *Manchester Evening News*, 9th March 2007 http://menmedia.co.uk/manchestereveningnews/news/education/s/1001/1001469_400_university_jobs_could_go.html

212 *This is Plymouth* website, 18th September, 2008 http://www.thisisplymouth.co.uk/University–s–building–programme–blamed–job–losses/story–12683692–detail/story.html

213 *THES*, 29th October 2009 http://www.timeshighereducation.co.uk/story.asp?storycode=408844

214 *Salford Star*, 18th March 2013 http://www.salfordstar.com/article.asp?id=1735

215 BBC Website, 30th March 2015 https://www.pressandjournal.co.uk/fp/news/aberdeen/534570/150–jobs–could–go–at–aberdeen–university–in–bid–to–save–10–5m/

216 *The Press and Journal* Website, 19th May 2015 http://www.bbc.co.uk/news/uk-england-devon-32787198

217 Chronicle Live Website, 6th May 2016 http://www.chroniclelive.co.uk/news/north-east-news/northumbria-university-slash-up-112-11293969

218 BBC Website, 19th April, 2010 http://news.bbc.co.uk/1/hi/england/cumbria/8623536.stm

219 *Guardian*, 15th April 2005 http://www.guardian.co.uk/uk/2005/apr/15/highereducation.freedomofinformation

220 *Times*, 27 April 2018

221 *THES*, 10th October, 2014 https://www.timeshighereducation.com/news/mental-health-problems-affect-work-of-two-thirds-of-he-staff/2016294.article

222 *Guardian*, 2nd November, 2006 http://www.guardian.co.uk/education/2006/nov/02/highereducation.uk UCU 26

223 Universities and Colleges Union (2010) "The growing epidemic Work-related stress in post-16 education" http://www.ucu.org.uk/media/pdf/5/8/Work-related_stress_report.pdf

224 Universities and Colleges Union (2008) "Stress Survey" http://www.ucu.org.uk/media/pdf/d/0/ucu_hestress_dec08.pdf

225 UCU Website, 1st March, 2013 https://www.ucu.org.uk/article/6531/Unpaid-overtime-by-teaching-professionals-shoots-up

226 National Association of Teachers in Further and Higher Education (2002) "Core Funding Must Tackle University Basic Needs: Building and Teaching"

227 Universities and Colleges Union (2008) "Stress Survey" http://www.ucu.org.uk/media/pdf/d/0/ucu_hestress_dec08.pdf

228 Universities and Colleges Union (2008) "Stress Survey" http://www.ucu.org.uk/media/pdf/d/0/ucu_hestress_dec08.pdf

229 Universities and Colleges Union (2008) "Stress Survey" http://www.ucu.org.uk/media/pdf/d/0/ucu_hestress_dec08.pdf

230 *THES*, 26th January 2007 http://www.timeshighereducation.co.uk/story.asp?sectioncode=26&storycode=207598

231 *Guardian*, 25th May 2008 http://www.guardian.co.uk/education/2008/may/25/highereducation.students

232 *THES*, 26h February 2017 https://www.timeshighereducation.com/features/the-teaching-survey-2017-results-and-analysis#survey-answer

233 UCU Website 3rd November 2011 http://www.ucu.org.uk/index.cfm?articleid=5809

234 AcademicFOI.Com: "Workplace Bullying & Harassment" http://www.academicfoi.com/bullyingharassment/index.htm

235 *Guardian*, 9th June, 2004 http://www.guardian.co.uk/education/2004/jun/09/highereducation.research AUT

236 Universities and Colleges Union (2008) "Stress Survey" http://www.ucu.org.uk/media/pdf/d/0/ucu_hestress_dec08.pdf

237 Universities and Colleges Union (2008) "Stress Survey" http://www.ucu.org.uk/media/pdf/d/0/ucu_hestress_dec08.pdf

238 *Guardian*, 6th November, 2007 http://www.guardian.co.uk/education/2007/nov/06/highereducation.uk UCU

239 UCU (2008) "Stress Survey" http://www.ucu.org.uk/media/pdf/d/0/ucu_hestress_dec08.pdf

240 *THES* 12 May 2011 www.timeshighereducation.co.uk/story.asp?storyCode=416117

241 HESA Website

242 Universities UK (2008) "Recruitment and Retention HE" http://www.universitiesuk.ac.uk/Publications/Documents/Recruitment_and_Retention_2008.pdf

243 Universities UK (2007) "Policy Brief 2007 Talent wars" http://www.guardian.co.uk/education/2007/jul/19/highereducation.uk1

244 Universities UK (2007) "Patterns of Higher Education institutions in the UK: Seventh report" http://www.universitiesuk.ac.uk/Publications/Documents/patterns7.pdf

245 HESA website

246 HESA website

247 Universities UK (2011) "Facts and figures 2011" http://www.universitiesuk.ac.uk/Publications/Documents/HigherEducationInFactsAndFiguresSummer2011.pdf

248 *THES*, 13th March, 2008 http://www.timeshighereducation.co.uk/story.asp?storycode=401025

249 BBC Website, 31st March, 2009 http://news.bbc.co.uk/1/hi/health/7974945.stm

250 Ministry of Justice Website http://www.justice.gov.uk/downloads/publications/corporate-reports/MoJ/salaries-schedule-2011-12.pdf

251 *Guardian*, 4th July, 2007 http://www.guardian.co.uk/education/2007/jul/04/postgraduate.highereducation

252 *Telegraph*, 23rd October 2010 http://www.telegraph.co.uk/news/worldnews/8080644/China-The-Ultimate-Brain-Drain.html

253 House of Commons Innovation, Universities, Science and Skills Committee Students and Universities (2009) Evidence British Medical Association http://www.publications.parliament.uk/pa/cm200809/cmselect/cmdius/170/170ii.pdf

254 House of Commons Innovation, Universities, Science and Skills Committee Students and Universities (2009) Evidence Engineering

Councils UK (ECUK) http://www.publications.parliament.uk/pa/
cm200809/cmselect/cmdius/170/170ii.pdf

255 *Independent*, 29th January 1996 http://www.independent.co.uk/
news/huge-gulf-found-in-university-chiefs-pay-1326395.html

256 *THES*, 19th May 2016 https://www.timeshighereducation.com/
features/times-higher-education-pay-survey-2016

257 *THES*, January 2012 www.timeshighereducation.co.uk/story.
asp?storycode=418661

258 HESA Website

259 *THES*, 10th May, 2012 http://www.timeshighereducation.co.uk/
story.asp?sectioncode=26&storycode=419851&c=2

260 *THES*, 7th August 2014 https://www.timeshighereducation.com/
news/v-cs-pay-rises-even-if-student-demand-falls/2015025.article

261 *Guardian*, 7th August 2014 http://www.
theguardian.com/education/2015/mar/15/
rises-for-university-chiefs-cannot-be-justified

262 *Guardian*, 8th February 2002 http://www.guardian.co.uk/educa-
tion/2002/feb/08/administration.highereducation

263 House of Commons Innovation, Universities, Science and Skills
Committee Students and Universities (2009) Report http://www.publi-
cations.parliament.uk/pa/cm200809/cmselect/cmdius/170/17005.htm

264 *THES*, 10 May 2012 www.timeshighereducation.co.uk/story.
asp?storycode=419890

265 *Guardian*, 15th March, 2015 http://www.guardian.co.uk/educa-
tion/2009/mar/19/brian-roper-resignation-london-met 24

266 BBC Website 29th October 2012 http://www.bbc.co.uk/news/
uk-england-kent-20125965

267 *THES* 22nd November 2012 http://www.timeshighereducation.co.uk/story.asp?storycode=421915

268 Wales Online 17th July 2012 http://www.walesonline.co.uk/business-in-wales/business-news/2012/07/17/former-vice-chancellor-of-the-university-of-wales-marc-clement-takes-up-new-role-with-swansea-university-91466-31411275/#sitelife-commentsWidget-bottom#ixzz2CQdhbvLV

269 *THES* 3rd March 2011 http://www.timeshighereducation.co.uk/story.asp?storycode=415393

270 Holyrood 26th July 2011 http://www.holyrood.com/2011/07/abertay-principal-retires-following-dispute/

271 *THES,* 5th March 2009 http://www.timeshighereducation.co.uk/story.asp?storyCode=405665&sectioncode=26

272 *Guardian* 19th March 2009 http://www.guardian.co.uk/education/2009/mar/19/brian-roper-resignation-london-met

273 BBC Website 14th January 2009 http://news.bbc.co.uk/1/hi/england/west_yorkshire/7827966.stm

274 *Guardian* 10th January 2006 http://www.guardian.co.uk/education/2006/jan/10/highereducation.uk4

275 *THES* 2nd August 2002 http://www.timeshighereducation.co.uk/story.asp?storyCode=170814&sectioncode=26

276 *THES* 20th November 1998 http://www.timeshighereducation.co.uk/story.asp?storyCode=109930&sectioncode=26

277 *THES* 27th March 1998 http://www.timeshighereducation.co.uk/story.asp?storyCode=106477&sectioncode=26

278 *THES* 19th July 1996 http://www.timeshighereducation.co.uk/story.asp?storyCode=99918&sectioncode=26

279 *Independent* 2nd November 2000 http://www.independent.co.uk/news/education/education-news/blowing-the-whistle-on-a-vicechancellors-fiddle-621901.html

280 *THES* 13th January 1995 http://www.timeshighereducation.co.uk/story.asp?storyCode=98418&sectioncode=26

281 BBC Website, 17th August, 2004 http://news.bbc.co.uk/1/hi/education/3573910.stm

282 *Telegraph* 12th September 2013 http://www.telegraph.co.uk/education/educationnews/10306211/University-leavers-lack-the- essential-skills-for-work-employers-warn.html

283 Total Jobs (2011) "Graduate survey" http://recruiterspace.totaljobs.com/downloads/general/Graduate%20audience%20profile.pdf

284 *Guardian*, 14th August, 2006 http://www.guardian.co.uk/politics/2006/aug/14/science.schools

285 Association of Graduate Recruiters, 4th February, 2008 http://www.agr.org.uk/Content/Recruiters-predict-highest-increase-in-graduate-vacancies-in-ten-years

286 *Guardian*, 3rd June 2008, http://www.guardian.co.uk/commentisfree/2008/jun/03/maths.education

287 Confederation of British Industry (2015) Education and Skills Survey http://www.cbi.org.uk/index.cfm/_api/render/file/?-method=inline&fileID=92095A98-3A90-4FBD-9AF891997B103F5

288 *THES*, 18th March 2013 https://www.timeshighereducation.com/news/graduates-in-stem-need-to-rise-by-half/2002594.article

289 *Guardian,* 17th September 2008 http://www.guardian.co.uk/education/2008/sep/17/graduates.business

290 *Telegraph*, 2nd April September 2013 http://www.telegraph.co.uk/finance/comment/9967240/

Tell-youngsters-the-truth-the-UK-needs-you-to-work-not-go-to-university.html

291 Institute of Education Website 15th October 2010 http://www.ioe.ac.uk/45855.html

292 *Guardian*, 19th April 2016 http://www.theguardian.com/commentisfree/2016/apr/19/degree-graduates-low-pay-high-debt-students

293 Oxford Review of Economic Policy Vol 20, No2 "The economic and distributional implications of current policies on Higher Education" Ewart Keep & Ken Mayhew http://www.colinwatsonleeds.co.uk/MTEArticles/EwartkeepDistrib.pdf

294 *Guardian*, 14th August 2002 http://www.guardian.co.uk/politics/2002/aug/14/highereducation.publicservices

295 BBC Web site 22nd July 2002 http://news.bbc.co.uk/1/hi/education/2143441.stm

296 *Guardian*, 14th March, 2011 http://www.guardian.co.uk/education/2011/mar/14/forensics-science-students-job-market

297 *Guardian*, 26th October, 2006 http://www.guardian.co.uk/money/2006/oct/26/graduates.highereducation

298 Ibid

299 Centre for Workforce Intelligence, 1st September 2011 http://www.cfwi.org.uk/points-of-view/forums/moving-towards-integrated-care-with-a-specific-focus-on-older-people/166773810

300 HESA website

301 HESA Website

302 University of West London Website Graduate Diploma and Psychology http://courses.uwl.ac.uk/CourseDetails.aspx?CourseInstanceID=30198

303 The Lawyer Website, 4th July 2011 http://www.thelawyer.com/1008470.article

304 Thomson Reuters, 2nd February 2002 http://newsandinsight.thomsonreuters.com/Legal/News/2012/02 – February/Twelve_law_schools_sued_by_graduates_over_misleading_employment_data/

305 House of Commons Select Committee on Science and Technology Seventh Report http://www.publications.parliament.uk/pa/cm200405/cmselect/cmsctech/96/9608.htm

306 *Guardian,* 24th June, 2008 http://www.guardian.co.uk/education/2008/jun/24/highereducation.uk2

307 *Guardian*, 22nd October, 2007 http://www.guardian.co.uk/education/2007/oct/22/students.uk

308 *THES*, 27th Oct 2011 www.timeshighereducation.co.uk/story.asp?storycode=417898

309 Chartered Institute of Personnel and Development, (2010), Labour Market Outlook: Quarterly Survey Report, Summer 2010

310 Confederation of British Industry (2010) "Ready to Grow: business priorities for education and skills. Education and skills survey"

311 HOC Select Committee (2009) Universities and Students Evidence Institute of Physics http://www.publications.parliament.uk/pa/cm200809/cmselect/cmdius/170/170ii.pdf

312 *Guardian* 5th July, 2001 http://www.guardian.co.uk/education/2001/jul/05/highereducation.uk

313 Wellcome Trust (2001) "Review of Wellcome Trust PhD Research Training" http://www.wellcome.ac.uk/stellent/groups/corporatesite/@policy_communications/documents/web_document/wtd003206.pdf

314 "David Craig (2008) *"Squandered"* Constable, London

315 *Daily Mail* 3rd January 2008 http://www.dailymail.co.uk/news/article–505798/

How–doctors–lie–death–certificates–hide–true–scale–toll–hospital–
infections.html

Evening Telegraph, 18th February 2010 http://www.eveningtelegraph.
co.uk/output/2010/02/18/story14569447t0.shtm

Daily Mail, 13th October 2007 http://www.dailymail.co.uk/health/arti-
cle–487375/Cover–ups–lies–cynical–conspiracy–let–superbug–claim–
90–lives.html

316 *Guardian,* 6th July 2000

317 *Daily Mail,* 28th August, 2009 http://www.dailymail.co.uk/debate/
article–1209573/The–harsh–truth–We–nurses–just–forgotten–care.
html#ixzz1gpzCr5Gs

318 *Daily Mail,* 9th November, 2010 http://www.dailymail.co.uk/news/
article–1327766/Mid–Staffordshire–NHS–hospital–scandal–left–1–
200–dead–happen–again.html#ixzz1wLpXgMVk

319 *Telegraph,* 9th November 2011 http://www.telegraph.co.uk/health/
healthnews/8877991/Age–discrimination–within–NHS–leaves–elderly–
neglected.html

320 *Telegraph,* 28th August 2011 http://www.telegraph.co.uk/
health/8728849/Nursing–is–no–longer–the–caring–profession.html

321 Adam Smith Institute (2009) "The *Broken University*" www.
adamsmith.org/images/stories/the–broken–university.pdf

322 Ibid

323 Ibid

324 *Guardian,* 25th November 2009 http://www.guardian.co.uk/news/
datablog/2009/nov/25/gdp–uk–1948–growth–economy#data

325 House of Commons Research Paper (1999) "A Century of
Change:Trends in UK statistics since 1900" http://www.parliament.uk/
documents/commons/lib/research/rp99/rp99–111.pdf

326 ONS statistics

327 ONS statistics

328 Alison Wolf (2002) *"Does Education Matter"* Penguin, London

329 *Telegraph,* 29th March 2012 http://www.telegraph.co.uk/education/educationnews/9173784/University-drop-out-rate-soars-by-13pc-in-a-year.html

330 *Daily Mail*, 20th March 2012 http://www.dailymail.co.uk/news/article-2122591/More-fifth-university-students-fail-finish-degree.html#ixzz24wO3Y7J2

331 HESA website http://www.hesa.ac.uk/index.php?option=com_content&task=view&id=2064&Itemid=141

332 House of Commons Select Committee on Education (2001) http://www.parliament.the-stationery-office.co.uk/pa/cm200001/cmselect/cmeduemp/124/12404.htm

333 *THES* website, 16th February 2017 https://www.timeshighereducation.com/features/the-teaching-survey-2017-results-and-analysis#survey-answer

334 *Telegraph,* 5th March 2012 http://www.telegraph.co.uk/education/educationnews/9124555/Bright-students-cannot-write-essays-say-Cambridge-dons.html

335 *Telegraph*, 5th March 2012 http://www.telegraph.co.uk/education/educationnews/9124555/Bright-students-cannot-write-essays-say-Cambridge-dons.html

336 Ibid

337 House of Commons Innovation, Universities, Science and Skills Committee Students and Universities (2009) Report http://www.publications.parliament.uk/pa/cm200809/cmselect/cmdius/170/17005.htm

338 Ibid

339 *Telegraph*, 10th December 2010 http://www.telegraph.co.uk/education/educationnews/8194038/Spoon-fed-students-lack-resilience-needed-at-Oxbridge.html

340 House of Commons Innovation, Universities, Science and Skills Committee Students and Universities (2009) Report http://www.publications.parliament.uk/pa/cm200809/cmselect/cmdius/170/17005.htm

341 *Guardian*, 17th June 2009 http://www.guardian.co.uk/education/2009/jun/17/a-levels-on-satnav

342 *London Evening Standard*, 3rd April 2012 http://www.standard.co.uk/panewsfeeds/remedial-classes-for-undergraduates-7609131.html

343 *Telegraph*, 1st August 2012 http://www.telegraph.co.uk/education/educationnews/9444360/Spoon-fed-students-struggling-with-university-maths.html

344 *Telegraph*, 3rd April 2012 http://www.telegraph.co.uk/education/educationnews/9180982/Spoon-fed-students-given-tuition-in-basic-skills-at-university.html

345 *Guardian*, 25th April 2007 http://www.guardian.co.uk/uk/2007/apr/25/highereducation.education

346 *Guardian*, 9th February 2006 http://www.guardian.co.uk/education/2006/feb/09/highereducation.uk1

347 House of Commons Innovation, Universities, Science and Skills Committee Students and Universities (2009) Evidence Institution of Engineering and Technology http://www.publications.parliament.uk/pa/cm200809/cmselect/cmdius/170/170we51.htm

348 *Guardian*, 10th December, 2006 http://www.guardian.co.uk/news/2006/dec/10/letters.highereducation

349 House of Commons Innovation, Universities, Science and Skills Committee Students and Universities (2009) Report

http://www.publications.parliament.uk/pa/cm200809/cmselect/cmdius/170/17005.htm

350 Conservative Home Website, July 10th 2009 http://conservative-home.blogs.com/centreright/2009/07/elizabeth-truss-the-misuse-of-maths.html

351 BBC Website 11th February 2002 http://news.bbc.co.uk/1/hi/education/1815073.stm

352 Barry Stubbs Website A level and GCSE grades http://www.bstubbs.co.uk/natfig.htm

353 Barry Stubbs Website A level and GCSE grades http://www.bstubbs.co.uk/natfig.htm

354 Barry Stubbs Website A level and GCSE grades http://www.bstubbs.co.uk/natfig.htm

355 *Guardian,* 20th January 2010 http://www.guardian.co.uk/education/2010/jan/20/languages-become-twilight-subjects CILIT

356 RSA Website https://www.thersa.org/about-us/media/2015/students-in-deprived-neighbourhoods-being-denied-access-to-tough-subjects

357 House of Commons Innovation, Universities, Science and Skills Committee Students and Universities (2009) Evidence Roger Brown http://www.publications.parliament.uk/pa/cm200809/cmselect/cmdius/170/170we101.htm

358 *Guardian*, 22nd May 2002 http://www.guardian.co.uk/uk/2002/may/22/highereducation.education

359 *Telegraph*, 22nd February 2005 http://www.telegraph.co.uk/news/uknews/1484084/Over-10000-Oxbridge-rejects-went-on-to-gain-straight-As.html

360 *Guardian*, 2nd May 2003 http://www.guardian.co.uk/education/2003/may/02/students.uk

361 *Guardian,* 12th June 2008 http://www.guardian.co.uk/education/2008/jun/12/highereducation.uk ,

362 Ibid

363 House of Commons Innovation, Universities, Science and Skills Committee Students and Universities (2009) Evidence Engineering Councils UK http://www.publications.parliament.uk/pa/cm200809/cmselect/cmdius/170/170we77.htm

364 *Guardian,* 27th August 2004 http://www.guardian.co.uk/education/2004/aug/27/alevels2004.alevels1

365 House of Commons Innovation, Universities, Science and Skills Committee Students and Universities (2009) Evidence Institute of Physics http://www.publications.parliament.uk/pa/cm200809/cmselect/cmdius/170/170we31.htm

366 Reform (2009) "The Misuse of Maths" http://www.reform.co.uk/client_files/www.reform.co.uk/files/the_misuse_of_maths.pdf

367 Channel Four Website, 9th July 2009 http://www.channel4.com/news/articles/science_technology/introducing+the+apossat-navapos+maths+exam/3257252.html

368 *Telegraph,* 8th December 2011 http://www.telegraph.co.uk/education/secondaryeducation/8943954/Exam–chief–you–dont–have–to–teach–a–lot–for–our–tests.html

369 *Telegraph* 31st January 2012 http://www.telegraph.co.uk/education/educationnews/9052181/Exam–boards–accused–of–marketing–easy–GCSEs–to–schools.html

370 Oxford University Website www.ox.ac.uk/about_the_university/facts_and.../index.html

371 Barry Stubbs Website A level and GCSE grades http://www.bstubbs.co.uk/natfig.htm

372 Bruce Choppin (1981). "Is Education Getting Better?" British Educational Research Journal 7 (1): 11.

373 House of Commons Innovation, Universities, Science and Skills Committee Students and Universities (2009) Report http://www.publications.parliament.uk/pa/cm200809/cmselect/cmdius/170/17005.htm

374 House of Commons Innovation, Universities, Science and Skills Committee Students and Universities (2009) Report http://www.publications.parliament.uk/pa/cm200809/cmselect/cmdius/170/17005.htm

375 *Guardian*, 20th August 2002 http://www.guardian.co.uk/education/2002/aug/20/highereducation.alevels2002

376 *Guardian,* 11th May 2005 http://www.guardian.co.uk/uk/2005/may/11/accesstouniversity.politics

377 *Telegraph*, 14th August 2008 http://www.telegraph.co.uk/news/uknews/1484084/Over-10000-Oxbridge-rejects-went-on-to-gain-straight-As.html

378 BBC Website, 28th August 2010 http://www.bbc.co.uk/news/education-11112169

379 *THES* 11th Aug 2011 www.timeshighereducation.co.uk/story.asp?storyCode=417088

380 *Telegraph* 13th November 2010 http://www.telegraph.co.uk/education/universityeducation/8130726/Number-of-universities-requiring-A-triples.html

381 Civitas (2005) Education: Better results and declining standards? Online Briefing David Green, Anastasia de Waal and Ben Cackett http://www.civitas.org.uk/pdf/educationBriefingDec05.pdf

382 Fact Check 19th August 2010 http://fullfact.org/factchecks/grade_inflation_rising_results_falling_standards-1538

383 Ibid

384 BBC Website, 24th January 2013 http://www.bbc.co.uk/news/education-21162960

385 Guardian, 30th January 2001 http://www.guardian.co.uk/uk/2001/jan/30/education.oxbridgeandelitism

386 BBC Website, 15th March 2008 http://news.bbc.co.uk/1/hi/education/7297143.stm

387 Guardian, 10th January 2012 http://www.guardian.co.uk/education/2012/jan/10/how-cambridge-admissions-really-work

388 TES, 20th August 1999 http://www.tes.co.uk/teaching-resource/Cambridge-moves-to-scrap-entrance-exam-308734/

389 Oxford University website http://www.ox.ac.uk/about_the_university/facts_and_figures/undergraduate_admissions_statistics/school_type.html

390 Cambridge University website http://www.study.cam.ac.uk/undergraduate/publications/docs/admissionsstatistics2011.pdf

391 Sutton Trust (2008) "Individual University Admissions by School" http://www.suttontrust.com/research/university-admissions-by-individual-schools/

392 Telegraph, 12th July 2008 http://www.telegraph.co.uk/education/2403623/Cambridge-is-too-posh-say-state-schools.html

393 *THES*, 12th August 2009 http://www.timeshighereducation.co.uk/story.asp?storyCode=407750&sectioncode=26

394 *Telegraph*, 27th Apr 2012 http://www.telegraph.co.uk/education/educationnews/9228674/State-school-teachers-biased-against-Oxbridge-study-finds.html

395 Sutton Trust Website, 27th April 2012 http://www.suttontrust.com/news/news/less-than-half-of-state-teachers-oxbridge/

396 House of Commons Business, Innovation and Skills Committee Government reform of Higher Education Twelfth Report of Session 2010–12

397 Student Media Wire Website 7th October 2008 http://www.student-mediawire.co.uk/news/1971/one–in–three–graduates–earn–under–15k/

398 Source SLC statistical first release 1/2015 Student loans for higher education in England – financial year 2014–15 and earlier editions dera.ioe.ac.uk/22709/1/SN01079.pdf

399 House of Commons Library (2016) "Students Loans Statistics" www.parliament.uk/briefing–papers/sn01079.pdf

400 House of Commons Business, Innovation and Skills Committee Government reform of Higher Education Twelfth Report of Session 2010–12 http://www.publications.parliament.uk/pa/cm201012/cmselect/cmbis/885/885.pdf

401 Student Loan Company (2012) "INCOME CONTINGENT REPAYMENTS BY REPAYMENT COHORT AND TAX YEAR 2000/01TO 2010/11 INCLUSIVE (PROVISIONAL)" http://www.slc.co.uk/media/333189/slcosp032012.pdf

402 House of Commons Business, Innovation and Skills Committee Government reform of Higher Education Twelfth Report of Session 2010–12 http://www.publications.parliament.uk/pa/cm201012/cmselect/cmbis/885/885.pdf

403 *Independent* 8th November 2012 http://www.independent.co.uk/news/education/education–news/half–of–graduates–could–have–their–student–loans–written–off–admits–government–8297216.html

404 Skandia (2012) "First steps to wealth" http://www2.skandia.co.uk/Documents/Literature%20Library/212–5003–first–steps–to–wealth.pdf

405 BBC Website, 21st March 2012 http://www.bbc.co.uk/news/business–17459856

406 Ibid

407 *THES*, 26th May 2011 www.timeshighereducation.co.uk/story.asp?storycode=416257

408 BIS (2011) "The Returns to Higher Education Qualifications" http://www.bis.gov.uk/assets/biscore/higher-education/docs/r/11-973-returns-to-higher-education-qualifications.pdf

409 HEPI (2011) "The government's proposals for Higher Education funding and student finance – an analysis" http://www.hepi.ac.uk/466-1875/The-government's-proposals-for-higher-education-funding-and-student-finance-%E2%80%93-an-analysis.html

410 Intergenerational Foundation (2012) "False Accounting" http://www.if.org.uk/wp-content/uploads/2012/05/False-Accounting_-Why-Higher-Education-Reforms-dont-add-up.pdf

411 *Telegraph* 6th November 2012 http://www.telegraph.co.uk/news/politics/9659949/UK-facing-middle-class-brain-drain-as-professionals-seek-better-lives-abroad.html

412 *Spectator*, 20th October 2012 http://www.spectator.co.uk/the-week/diary/8689311/diary-562/

413 *Telegraph* 23rd November 2012 http://www.telegraph.co.uk/education/educationnews/9699524/Britain-being-hit-by-rise-in-graduate-brain-drain.html

414 *Guardian*, 8th November 2017 https://www.theguardian.com/education/2017/nov/08/student-loans-company-sacks-chief-executive-steve-lamey

415 Yahoo Website – Telegraph 17th November 2017 https://www.yahoo.com/news/hmrc-blame-student-loan-errors-100508879.html

416 Varsity Website – 16th November 2017 https://www.varsity.co.uk/news/14118

417 Demos (2010) "*A report into the attitudes and aspirations of this year's graduates.*"

www.endsleigh.co.uk/Student/.../Demos_Report_2010_screen.pdf

418 *Guardian*, 10th May, 2002 http://www.guardian.co.uk/money/2002/may/10/studentfinance.education

419 *Guardian*, 6th October, 2006 http://www.guardian.co.uk/money/2006/oct/06/houseprices.studentfinance Scottish Widows

420 *Guardian*, 24th July, 2006 http://www.guardian.co.uk/money/2006/jul/24/studentfinance.graduates

421 *Independent*, 25th February, 2013 http://www.independent.co.uk/student/postgraduate/the-boomerang-generation-why-are-so-many-more-graduates-moving-back-in-with-mum-and-dad-8509575.html

422 *Independent*, 25th February, 2013 http://www.independent.co.uk/student/postgraduate/the-boomerang-generation-why-are-so-many-more-graduates-moving-back-in-with-mum-and-dad-8509575.html

423 *Telegraph*, 10th September, 2012 http://www.telegraph.co.uk/finance/personalfinance/borrowing/mortgages/9529249/Student-loans-will-make-it-harder-for-graduates-to-get-a-mortgage.html

424 Mintel, July 2011 http://www.mintel.com/press-centre/press-releases/730/boomerang-kids-return-to-the-nest-3-million-aged-20-now-living-back-with-parents

425 *Independent*, 25th February, 2013 http://www.independent.co.uk/student/postgraduate/the-boomerang-generation-why-are-so-many-more-graduates-moving-back-in-with-mum-and-dad-8509575.html

426 *Telegraph*, 2nd November, 2015 http://www.telegraph.co.uk/finance/personalfinance/borrowing/mortgages/11960805/The-charts-that-show-its-not-THAT-hard-for-first-time-buyers.html

427 *Independent*, 25th February, 2013 http://www.independent.co.uk/student/postgraduate/the-boomerang-generation-why-are-so-many-more-graduates-moving-back-in-with-mum-and-dad-8509575.html

428 Collegiate Times, 13th February 2012 http://www.collegiatetimes.com/stories/19244/law-students-suing-schools

429 HEPI (2006) "Demand for HE to 2020" http://www.hepi.ac.uk/files/22DemandforHEto2020.pdf

430 HEPI (2008) "Demand for Higher Education to 2029 HEPI" http://www.hepi.ac.uk/466-1366/Demand-for-Higher-Education-to-2029.html

431 Telegraph, 23rd October 2010 http://www.telegraph.co.uk/news/worldnews/8080644/China-The-Ultimate-Brain-Drain.html

432 THES, 29th July 2010 http://www.timeshighereducation.co.uk/story.asp?storycode=412760

433 Guardian, 6th March 2011 http://www.guardian.co.uk/education/2011/mar/06/university-europe-no-debt

434 Fulbright Commission Website http://www.fulbright.org.uk/study-in-the-usa

435 Guardian, 17th December 2012 https://www.theguardian.com/education/2012/dec/17/american-universities-lure-british-students

436 Guardian, 2nd February 2010 http://www.guardian.co.uk/education/2010/feb/02/chinese-universities-will-rival-oxbridge

437 Guardian, 29th January 2009 http://www.guardian.co.uk/education/2009/jan/29/overseas-students-british-degrees

438 Telegraph, 23rd October 2010 http://www.telegraph.co.uk/news/worldnews/8080644/China-The-Ultimate-Brain-Drain.html

439 Universities UK (2007) "Policy Briefing: Talent Wars" http://www.universitiesuk.ac.uk/Publications/Documents/Policy%20Brief%20Talent%20Wars.pdf

440 Sydney Morning Herald 16th January 2011 http://www.smh.com.au/national/ageing-academics-set-university-timebomb-20110115-19ry1.html

441 Universities UK (2007) "Policy Briefing: Talent Wars" http://www.universitiesuk.ac.uk/Publications/Documents/Policy%20Brief%20Talent%20Wars.pdf

442 *Telegraph*, 23rd October 2010 http://www.telegraph.co.uk/news/worldnews/8080644/China-The-Ultimate-Brain-Drain.html

443 *Guardian*, 22nd February 2010G http://www.guardian.co.uk/science/2010/feb/22/funding-cuts-brain-drain-scientist

444 *THES*, 14th Jun 2012 www.timeshighereducation.co.uk/story.asp?storyCode=420231

445 *THES*, 15 December 2011 http://www.timeshighereducation.co.uk/story.asp?storycode=418436

446 *Chronicle*, 2nd January 2011 http://chronicle.com/article/University-Mergers-Sweep/125781/

447 *Guardian*, 5th July 2007 http://www.guardian.co.uk/education/2007/jul/05/highereducation.news

448 Shanghai University Ranking Website http://www.shanghairanking.com/

449 *Guardian*, 3rd October 2012 http://www.guardian.co.uk/education/2012/oct/03/british-universities-set-collapse-mediocrity

450 OECD (2007) "How do rankings impact on higher education?" www.oecd.org/edu/imhe/39802910.pdf

451 *Guardian*, 17th August 2017 https://www.theguardian.com/education/2017/aug/17/former-theresa-may-aide-attacks-tuition-fees-ponzi-scheme-nick-timothy

452 *THES*, 15th November 2017 https://www.timeshighereducation.com/news/uk-universities-forced-axe-misleading-rankings-claims#-survey-answer

453 Martin Trow (2005) "An American Perspective on British Higher Education: The Decline of Diversity, Autonomy and Trust in Post-war

British Higher Education" Working Papers, Institute of Governmental Studies, UC Berkeley http://escholarship.org/uc/item/1mg88095

454 Law Society Website http://www.lawsociety.org.uk/careers/becoming-a-solicitor/entry-trends/

455 Skandia (2012) "First Steps to Wealth" http://www2.skandia.co.uk/understanding-investment/skandia-insights/first-steps-to-wealth/

456 The Open University Website http://www.open.ac.uk/courses/fees-and-funding

457 *Telegraph*, 27th Aug 2012 http://www.telegraph.co.uk/finance/economics/9501874/Despite-the-crisis-Britons-are-still-spending-like-drunkards.html

458 CentreForum (2011) "*Universities challenged: making the new university*" www.centreforum.org/assets/pubs/universities-challenged-web.pdf

459 *Telegraph*, 27th October 2012 http://www.telegraph.co.uk/education/educationnews/9636721/English-students-can-take-cheaper-courses-abroad.html

460 *THES*, 3rd May 2012 www.timeshighereducation.co.uk/story.asp?storycode=419824

461 Top Universities in the World Website http://www.university-list.net/rank/univ-110066.html

462 CUCAS Website http://www.cucas.edu.cn/HomePage/content/content_412.shtml

463 Adam Smith Research Trust (2009)"The Broken University *What is seen* and *what is not seen* in the UK Higher Education sector" James Stanfield